Reach Out, Build Up, Send Back

The unfolding story of the Overseas Christian Fellowship Australia, established in 1959

An initiative of the OCF Heritage Project

Written by Lim May Kuan

Reach Out, Build Up, Send Back; The unfolding story of the Overseas Christian Fellowship Australia, established in 1959

Copyright: © Lim May Kuan, 2023

All rights reserved. No part of this book may be copied, reproduced or transmitted by any means without prior permission of the author, except in the case of brief quotations embodied in review articles.

Cataloguing-in-Publication entry is available from the National Library of Australia http:/catalogue.nla.gov.au

First published in Hackham, South Australia, November 2023
by Immortalise via Ingram Spark. www.immortalise.com.au

ISBN   paperback   978-0-6457721-3-5
       ebook   978-0-6457721-4-2

Artwork concept by Naw Day Day. The grey location icons on the map indicate OCF centres that once existed, while coloured pins indicate OCF centres in existence at the time of publication. Map on the cover: Image by flatart on Freepik. Icons on the cover: Image by Freepik. Road image and map on the inside pages: Image by Freepik.

All Scripture quotations, unless otherwise indicated, are taken from the Holy Bible, New International Version®, NIV®. Copyright ©1973, 1978, 1984, 2011 by Biblica, Inc.™ Used by permission of Zondervan. All rights reserved worldwide. www.zondervan.com The "NIV" and "New International Version" are trademarks registered in the United States Patent and Trademark Office by Biblica, Inc.™

FOREWORD	*1*
INTRODUCTION	*6*
How This Book Came to Be	6
PROLOGUE	*10*
SECTION 1: EARLY DAYS, 1950S TO EARLY 1970S	*21*
1. Formation of OCF Australia	23
Cowes Convention	24
Negotiations over name and affiliation	27
2. Training Ground	35
The first OCF Australia convention and AGM	35
Privilege of Planning, Great Honour of Chairing	39
3. Strong Supporters	46
Associate Members	46
Staff Workers	55
4. Vision and Leadership	65
Creation of the OCF Handbook	65
Formation of OCF Hobart	77
5. A Servant of the Church	80
Too many invitations	80
The OCF-church relationship	82
6. Early Bible College students	92
Wilfred Chee	92
Melville Szto	95
Yong Chen Fah	100
7. The Wider World	106
From Many Nations	106
Operation Welcome	110
8. Returnee Missionaries	116
Continued Exposure	117
Newsletters	121
Perkantas	124
SECTION 2: MIDDLE YEARS, MID 1970S–LATE 1990S	*130*
9. Melbourne	132
Three co-chairs: Parkville, Clayton, La Trobe	133
Declaration of the Priority to Serve Our Own People	140
Carlton	144
10. Sydney	147
Sydney's District Bible Study Groups	147
Adding to the Handbook	156

11. ADELAIDE **160**
   A Diaspora Church Funds a Staff Worker   160
   Guidelines on the Charismatic Movement   163
12. PERTH **171**
   Jarrahdale Leadership Camp   171
   The Formation of OCFs Murdoch and Curtin   176
   Bullsbrook Camp   181
13. STREAMS OF LIVING WATER **186**
   Promises for Parkville   186
   Geelong Blessed by Barrabool Hills Baptist   189
   Formation of OCF Flinders   193
14. VISION FOR EXPANSION **198**
   Formation of OCF Kew (Swinburne)   199
   Formation of OCF Melbourne Uni   203
   Formation of OCF Caulfield and Frankston   209
15. PRESSING INTERNAL AND EXTERNAL CONCERNS **213**
   The La Trobe convention   213
   A Question of Hermeneutics   218
   Pushback Against Experiential Emphasis   224
16. CATALYST AND SAFEGUARD: A BOARD ENVISAGED **230**
   The Help of Resource Persons and Local Advisors   230
   Crisis and Opportunity in Hobart   232
   Formation of OCF UniSA   237

SECTION 3: RECENT TIMES, 2000 AND BEYOND   243

17. FORMAL SUPPORT **245**
   No Consensus   246
   Western Australia Staffworker Organisation   248
18. INFORMAL SUPPORT **254**
   Sydney   255
   Armidale   260
   Newcastle   261
   Wollongong   265
   Canberra   266
19. SPIRITUAL MOTHERS AND FATHERS **270**
   A Board Established   271
   A Board Functions   274
20. THE STRUGGLES AND SIGNIFICANCE OF BEING SMALL ... **280**
   Strategic Growth Officer   280
   OCF Swinburne   282
   OCF Caulfield   283
   OCF Hobart   284
   OCF Curtin   285

    Vital Church Support   286

21. Drift Apart **289**
    Sydney Breaks Away   289
    Parkville Moves Out of Swanston Street COC   293
    Carlton Steps Aside   294

22. Regroup **297**
    Pass on Vision, Raise up Leaders   297
    Prioritise Overseas Student Leadership   301

23. The Essential Nature of the Fellowship **307**
    Staff Workers   307
    Staying true to our vision   318

24. Reset **323**
    The Sixtieth Convention   323
    Innovation and Increased Partnership   327
    The Blessing of Meeting Together   331

25. The Next Chapter **344**

EPILOGUE   *346*

ACKNOWLEDGEMENTS   *350*

APPENDIX A OCF AUSTRALIA CHAIRPERSONS   *353*

APPENDIX B ORAL HISTORY INTERVIEWS   *356*

BIBLIOGRAPHY   *362*

Acronyms

ABI	Adelaide Bible Institute
AACC	Austral-Asian Christian Church. After 2005, it refers to the English congregation known as the Austral-Asian Community Church
AOCCOS	Australian Organisational Coordinating Committee for Overseas Students
AF	Asian Fellowship
AFES	Australian Fellowship of Evangelical Students
AGM	Annual General Meeting
AOG	Assemblies of God
AUEU	Adelaide University Evangelical Union
BEM	Borneo Evangelical Mission
BOA	Board of Advisors
CMS	Church Missionary Society
COC	Church of Christ
CPC	Chinese Presbyterian Church
CU	Christian Union
DBSG	District Bible Study Group

ES	Evangelical Students
ESCCC	East Sydney Community Christian Church
EU	Evangelical Union
EXCO	Executive Committee of OCF Australia
GC	General Council of OCF Australia
GCF	Graduates Christian Fellowship
IVF	Inter Varsity Fellowship
MBI	Melbourne Bible Institute
MTC	Moore Theological College
MU	Melbourne University
NSWIT	New South Wales Institute of Technology
OCF	Overseas Christian Fellowship
PERKANTAS	*Persekutuan Kristen Antar Universitas*, or Christian Inter Varsity Fellowship
RMIT	Royal Melbourne Institute of Technology
QIT	Queensland Institute of Technology
QUT	Queensland University of Technology
SA	South Australia
SAIT	South Australian Institute of Technology

UNSW	University of New South Wales
UniSA	University of South Australia
UQ	University of Queensland
UWA	University of Western Australia
WA	Western Australia
WAIT	Western Australia Institute of Technology
YFC	Youth for Christ
YMCA	Young Men's Christian Association

Writing Conventions

Western names will be in the format of given name, followed by family name, for example, Harrold Steward and Christina Chew—Harrold and Christina are the given names. Unless otherwise specified, Chinese names will be in the format of family name followed by given name, for example, Yap Chin Far where Yap is the family name.

The year of the AGM and convention will be taken as the academic year just completed. For example, the 1959 convention was held in the summer of 1959/1960. Although part of the convention took place after the New Year, it will be referred to as the 1959 convention. Similarly, the 1964 Adelaide convention was held from 2 to 9 January 1965, but is referenced by the academic year that had just been completed.

Unless otherwise stated, AGM refers to the OCF Australia AGM, and the EXCO refers to the Executive Committee of OCF Australia. The leader of EXCO and local centres will be referred to as chairperson, even though some local centres use other names such as president.

Oral history interviews have for the large part been transcribed verbatim. However, there has been minor editing to remove false starts and improve readability. Interviewees have reviewed and approved their oral history transcript excerpts as being in accordance with their intended meaning. Minor corrections have also been made to some quotes taken from other sources, such as minutes, emails, or newsletters to improve readability.

TIMELINE

1. 1956 • Asian Fellowship formed
2. 1957 • OCF Sydney formed
3. 1958 • OCF Brisbane and OCF Melbourne formed
4. 2 Feb 1959 • OCF Australia formed
5. 1959 • OCF Perth affiliated
6. 1964 • OCF Geelong dissolved
7. 1967 • OCF Hobart affiliated
8. 1977 • OCF Newcastle affiliated
   • OCF Melbourne dissolved
9. 1979 • OCFs Parkville, La Trobe and Clayton affiliated
10. 1980 • OCF Geelong reaffiliated
11. 1982 • OCF Carlton affiliated
12. 1983 • OCF Canberra affiliated
13. 1984 • OCF Armidale affiliated
14. 1986 • OCF Flinders affiliated
15. 1987 • OCF Wollongong affiliated
16. 1988 • OCF Murdoch affiliated
17. 1989 • OCFs Kew (now known as Swinburne) and QUT affiliated
18. 1990 • OCFs Caulfield, Curtin, and Melbourne University affiliated
19. 1995 • OCFs Frankston and Griffith University affiliated
20.
21. 2000 • OCF Armidale dissolved
22. 2003 • OCF Launceston provisionally affiliated
23. 2008 • OCFs Wollongong and Newcastle dissolved
    • OCF Parkville renamed OCF Melbourne City
24. 2009 • OCF Berwick affiliated
25. 2015 • OCF Carlton disaffiliated
    • OCF Melbourne City renamed OCF RMIT
    • OCF Sydney renamed OCF UNSW

Foreword

Shen Dah Cheong addressing the 60th OCF Australia convention in Melaka, Malaysia.

In 1959, the Dalai Lama fled China. Fidel Castro came to power in Cuba. Billy Graham commenced his Australian tour. On 10 May 1959, 150 000 people gathered at the Sydney Cricket Ground to hear him preach. It was a time of spiritual awakening.

I came to Melbourne as an overseas student that year. During those next six years, the Overseas Christian Fellowship (OCF) played an important part in my life. OCF helped me to grow in my Christian faith and taught me to serve God and others.

Reach Out, Build Up, Send Back (1959-2022) contains information about the OCF drawn from the historical documents and from over 60 oral history interviews. It gives an overview of the formation and development of OCF over the last 63 years. Today, OCF's vision and legacy is still the same. God is still working amongst the overseas students who are called to share the love of God, to prepare themselves for their future vocation and to equip themselves to serve God.

In this book, we see the history and the growth of OCF. We also see that so many lives of the overseas students have been touched and changed. As we read this account, we need to look beyond the history and the people of OCF. We need to pause a while and lift up our eyes to see God's glory and majesty, and his love and goodness to us all these years.

In the year 1959, God began a ministry to reach out to the overseas students through OCF. Today in 2023, God continues this ministry amongst the overseas students. This book is a testament of God's leading hand in this movement. May this book also inspire and challenge us to continue this student work, so that the OCFers and alumni will be an impact and blessing to others in Australia and overseas.

Shen Dah Cheong
OCF Australia Chairperson 1963 and 1964
5 August 2023, Sydney

Foreword

From left: Thomas Tai, Donovan Koh, Andrea Ong, Lee Wei Lyn, members of the 2023 OCF Australia EXCO.

The account of the Overseas Christian Fellowship is not merely a chronicle of events or a list of names of the people involved, but a testament to the power of God at work through the individuals who stepped out in their passion and love for God. With the Great Commission as our guiding mission (Matt. 28:18-20), OCF has developed to have a rich history packed with accounts of God's faithfulness to the Fellowship. Through reading this book, you can expect to be transported back to a time when the seeds of this club were sown and witness God's goodness through and in the various OCF centres since 1959.

In the chapters ahead, you will come to hear from the pioneering founders who saw the need for students far from their homes to find community, belonging, and spiritual growth in a foreign land. You may even personally identify with those who have left their legacy in God's ministry—reaching out to students on their campus, stepping up in faithfulness to build disciples, and sending students back to spread the Good News. These visionaries understood that despite geographical distances and cultural differences, the common bond of faith could serve as a bridge, spanning oceans and transcending borders.

In the early days of OCF, the fellowship was characterised by international students who desired a community that shared a common foundation of faith, friendship, and a shared mission for God. Through the accounts of the early and more recent members, we witness the acts of compassion, the intellectual exchanges, and the heartwarming stories of lives touched by the spirit of this fellowship. Sharing similar backgrounds, they exercised their faith and acted out of conviction, resulting in fellowship and fun over the many years.

But this narrative is not confined to the past. It reverberates into the present and foreshadows an even more vibrant future. The Overseas Christian Fellowship has evolved and continued to thrive through the many years. There is no doubt that God's plan for OCF will only continue to prevail, and we hope that this book will be a lasting testament and encouragement to those curious to understand how God has used ordinary people for His mission. We hope that the stories from these OCF leaders will inspire you to reconnect

Foreword

with OCFers you may have lost touch with, and to be spurred on to continue living out the Great Commission in your current unique season.

> Donovan Koh, Andrea Ong, Thomas Tai, Lee Wei Lyn
> OCF Australia EXCO 2023
> 9 August 2023, Melbourne

Introduction

How This Book Came to Be

In December 2019, members and alumni of the Overseas Christian Fellowship (OCF) Australia gathered for their 60th annual convention in Melaka, Malaysia. There they realised the need to preserve the history of OCF Australia. Many founding members were in their seventies and eighties, and the history of the organisation as a whole had never been written. In view of this, several of us formed the OCF Heritage Project.

Initial members of this team were Seet Ai Mee, Joshua Sim, Bob Rick Looi, Christina Chew, Galven Lee, Jedidiah Watt and me (Lim May Kuan). Various ones left and joined the team over the next four years. Later members were Peh Yan Ting, Esther Siong, Eugene Rodrigo, Jerad Tan and Joshua Chan. To preserve our shared spiritual heritage, we decided on two outcomes for our project: one, create a digital OCF archive; two, publish a book. The digital archive would aid research necessary to write an OCF history book and capture far more than a book can contain. The digital archive has almost been completed. In the near future, we aim to deposit copies of this archive with the OCF Executive Committee (EXCO) and one or two theological colleges. The second goal, the book that we envisaged, is now in your hands.

We used both oral history and historical sources in our research. Thank you to all who responded to our call for OCF documents, photos and memorabilia. Joshua Sim and Bob

Rick Looi sorted and filed donated material into a digital archive, including AGM minutes, convention and camp booklets, and local centre histories. The team also received physical material such as slides and pamphlets. Some of this has been deposited at the Trinity Theological College in Singapore. The papers of Ian Burnard, the General Secretary of the Inter Varsity Fellowship (IVF) from 1962 to 1976, provided valuable information about the formative years of OCF Australia. These papers are archived at the Samuel Marsden Archive at the Moore Theological College (MTC) in Sydney. Where cited, it is referenced as MTC, followed by the box number and folder labels.

For oral history, we prioritised interviewing OCF Australia chairpersons, in line with the focus on OCF Australia as a national organisation. Although oral historians prefer in-person interviews, we conducted most of our interviews online because of our limited resources and the COVID-19 pandemic. Despite this, interviewers and interviewees could see one another, and great physical distances were bridged, through online platforms such as Zoom or Squadcast. We interviewed 41 of the 59 past EXCO chairpersons. These interviews conveyed a sense of the joys and struggles involved, often hard to grasp through written reports alone.[1] Although exact dates or details may have been forgotten, interviewees readily recalled the things that were important to them and communicated underlying truths through their

---

[1] A. Portelli, 'Living Voices: The Oral History Interview as Dialogue and Experience,' *The Oral History Review 45,* no. 2 (2018):247.

beliefs, feelings and attitudes.² The interviews were very profitable dialogues. Sometimes, younger alumni or current OCF students accompanied a more experienced interviewer. The oral history interviews have augmented information from written sources and have also been used to fill gaps in extant records.

In order to reconstruct the history of OCF Australia, we have pieced together, to the best of our ability, an account of OCF Australia from 1959 to 2022. Where the account relies on personal recollections, a second source has been sought for corroboration, as far as possible. Joshua Sim's guidance on historical methods has been invaluable. While I have tried to be as thorough and objective as possible, I recognise that all historians and writers process information through a lifetime of experience. OCF has been an integral part of my faith journey: I was in OCF Parkville in 1989 as a Year 12 student, and then in OCF Melbourne University from 1990 to 1994. My husband Lee Joon Chong and I are current advisors for OCF AU/UniSA. We have been blessed through the ministry of OCF and continue to invest in it. It has been a source of much joy to us.

For three and a half years, I travelled back in time to examine our shared OCF Australia story. I invite you to retrace my steps, with this book as my torch, shining a light on selected events. There were many possible ways to tell

---

² B.M. Robertson, *Oral History Handbook* (Adelaide: Oral History Association of Australia, South Australia, 2013), 4.

this story. I have selected one path out of many possibilities such as a collection of local OCF centre histories or personal testimonies. This route stops at events that, to me, have shaped OCF Australia at a national level. I have had to leave out many wonderful testimonies and stories. If that is your story, I apologise, and urge you to write it down, or tell someone, so that we will not forget things that ought to be remembered.

As the main interviewer, I have been blessed to speak with former leaders, members and supporters of the ministry. Many spoke at length about their time in OCF, when they were in their early twenties. Their stories have shown me that youth is not wasted on the young. It is a gift from God, a season of life full of possibilities, where He gives each one a choice: whom will you love, whom will you serve? The ministry of OCF Australia has been carried all these years by young people. So many of us laboured for a brief, but intense, period in OCF Australia. The ministry continues to this day to be a blessing and a tool in the hands of the Lord. That continuity, despite our inexperience and brevity of service, evidences the hand of God, who plans, shapes and sustains all things for His purposes.

Lim May Kuan
18 August 2023
Adelaide

Prologue

Adelaide

In 1952, soon after arriving in Australia, Yap Chin Far suffered a persistent pain in his stomach and began vomiting. At the Royal Adelaide Hospital, he was diagnosed with appendicitis. Dr Harrold Steward operated on him. On subsequent ward rounds, Dr Steward noticed that Chin Far's only visitors were other overseas students. When Chin Far was discharged, Dr Steward invited him for a home-cooked meal.

Mrs Gwenda Steward fretted that their home might seem plain to someone who must come from a wealthy family, given that he could study abroad. But Chin Far's politeness and sincerity dispelled her worries. He thoroughly enjoyed her cooking, though not the rice pudding! After doing the dishes, Gwenda found Chin Far romping around the lounge with the Steward children, laughing as if they were the best antidote to homesickness. The children used Chin Far's European name, Dicky, and he became a regular visitor to their home.

Sometime later, Dr Steward brought Dicky, a Buddhist, to a Youth for Christ rally at the Adelaide Town Hall. That night, Chin Far became a Christian. Gwenda recalled, 'He became burdened for his fellow students. Many of them came to our home. Yap never asked for entertainment, for lavish food, or even outings. His one desire was for them to come into a Christian home and learn the ways of the Lord

Jesus.'³ In 1954, the Stewards left for Indonesia where Dr Steward was to take up a position in a missionary hospital. Gwenda wrote, 'Our biggest heartbreak was to leave behind the Asian students who had become part of our family.'

Dicky invited his friends Robert Oh and Shirley Au Yong to Youth for Christ rallies. (They had all studied at Victoria Institute in Kuala Lumpur previously.) Robert and Shirley became Christians and were baptised at the Parkside Baptist Church in 1954.⁴ When Dicky bought a motorbike, he brought Charles Aw to church. Charles studied accountancy at a commercial institute. Charles also became a Christian. Dicky, Robert, Shirley and Charles began attending Adelaide University Evangelical Union (EU) meetings. The EU had been trying to reach Asians but with little success. The EU president Ian Burnard encouraged Chin Far and his friends to form their own group to reach fellow Asians.

In 1956, Chin Far and his friends formed the Asian Fellowship (AF). They met on Saturday afternoons at the Church of England on North Terrace, now known as Holy Trinity. The church gave them free use of the hall, asking only that they keep the place tidy. The Church of England minister Reverend Lance Shilton, and a Baptist minister Reverend Allan Tinsley, gave Bible talks. Sometimes, Robert also shared from the Scriptures.

---

³ Harrold and Gwenda Steward, 'Invite the World into Your Home,' *His*, 1957, 9, 10.
⁴ Shirley Au-Yong, Email to author, July 2020.

The following year, the AF welcomed new overseas students and shared tips on living abroad. Charles and Shirley introduced badminton and table tennis games at AF to sustain interest. Some freshers became members: Indonesians Panusunan Siregar and Benny Theng, and Malayans Tan Eng Seong and Daniel Gunaratnam. Every year in December, the AF hosted an Asian Christmas dinner free of charge. Many non-AF members came. Shirley was the chief chef, while the boys served as her assistants and waiters. Back in Malaya, Shirley's family had servants and a cook. From memory of watching food preparation in her home kitchen, Shirley recreated curry and rice dishes. The event was a huge success and became an AF tradition. Shirley later said that she found the joy of serving the Lord at the AF and it never left her.

In 1958, the AF formed a committee: Robert president, Shirley secretary, Charles treasurer, Chin Far and others committee members. In early 1959, just before returning home after graduation, Robert represented the AF at a gathering of other overseas Christian fellowship groups at Cowes on Philip Island in Victoria. At this conference, the AF was asked to change its name to OCF Adelaide, to conform to the naming convention of similar groups in Brisbane, Sydney and Melbourne.

Brisbane

Timothy Sim, a final-year engineering student with boundless energy, had been thinking about how to bring overseas students to Christ and to train them as leaders with deep evangelical faith. On 14 June 1958, he gathered six other overseas Christian students in a small room in the centre of Brisbane.[5] They formed the Overseas Christian Fellowship (OCF) Brisbane and elected Timothy as chairperson.

Eighteen people attended their first meeting at the Vulture Street Baptist Church Hall in South Brisbane. Thereafter, OCF Brisbane met fortnightly and invited speakers from the China Inland Mission, the Graduates Fellowship and a general practitioner who clearly pointed to Christ. Regular attendance grew to forty people. They had Sunday afternoon Bible studies, picnics, boat outings, and tennis afternoons. Scripture Union and various churches hosted fellowship teas for overseas students and invited them to church camps.[6]

Sydney

In the mid-1950s, none of the student clubs appealed to Vincent Chia, a Sydney University architectural student. So, he

---

[5] *Overseas Christian Fellowship (Australia) Handbook* (1 ed., 1964), 14.
[6] *Year by Year: A Reverie by an Ancient OCFer* (Pamphlet), Produced by OCF Brisbane, June 1960. MTC/IVF 159-10-11/OCF2.

gathered other overseas students whom he had befriended on his sea voyage to Australia. They started a Christian fellowship group for overseas students, and organised it around singing, outings and Bible camps. As the first Christian in his family, Vincent had enjoyed these activities at the Bethesda Church in Singapore.

Gordon Blair had once attended Bethesda Church during his posting in Singapore. Likely through a Brethren church in Sydney, Gordon met Vincent and offered him free use of a hall near Sydney University for the club. Vincent asked if students would be required to attend any church or organisation in return. Gordon said there were no such requirements, and his offer was accepted. Vincent had a deep desire for independence due to the national movement in Singapore. His resolve was strengthened by the White Australia Policy. This policy had been introduced in 1901 'to limit non-British migration to Australia'.[7] Although laws were not as overtly discriminatory as they had once been, foreign property ownership was still forbidden, and some restaurateurs refused to serve Asians. At OCF, however, everyone was welcomed. Both overseas and local students enjoyed fellowship together, with much practical support from the Brethren church.

On 3 March 1957, Vincent and five other students officially formed the Overseas Christian Fellowship (OCF) of Sydney. Vincent Chia was elected as president and Eva Guan

---

[7] 'White Australia Policy,' National Museum Australia, accessed 19 Sept 2023, https://www.nma.gov.au/defining-moments/resources/white-australia-policy.

Chew, also from Singapore, as secretary. Guan Chew was studying Arts on a Colombo Plan scholarship, a British Commonwealth initiative.

Overseas students often came from the same cities in South East Asia, or met each other on the voyage to Australia. Somehow, through these informal connections, OCF Sydney invited other interstate overseas Christian student groups to their 1957 Bible Camp at Toukley.[8] The delegates from around Australia had such a wonderful time that the idea of working together was born.[9]

First OCF Sydney committee. Vincent Chia is in the back row, on the far right.

In mid-1958, Eva wrote in the OCF Sydney newsletter, 'Gordon Blair: A very dear friend of the OCF has been called home to be with the Lord. Mr Blair has been a great help in

---

[8] *OCF Sydney 1957-2007* (OCF Sydney Alumni, Sydney, 2007) 2.
[9] Edward Cheah, 'Hitherto and whither to?' *Search*, OCF Melbourne, 1959.

the formation of the OCF (Sydney) and also a great encourager. The group would like to express our deepest sympathy to the Blair family.'[10]

In 1958, medical student Edmund Lim became chairperson. OCF Sydney formalised its structure and adopted a constitution with a more missional focus. They had excellent speakers, many from the Inter Varsity Fellowship (IVF). Members grew in their faith. By the end of the year, meetings drew over fifty people. Although most were university students, there were also nurses, matriculation and college students.[11]

Melbourne

In the early-1950s, engineering student Edward Cheah regularly attended lunchtime Evangelical Union (EU) lectures on Tuesdays. He had been raised by godly Christian parents in Penang. Part-way through his university studies, Edward moved into the Overseas Students' Hostel, an old Victorian mansion on Queensberry Street, Carlton. The Church Missionary Society (CMS) had opened the hostel in 1954 to provide a centre for overseas students to live and study in a homely Christian atmosphere.[12] In the evenings, students

---

[10] Eva Chew, *OCF Sydney Newsletter*, 1958. MTC /IVF 159-11-12/ Overseas Students.

[11] Colin Lee, 'The History of OCF,' *The Mustard Seed*, OCF Sydney, 1983.

[12] Keith Cole, *The History of the Church Missionary Society of Australia* (Melbourne: Church Missionary Historical Publications Trust, Victoria, 1971), 250.

often gathered in the lounge for a warm drink before bed. The warden and his wife would read a portion of Scripture and pray with Christian students.[13] At this time, Edward felt that something should be done to care for the overseas Christians in Melbourne.

In 1957, Ian Burnard, formerly from Adelaide University Evangelical Union, joined the IVF staff team at Melbourne Uni. He befriended Edward Cheah and some students, including Betty Tan. On 8 March, ten overseas students met informally with Ian. The students decided to gather regularly for Bible studies and prayer as the best way to reach other overseas students. They called themselves OCF Melbourne and met at the CMS Hostel. The Anglican minister at St Jude's Carlton, Rev Jock Ryan, was a great friend and spiritual supporter. He often ate with them and would share devotions before their meals.

One of the earliest outings of OCF Melbourne, an outing to Geelong. Photo supplied by Clive Murdoch.

---

[13] Edward Cheah, Interview by Joshua Sim and author, 2021.

Daniel seated in the centre. Photo taken at his farewell at St Jude's church. Photo supplied by Clive Murdoch.

At OCF Melbourne's second meeting, a Vietnamese commerce student, Daniel Vu, announced that he had decided to follow Jesus. This encouraged the group tremendously. Yang Soo Suan, a Singaporean architectural student at the time recalled:

> He [Daniel] came to OCF during its formative years when the number [of members] was small. He participated wholeheartedly in most, maybe all activities of worship, fellowship, talks and Bible studies. From memory, he could be the only Vietnamese among the tight-knit community of overseas students. Because of the growing conflicts in Vietnam, he was singled out for special attention and care. He was well-liked within the fellowship and was

given an extraordinary farewell party (as seen in the photo), when he decided to return home amidst the escalating conflict between north and south Vietnam, when many of his compatriots chose to stay [in Australia].[14]

Many years after south Vietnam fell to the north, Soo Suan reconnected with Daniel who had managed to escape to the United States.

Some Australians also became Christians through OCF Melbourne, including a young man from rural Victoria, Clive Murdoch. He attended the meetings because they were held at the CMS hostel where he boarded. He remembered that as the OCF meetings became more popular, desks had to be pushed back to the rear of the room to make more space.[15]

When OCF Melbourne outgrew the CMS hostel, they moved to the Campaigners for Christ's fellowship room in Carlton. Regular Sunday afternoon meetings drew Christians and non-Christians. Occasional picnics and snow trips attracted even more people. At the end of these outings, a speaker would deliver a short message and give thanks for their enjoyable time together. At the start of each academic year, members met as many new arrivals as possible at the train station and invited them to the special Freshers' Welcome. Eventually, OCF Melbourne elected a committee. On 22 March 1958, Rev Jock Ryan prayed for the nine newly elected committee members.

---

[14] Yang Soo Suan, Email to author, 14 October 2022.
[15] Clive Murdoch, Interview by author, 22 July 2022.

Some of these committee members then attended OCF Sydney's Easter Bible Camp at Toukley that year. They returned with an enlarged vision of what might be possible if overseas Christian students around Australia worked together. In the spirit of collaboration and fellowship, they invited interstate students to their summer camp to be held at Cowes in early 1959. Student leaders began thinking if this gathering might be an opportune time to form a national fellowship of overseas Christian students.

1957 gathering in Melbourne, in conjunction with visit of Malayan Prime Minister Tunku Abdul Rahman after the independence of Malaya. Front row, from left: Betty Tan (5th), Lilian Ho (7th, who later became an IVF travelling staff worker), Edward Cheah (9th). Photo supplied by the Betty Tan via the OCF Alumni Network.

Section 1: Early Days, 1950s to early 1970s

In 1959, when our story officially begins, the centre of world power and knowledge lay in the west. Situated in the east, but identifying as a western nation, Australia was well-positioned to become a key education provider in Asia. Soon, overseas students began arriving. Some of them were Christians. Others became Christians in Australia. As a result, overseas Christian student groups sprung up in several cities. The leaders of these groups wanted to form a fellowship as they found that they had been blessed by meeting together.

At this time, there were only two Christian clubs in universities across Australia: the older Student Christian Movement, and the Inter Varsity Fellowship (IVF). Both groups wanted overseas students to join them, but neither had considered the possibility of the overseas students forming a separate group before. Indeed, most Australian Christians could not imagine any need that existing groups or churches could not meet. As such, there was scepticism towards the idea of an overseas Christian student group. Fortunately, students had the encouragement and support of a few key Australians, including early staff workers of the IVF. Once formed, the ideas and efforts of overseas students, with the input from Australian Christians, shaped the character of the new group.

This section tells the story of how OCF Australia grew from a handful of students to an established fellowship within roughly fifteen years. By the early 1970s, OCF had become well-known as a group that helped overseas students and equipped them for future service. Through service opportunities and participation at annual conventions, early members formed long-lasting friendships across Australia. The fruit of the ministry in this period has probably exceeded the expectations of even the most visionary of its founders.

1. Formation of OCF Australia

From 1956 to 1958, four overseas Christian student groups were established in Australia: Asian Fellowship in Adelaide, and Overseas Christian Fellowships in Brisbane, Sydney and Melbourne. These groups had little to do with each other until OCF Sydney invited the others to their camp at Toukley.[16] The students had such a great time of fun and fellowship that they began to imagine a national fellowship group to link all four groups.

OCF Melbourne returned Sydney's hospitality by inviting all interstate groups to their 1959 summer camp in Cowes, Philip Island. Student leaders wanted to create and formalise a national fellowship during the week-long camp. Each group came with ideas, some very strongly held, of what the group should be called and whether it should be affiliated with the Inter Varsity Fellowship (IVF). Achieving consensus in such a short time would prove a challenge.

---

[16] On p. 2 of *OCF (Sydney) 1957-2007* written by Colin Lee in 1982, the date of this first interstate camp is recorded as December 1957. However, p.6 of *Historical Notes—OCF (Melbourne) 1957-1977* compiled by Donald Burke, written by Loh Hoe Peng in 1969, records it as 1958. The Melbourne record further states 'As a result of the invitation of OCF in Sydney to join them at their Bible Camp in Easter, the adoption of the drafted Constitution was delayed until March, 1958.' Because of the earlier date of writing, and the detail about the commissioning, it is more likely that the interstate camp was in Easter 1958.

Cowes Convention

On Saturday, 31 January 1959, at Cowes on the southern tip of Victoria, over a hundred students, nurses and workers arrived for a week-long convention. Excited chatter filled the Cora Lynn guest house. After finding their rooms, students explored the beautiful beach nearby. Most of the young people were part of overseas student fellowship groups in Brisbane, Sydney, Melbourne and Adelaide.

Ian Burnard was in the crowd. He was an IVF staff member. The IVF General Secretary Charles Troutman regarded that it was essential that Ian attend. Charles hoped that any new overseas student group would seek affiliation with the IVF. They wanted to safeguard any new group against theological liberalism on one hand, and isolationism or exclusivism on the other. Some Australians felt that it was not good for the Asians to form their own group. However, in the short space of less than a year, Charles had been persuaded that God was at work. As recently as April 1958, Charles had written to Ian, 'this OCF is a mystery to me... I am doing my level best to find out who is behind it.'[17]

---

[17] Charles Troutman, Letter to Ian Burnard, 16 April 1958. MTC/Hercus Burnard 278-6/Burnard Correspondence from Troutman 1956-61.

Section 1: Early Days, 1950s to early 1970s

Registration Form for Cowes Convention 1959. MTC/IVF-159-10-11/OCF2.

Here are the three proposals which Oh and Charlie asked me to pass on to you. It was felt that at this stage it should be done unofficially, with the initiative coming from the A.F.. As the wording of these proposals were made up on the spur of the moment, I doubt whether they would remember the exact wording. However the thoughts expressed in them are held very firmly by the A.F. leaders.

Well here they are:
(1) Adelaide A.F. is ready to formally link up into an Australia wide organisation of Asian Christians.
(2) It is their wish that this organisation should be a member of the I.V.F. family.
(3) It is considered that (1) × (2) would have to take place at the same time.

They would very much like your advice as to what they should do. Oh in particular appreciates the problem very clearly. As he is leaving for home about March 59, it would be good if the details of the proposed organisation

could be thrashed out before then. His advice and help would be invaluable.

Undated correspondence circa October 1958 from Michael Thomas to Charles Troutman, IVF General Secretary. Michael explained that the AF leaders wanted to finalise the formation of a national body before Robert Oh left Australia in March 1959. Robert Oh was one of the founding leaders of the Asian Fellowship in Adelaide. MTC/Hercus Burnard 278-6/Burnard Correspondence from Troutman 1956-61.

organisation to be called the Austral-Asian Christian Fellowship, but the others favoured the name OCF Australia. Secondly, views differed over affiliation with the IVF. Edward saw the need for a chairperson other than himself. He approached Lawrence Chia, an undergraduate from Sydney University. Lawrence agreed and Edward briefed him.

In fact, Lawrence already knew of some of the issues at hand. As the Sydney University Evangelical Union (EU) president, he had been privy to discussions within the IVF over the past year on the topic of affiliation. Lawrence had read Charles Troutman's draft letter to overseas student leaders on the topic of affiliation.

In Charles's words, Lawrence 'felt that the Asians might take exception to its bluntness. This of course, is simply the difference between East and West as I tried my level best to be clear and open.'[19] In reality, Lawrence understood how his people felt about Western colonialism and superiority, perceived or otherwise. He knew that the main barrier to affiliation was the fear of losing autonomy. Despite Lawrence's youth, Charles took onboard his feedback. (Later, he asked Lawrence to check his letters to the Asians beforehand.) The letter that Charles eventually sent Adelaide student leader Eng Seong contained the following five points.

1. An understanding that affiliation will be on the basis of OCF having the same Doctrinal Basis as IVF Australia, and the purpose of the organisation will be similar, to reach out to other students.

---

[19] Charles Troutman, Letter to Ian Burnard, 8 Dec 1958. MTC/Hercus Burnard 278-6, Burnard Correspondence from Troutman 1956-61.

In June 1958, Eva Guan Chew of Sydney wrote to Charles and raised the possibility of IVF and OCF working together. A few months later, in response to a letter from Tan Eng Seong in Adelaide, Charles had replied, 'Your suggestion that the OCF might be affiliated with the Australian IVF seems to be a very happy solution to the problem of Asian students in Australia. This matter has been exercising our minds and we have given a good deal of prayer to it for some time. When the Asian Fellowship was formed in Adelaide several years ago, we felt that the Lord was beginning to give an answer to our prayers for a more effective means of helping our Asian friends. There seems to be a limit to what Australian folk can do without the assistance of Christian Asians.'[18] In the lead-up to the convention, student leaders from other states had also been holding meetings, writing letters, and thinking about a national body. By January 1959, most of them had opinions on how this ought to be achieved.

Negotiations over name and affiliation

At Cowes, student leaders met at night after the official program to talk about the formation of a pan-Australia body of overseas Christian students. Edward Cheah from OCF Melbourne chaired the closed-door meeting. Each group sent two leaders as representatives. As the meeting dragged on, two obstacles became apparent. Firstly, Adelaide wanted the

---

[18] Charles Troutman, Letter to Tan Eng Seong, 21 Nov 1958. MTC/158/11-12.

2. The IVF felt that the OCF Australia should have actual representation on the IVF General Committee on the same basis as EU presidents, whereby the OCF Australia chairperson will automatically become a member of the IVF General Committee.

3. The IVF encouraged the OCF to focus on universities, colleges and hospitals (presumably for nursing students). The reason was because the IVF considered the universities to be the most difficult field, and other groups were already working in schools.

4. The IVF urged local OCF centres to work closely with local EUs, for example by having an OCF representative on EU committees and vice versa. 'Please understand that we are not asking that you cooperate with us, but as an equal member of the IVF family, that we cooperate together in order that the Spirit of God might work mightily in our midst.'

5. The IVF counselled OCF to keep OCF truly overseas and not dominated by any national group.[20]

With this contextual understanding, Lawrence sat down at the table with other student leaders. At this second meeting, Edward introduced Lawrence as a suitable chairperson: an Asian familiar with OCF, but not an OCF leader. Everyone accepted this. Lawrence's role as EU president had given him an understanding of how to work

---

[20] Charles Troutman, Letter to Tan Eng Seong, 21 Nov 1958. MTC/IVF 159-11-12/Overseas Students.

*Lawrence Chia, circa 1959.
Photo supplied by Clive Murdoch.*

with people, step by step, to bring them together. He began by saying, 'How wonderful it is that God has given you a common vision and burden to reach out to other overseas students and build them up in the faith.' They paused to rejoice in this. Then he continued, 'Your groups have been firmly evangelical from the start, and it will be good to ensure that any organisation that you form will remain evangelical. We all want to be faithful, but how will we know that we are faithful? Part of the constitution is the doctrinal statement, which are rules for us to test our thinking, to ensure that we remain faithful to the Word of God.' Most of the leaders had had encounters with the theologically liberal Student Christian Movement (SCM), which had been trying to win over overseas students. Despite this, Sydney did not see the need for a doctrinal statement or a constitution. Some were from the Brethren church that did not use such documents. Nonetheless, as the Sydney leaders saw its importance to the others, they acquiesced.

With consensus over the constitution and doctrinal statement, discussions moved on to the name. Adelaide felt very strongly that this should be the Austral-Asian Christian

Fellowship, and that it should be affiliated to the IVF. They regarded affiliation essential to the viability of a student organisation with transient membership. They believed that the IVF could provide experience, support, and maybe also a person to travel around the different local centres to establish close ties, something which would be beyond the capability and time available to most students.[21] Melbourne also wanted affiliation. Sydney opposed it. Brisbane was undecided. The leaders faced an impasse. In a 2020 interview, Lawrence recalled how he met with the Adelaide leaders privately to find a way through:

> We talked about our common EU background and all that. I talked to them about the challenges of liberalism. They know it because my cousin became the Adelaide Chairman of SCM and they knew about it, you see. They were burdened enough to recognise the nature of our evangelicalism. I pitched it to the strong Adelaide leaders that our real battle is to get OCF Australia affiliated to IVF, to have a provision for Australian affiliates. You and the leaders of Melbourne and Brisbane are up for it, but Sydney is against it. The only way to win them is for you guys to speak up. But before you guys speak up, you can score points over the others on your generosity. I said, you're uniquely placed to show how generous you guys are, by giving up on your name. After much prayerful persuasion outside of the committee, we agreed. That night when we talked about the name, Adelaide offered and said 'okay, we are willing'. We

---

[21] Tan Eng Seong, Letter to Charles Troutman, 23 Sept 1958. MTC/IVF 159/10-11/OCF1.

compromised. Adelaide OCF could continue to call themselves AF in South Australia, we won't insist that because you are affiliated to the parent body of OCF, your name must change.[22]

Agreement on the name was a big win. Discussions then moved on to the most contentious point: affiliation with the IVF. On Thursday, the second-last night of the convention, the student leaders invited Ian Burnard to give a ten-minute explanation of the structure of the IVF. Ian explained that the IVF was the umbrella body over Christian groups in institutes of higher learning around Australia. All affiliates retained their autonomy. The IVF supported them through appointed staff who travelled to minister to each group as requested.

That night, Ian wrote to Charles, 'We are having a good time here, although we are having to wait and see what the Lord is doing—though this is normal of course. There are quite a few non-Christians here and a joy to yarn with some and see the Lord at work. Merlin [an Australian student, soon to be staff worker] and I have kept in the background quite a lot and it has been good just to watch how the Asians are handling things. With reference to OCF Australia wide matters the Adelaide folk are having to take quite a battering, but they are tremendously gracious and I think that the Lord is giving all a vision of what He wants which will transcend differences.'[23]

---

[22] Lawrence Chia, Interview by Joshua Sim and John Kiew, 2020.
[23] Ian Burnard, Letter to Charles Troutman, 5 Feb 1959. MTC/IVF159/24/Burnard Ian 1959-60.

Finally, Sydney agreed to affiliation with the IVF. On the last night of the convention, Friday 5 Feb 1959, the AF President Charles Aw announced that OCF Australia had been formed with four founding centres: Brisbane, Melbourne, Sydney and Adelaide. All the convention delegates received the news with joy. With leaders working in humility and unity, OCF and AF members could look forward to more joint events.

Indeed, the past week had been memorable. Every morning, the Vice Principal of the Melbourne Bible Institute Rev R V Merritt had spoken on 'Who exactly is Jesus Christ?' Small-group discussions were enlivened by the varied backgrounds of the delegates: Christians and non-Christians; students and graduates; Malayans, Singaporeans, Hong Kongers, Ceylonese, Fijians, South Vietnamese, and Australians. Games and sport filled the afternoons. One night they watched fairy penguins come in from the sea, and another, they staged an impromptu concert. Evangelist Leighton Ford presented the gospel message on Thursday night. Five students and nine Cowes residents became Christians.

All this pointed to increased effectiveness of united Christian witness. In July that year, Edward Cheah wrote an article for the OCF Melbourne newsletter *Search*. He acknowledged the faithful support of Australians since the end of the war. The newsletter also went out to churches in Asia, and sought their prayers because, 'The Lord has, as it were, planted us as your outposts for Him in Melbourne. We are entering into the work for you, where otherwise you could not reach. Some who have come to Melbourne as non-Christians will now return to you as Christians who shall take their stand with you in the service of Christ.'

God enabled founding student leaders to work through their differences to find common ground on what truly mattered. Asian Fellowship's early compromise on their preferred name paved the way for OCF Australia to be affiliated with the IVF. This affiliation connected OCF Australia to a widespread network of Christian churches, pastors and staff workers. Their early support and guidance ensured that OCF Australia was founded and centred in the person and work of Jesus Christ. This was achieved through wisdom, meekness and humility befitting of Christ's disciples, so that barriers were broken to bring about fellowship across Australia, between overseas students from different counties, studying in different states, and between Anglo-Celtic Australians and overseas students. Indirectly, it also connected Australian churches with churches around the world, but the full extent of this had yet to be realised.

2. Training Ground

OCF Australia had been formed on the last night of the 1959 Cowes Convention in February. Adelaide had been given the honour of hosting the first official OCF Australia convention and AGM, but office bearers would not be elected for another month. This was left up to the Asian Fellowship in Adelaide to arrange among themselves.

The administration processes and people required to run OCF Australia had yet to be put in place. This meant that a great deal of work remained to be done. For this, God had already prepared willing servants—young, inexperienced students to carry out the work, and older wiser mentors who saw their potential and guided them patiently. The mentors did not prescribe a particular way of doing things, rather, they accepted invitations to AGMs and conventions, gave counsel when asked, and modelled godly character.

The first OCF Australia convention and AGM

In December 1959, at the Adelaide Bible Institute in Victor Harbor, around twenty delegates gathered for the first OCF Australia Annual General Meeting (AGM). Panusunan Siregar, or Soen as he was known to friends, chaired the meeting. He had succeeded Charles Aw as the OCF Australia chairperson in mid-August, after the Asian Fellowship AGM. (The leader of the AF and the leader of OCF Australia were one and the same in this first year.)

Charles Aw in Adelaide, 25 February 1961. Photo supplied by Helena Stretton.

Soen was a fourth-year engineering student. Less than two weeks before the AGM, he wrote to Charles Troutman, asking if one of the IVF staff workers could attend the OCF AGM: 'We feel strongly the need of an experienced person to help us. We are thinking of the possibility of an IVF staff worker to join us. … I realise now that I should have written to you much earlier about this matter. This is part of my inexperience, and I am sure that you will understand and forgive.'[24] Soen's confidence in a gracious response was likely due to prior positive experience in relating to Charles and Ian, but also because he believed that this role was God's chosen means to train him.

A highlight of the first AGM was welcoming OCF Perth to fellowship. Two brothers, Paul Phua and Phua Seng Min, represented the new centre. Since May, a small group had been meeting fortnightly on Saturday afternoons. The impetus had come from awakened concern for Asians in

---

[24] Panusunan Siregar, Letter to Charles Troutman, 15 Dec 1959. MTC/IVF 159/10-11/OCF1.

Perth after the Billy Graham evangelistic rallies. The brothers had organised a meeting with eight other overseas students and six Australians from local churches and the Perth Evangelical Union. All shared a desire to reach out to overseas students, not only in universities, but also those in secondary schools, and technical and nursing colleges. [25]

After the AGM, the delegates returned to Adelaide for the first official OCF convention held in the magnificent surrounds of St Peter's College. The convention theme was 'Preparing now in Australia to serve Jesus Christ overseas'. For the past year, the convention planning team had met in the home of Dr Harrold and Gwenda Steward who had returned from Indonesia. Dr Steward was the Honorary Secretary of the planning committee. The experience and local connection of the Stewards helped greatly. Gwenda insisted that the convention begin no earlier than 29 December when markets reopened after Christmas, 'otherwise fruit and vegetables would barely be edible'. China Inland Missions (CIM) home director, J Oswald Sanders, and Adelaide Bible Institute (ABI) principal, Rev Allan Burrow, delivered the main messages. The Australian Broadcasting Commission recorded the OCF choir under the direction of Lilian Ho and broadcasted it during their Sunday half-hour segment 'Hymns We Love.'

At the end of the convention, students came forward before the whole group to share what the Lord had done for them. This Testimony Meeting made a strong impression on Charles Troutman. He wrote to thank Harrold and Gwenda

---

[25] Paul Phua and Phua Seng Min, Written interview, July 2021.

The first OCF Australia convention at St Peter's College, Adelaide in the summer of 1959/1960.

for their help and expressed gratitude over 'how much the Spirit of God was doing in so many lives'. Troutman also wrote, 'In spite of the Colombo Plan officials and the statements of the SCM, I believe that God has a work to do among Asians through Asians that cannot be done by their assimilation in the life of Australians. I was particularly impressed by the way in which a number of the men whom I knew to be shy in the presence of the Sydney EU were leaders and their freedom was wonderful to behold.'[26]

---

[26] Charles Troutman, Letter to Harrold and Gwenda Steward, 18 Jan 1960. MTC/IVF 159/10-11/OCF1.

Section 1: Early Days, 1950s to early 1970s

Privilege of Planning, Great Honour of Chairing

For a student's perspective, we have an article by Soen Siregar. He won a prize in an OCF essay competition for this article, which was published in the OCF Australia newsletter of 1964.

Asian Fellowship Committee Retreat 26 August 1961. Soen Siregar is seated in the front row, far right. Photo supplied by Helena Stretton (standing, far left).

A Time to Seek and A Time to Discover
By Panusunan Z. Siregar

Adelaide, Australia

31 August 1963

Until something happened that winter afternoon in 1958, I had no serious ambition. Sitting beneath a rugged eucalyptus tree in a rich farming district, 60 miles from Adelaide, South Australia, suddenly I knew: I wanted to be a dog ...

At the top of a hill on that sunny afternoon, I watched a middle-aged farmer directing his sheepdogs which controlled and guided hundreds of sheep moving along the green wide valley. As the farmer raised his hand he whistled, and the dog ran ahead to restrain a group of sheep from wandering. At another signal the dog moved quickly to the front to prevent the whole flock from going in a wrong direction. I noticed, too, that a dog would just rest, observe, and wait for instruction from the master. Hearing a whistle, the dog jumped to his feet and chased those sheep lagging behind eating grass.

It was the first time I had seen sheepdogs in action. They had been properly trained to understand the master's instructions because they knew just what to do. With their ability to run and bark, the instructions were carried out efficiently. They were so faithful, yet it seemed they were so content and free in their tasks, obviously enjoying themselves. So fascinated was I, that I forgot to read the Bible open beside me. I had been praying with the Psalmist from Psalm 25:

Show me your ways, LORD,

　teach me thy paths.

Guide me in your truth and teach me,

　for you are God my Savior,

and my hope is in you all day long.[27]

Twenty months before, I had received Jesus Christ as my Saviour and Lord, at a suburban church in Adelaide. I thought back further to my childhood, spent at a small town nestling 5000 feet above sea level on the western slope of the 'Barisan' Ranges in North Sumatra. In this predominantly strict Moslem region, I was brought up by my godly Christian parents. Most of our relatives were Moslem. There I learned that to be a Christian meant persecution. On Sundays as we passed the Moslem district on our way to Sunday School, the children often scorned and blasphemed the Name of Jesus. At school, children of Christians were sometimes abused, and I was always frightened of walking past the huge dominating mosque on my way to school every morning.

At the prime of his life, my father turned down an offer from the Dutch 'Controlleur', who wanted him to be the mayor of our town. It would be wonderful, of course, to have a capable Christian mayor to rule a predominantly Moslem town. And with this important position and a high salary, he would be able to send his children to Dutch schools. But my father realised that

---

[27] Psalm 25:4-5.

this was Satan's temptation, because he had heard the call to full-time Christian service.

At the age of 35, he entered a theological seminary to be trained as a pioneer pastor. From my father, I learned that being a Christian does not only mean suffering persecution for the Saviour, but also renouncing those things the world holds precious. Even in my childhood, I saw the reality of the cross a Christian must bear. It seemed heavy and costly.

It was only three weeks after my fifteenth birthday, on his deathbed after a year of illness, that my father comforted my mother for the last time. My father told me how he had seen the Lord, and he knew he was going to be with him. Father assured mother of the Lord's promise that he would take care of her and all the children. There in that room, where as a small boy I used to sleep, I sensed the reality of eternal life. My father had gone to a better Home and we will meet him again. I did not cry; I even went to school to sit for an examination for the Intermediate High School certificate.

Three years later I returned home from the provincial capital with the Senior High School certificate and a promise of a scholarship to study at any University in Indonesia or perhaps overseas. The first thing my mother did was to gather everyone in the house for a prayer and thanksgiving meeting.

In late Spring 1955 I arrived in Adelaide to study engineering. For two years the Lord steered my life. Members of the Evangelical Union at the university invited me to their meetings and conferences. The Asian Fellowship (the Adelaide OCF) welcomed me warmly to their group. Another Christian *took me to church regularly. One afternoon at the university library I was struggling with a mathematics problem. The student sitting next to me came to my rescue. Then he took the opportunity to whisper a gospel verse, which even today speaks to me with great meaning and depth. Here it is paraphrased by Hugh Redwood:*

> *'God loves the world, Nicodemus; loves it so much that He has given His only Son to save it, so that no one who accepts Him shall be lost, but that this life which lasts, <u>which begins here and now bridges the grave,</u> should be open to all. God did not send His Son here to pronounce the world's doom: He has come so that the world, <u>if it will</u>, may be saved.' John 3:16.*

God's love overcame me. Three weeks before an annual examination, as I could no longer resist the Spirit of God, I faced the fact that before God I was a sinner. On that decision night, I received the Lord Jesus as my personal Saviour (John 1:12) and confessed him as my Lord (Rom. 10:9). As the preacher led us in prayer in that old stone building, for the first time in my life, I knew the reality of sins forgiven.

Under the eucalyptus tree the Holy Spirit showed me how unwilling I was to surrender my whole future to Jesus Christ. I wanted to know his plan for my life before I handed my future to him. The Lord wanted me to trust him completely. That afternoon I confessed this sin, asking him to forgive me, and to steer my life and my future. Then I realised that the Lord's service is not a burdensome but a joyous one. My relationship with my

Master would be like that of the sheepdog with the shepherd. I asked him to train me.

He took me at my word, for immediately he began to train me. In the same year with little experience in organisation and limited knowledge of English, the Lord entrusted me with the task of being president of our local OCF, and president of OCF Australia for several months. I had the privilege of helping to plan and organise the first OCF Australia annual convention in Adelaide, and the great honour to chair the first OCF Australia General Committee Meetings prior to the convention. The Lord taught me many lessons, which otherwise I would never have learned.

For the Saviour's sake Christians may face persecution. Many legitimate practices have to be given up for something more urgent. Likewise habits and practices not honouring to the Lord. Hobbies, time and money, friendship, reputation and the choice of a life partner, everything has to be laid on the Altar of God. When this you do, you will find as I have found, that the burden is light. Did not our Lord Himself say, 'Come to me. ... for my yoke is EASY and my burden is LIGHT'? (Matt. 11:29-30)

I still clearly remember what I learned on that warm winter afternoon five years ago. The sheepdogs were able to muster the sheep, because they were completely submissive to every command of their master. And every time I think of sheepdogs, they preach a sermon on 'Service' ... with their fascinating dog accent.

Soen Siregar's testimony points to a God who hears private prayers and sees surrendered hearts. OCF became a tool in God's hands to give students many opportunities to serve him. Through this, they developed in godly character and ministry skills. More mature Australian Christians mentored them. These older Christians recognised that the young overseas students had insights that they did not. Ian Burnard, for example, believed in learning from the students, before trying to teach them. He had observed how paternalism too often scuppered good intentions.[28] This understanding that both teacher and learner contribute to God's work caused genuine friendships to develop across age and cultural differences. And so, service to God in this training ground called OCF Australia became soul-enriching and deeply rewarding.

---

[28] Ian Burnard, Letter to Charles Troutman, 1961.

3. Strong Supporters

In the 1950s and 60s, overseas students in Australia did not own houses and not many had cars. They had little by way of assets and earthly resources. Although supportive, the IVF was also facing budgetary pressures.[29] The practical help of many Australian Christians provided valuable support, opening up many church halls and family homes where the overseas students could experience genuine Christian hospitality and friendship. However, it was not immediately apparent how the contribution of Australians could be welcomed while safeguarding OCF's commitment to overseas students.

Associate Members

In 1960, the OCF Sydney leadership made provisions for Australians to become associate members. This would enable Australians to contribute to the ministry. Associate members could participate in all aspects of the fellowship apart from taking up formal leadership positions.[30] This provision eventually became available in all centres.

In 1961, Charles Troutman wrote to the OCF Australia chairperson, Deo Narayan. Charles explained that the IVF feels 'the associate membership idea of the OCF is a very excellent one ... used of those individuals who are in hearty

---

[29] John and Moyra Prince, *Out of the Tower* (Sydney: ANZEA Publishers, 1987), 42.
[30] *OCF Sydney 1957-2007*, 4.

sympathy with the aims, purpose and basis of the OCF and whom the OCF wishes to assist them in their work of witness for Christ'.[31] This constitutional provision formalised a close working relationship that already existed. For example, the 1959 Cowes Convention committee comprised of three Australians and three Asians. Some of the Australians who were a great support in the OCF ministry are listed below.

Sydney

Since 1952, Mrs Irene Young had given herself wholeheartedly to the welfare of overseas students in her role as the honorary IVF Overseas Student Secretary. She and her husband Dr Geoffrey Young opened their Cheltenham home to new arrivals and hosted many gatherings there. She

Mrs Irene Young and the Young home at Cheltenham. Photos supplied by the OCF Alumni Network.

---

[31] Charles Troutman, Letter to Deo Narayan, 5 April 1961.

adapted and widely distributed a four-page booklet to help IVF students and graduates to connect with international students. It advocated personal friendship as the best way to connect, warned against a patronising manner, and suggested learning how to cook rice properly—even Australians would prefer this to glue![32] After OCF was formed, Mrs Young actively supported the ministry. An updated edition of the friendship booklet suggested that members of the Graduates Fellowship and Evangelical Union introduce overseas students to OCF meetings in whichever city they were in. She mobilised the Graduate Fellowship of NSW to host monthly Asian Teas at Moore College. After tea, some of the students walked to St Barnabas Church in Broadway for the evening university service. Through Irene, respected Australian Christians such as Bishop Marcus Loane, Harold Knight and Dr John Hercus became interested in OCF and spoke at meetings. Many OCF Sydney leaders, such as Bill Lee and Dante The, became family friends of the Youngs.

Martin and Helen Bullock came to know the Lord in January 1965. They felt that they needed to do more and expanded their Christian ministry to OCF. Martin was a railroad engineer and would try to get a good seat on the train for IVF travelling staff workers. The Bullocks hosted them at their Eastwood home. They befriended, counselled, and journeyed with many generations of OCF members. Other Anglo-Celtic Australians who supported OCF Sydney

---

[32] *Suggestions for Work with International Students* (Booklet prepared by IVCF, adapted by Mrs Irene Young, n.d.).

were Tony Nichols, Dr and Mrs Samuel Tout, Mr and Mrs John Sinclair, Alex Gilchrist, Eric Norgate and Eugenie Koppen.

Martin and Helen Bullock. Photo supplied by the OCF Alumni Network.

Several Australian-born Chinese also became associate members. A large cohort came from the Chinese Presbyterian Church Youth Group. Their youth leader Gilbert Sun gave his testimony at the 1959 convention in Adelaide, saying that unless you were born again, it was no good being on the church roll—you might as well be a sausage roll! Other CPC youth group members in OCF were John Ting and his cousin Jeannette Lin. Their families had migrated to Australia from Swatow, China.

In 1966, associate member Andrew Lu was serving actively in OCF Sydney but never considered the post of OCF Sydney president because he was not a full member. An introduction to the OCF Sydney committee described him in his role as the Men's Vice-President: '[Andrew] has often been accused of being an ABC (Australian-born Chinese), but in fact is an HKBCBUIA (Hong Kong born Chinese, brought up in Australia)'.[33] Australian demographics—nationality and ethnicity, countries of origin and upbringing—were becoming more complex.

Brisbane

In 1960, OCF Brisbane had twenty-six full members and fourteen associate members, including Bruce Winter who worked with the Queensland government.[34] From the mid-

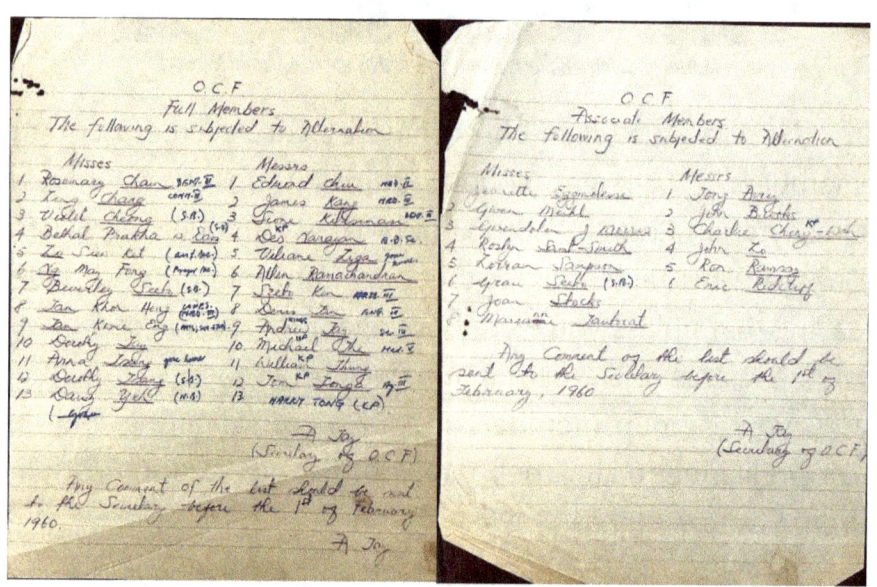

The 1960 OCF Brisbane full and associate membership lists. From the papers of Lawrence Chia.

---

[33] 'Notes of the 1966 Executive Committee,' *OCF Sydney News Magazine*, August 1966, 7. Note that this refers to the OCF Sydney committee, not the OCF Australia EXCO. MTC/1VF 159-11a/OCF 1965-7.

[34] Andrew Tay, Secretary of OCF Brisbane, 'Membership List 1960'.

60s, OCF Brisbane used to meet at Bruce Winter's flat, which was opposite the church in Kangaroo Point. Bruce was not a clergyman but worked with the Queensland government. OCF members would have fellowship tea after Bible studies at Bruce's flat, then adjourn to the church for their service.[35] Several lecturers at the University of Queensland were regular speakers at OCF Brisbane and great supporters: Professor Wilson (Geology), Professor Randle-Short (Child Health), and Dr O'Connor (Engineering).

Adelaide

In Adelaide, there was a particularly close relationship between the Asian and Australian students. Many Christian university students were members of both the EU and the AF. As the EU met on weekdays, and the AF on weekends, there were no program clashes.

When Adelaide organised the 1964 convention, six out of the nineteen convention committee members were Australians. Graeme Swincer was the transport officer. He had previously served as the overseas student secretary on the AF committee. His parents had a farm near Victor Harbor where they hosted large picnics for overseas students. Graeme's mother Mrs Joyce Swincer even took in students, overwhelmed by the anxieties and pressures of study, to recuperate at the farm.

---

[35] Wong Toh Sing, Interview with author, 2021.

Doug Swincer and Joyce Swincer hosting Asian Fellowship students at their farm in Victor Harbor.

The domestic supervisor on the convention committee was Helena Stretton. She found it exciting to work with so many overseas students. In the first Bible she had been given as a child, she had pasted a picture of Jesus surrounded by children from various countries. However, the world she grew up in bore little resemblance to that picture. In her primary school, she had known only one person from a different culture, a Chinese girl, whose family owned a grocery shop. Try as Helena did, she was unable to get to know the girl very fully. For Helena, it was a joy to meet so many Asians at university, and then to work closely with them.[36] Graeme and Helena continued in cross-cultural ministry beyond their university days.

Melbourne

Don Burke and Clive Murdoch were associate members who were firm friends with many OCF Melbourne members and an integral part of the group for many years. Both were keen photographers. Don compiled the history of OCF Melbourne into the 1970s, while Clive often recorded messages or AGM proceedings.

Harold McCracken and his wife Beth met several OCF members when they offered to drive students to a picnic at the Maroondah Dam organised by the Australian Asian Society in Victoria. One of the students, Jennie Ong, wrote that it opened up a friendship of more than thirty years with

---

[36] Helena Stretton, Interview with author and Goh Shu Xuan, 2020.

From left: Heather McCracken, Beth McCracken, Harold McCracken, Mrs Yap, Mrs Choo, Choo Seow Hung.

OCF Melbourne Committee circa 1960s. Clive Murdoch is in the front.

the couple. Harold would help students who faced any hiccups with their visas. Other Australians who were involved in OCF Melbourne were Rodney and Janet Lee, and Ralph Davies, a successful businessman in Melbourne who was also on the Borneo Evangelical Mission Home Council.

Australian associate members included students and non-students. Many of the people listed above were associate members, though it is not known if all of them formally took up membership. The Australian supporters of the ministry related to overseas students on the basis of Christian friendship, and often through the family unit. These friendships often continued well beyond student days, even to the end of their earthly lives. Many overseas students called them their Australian mum and dad.

Staff Workers

In 1960, the IVF had five staff workers. The General Secretary Charles Troutman was based in Sydney, and the other four staff workers including Ian Burnard travelled around Australia to minister to affiliate fellowship groups. Because of this, they were sometimes called travelling staff workers, to distinguish them from residential staff workers based in one city.

OCF leaders as honorary IVF travelling staff workers

In view of the growing work among overseas students, the IVF sought to employ an additional staff worker from India, through their connection with the International Fellowship of Evangelical Students. When that proved unsuccessful, they invited Lawrence Chia to fill the role during the holidays. Lawrence agreed but declined a salary. He asked only for the reimbursement of travel expenses.

Lawrence spent the summer of 1959/60 helping OCF committees in the various states. Since October 1959, a small group of overseas students had been meeting in Geelong. Lawrence travelled there to encourage them. He advised them on effective organisation and encouraged them to consider affiliation with OCF Australia. He put them in touch with Australian Christians. They were eventually affiliated in 1961. However, low attendance and a high leadership turnover led to its dissolution three years later. In the 1980s, OCF Geelong was reaffiliated, enjoyed a period of remarkable Spirit-filled gospel life, and then dissolved again. In the years to come, it would become evident that this was the nature of OCF: transient and affected by many internal and external factors. Despite this, like flowers in the desert, the possibility of new life was ever present.

The arrangement with Lawrence worked so well that the IVF also appointed Tan Eng Seong and Eva Chew as travelling staff workers in 1960. Eng Seong had recently graduated as an engineer and travelled when his work schedule permitted.

(The Australian government allowed overseas graduates to stay on for a year for internships and to gain work experience.) The precedence of not drawing a salary, made it possible for the IVF to make more appointments, as staff worker salaries were the responsibility of IVF members. (Ian used to encourage every student to donate one day's wages each year for this purpose.) The salaries were modest, and staff workers were guests of whichever fellowship group that invited them. It was their responsibility and privilege to meet staff workers at the station, house them and exercise Christian hospitality. Although the OCF appointees were not dedicated OCF staff workers, Ian recognised their giftings, and freed them to spend most of their time with OCF. Still, wherever possible, they met up with EU committees and leaders.

Later, Lilian Ho and Judy Ho (not related) from OCF Melbourne also served as travelling staff workers. Lillian was a Colombo Plan scholar, studying to be a music teacher. She wrote many of the early convention theme songs. In 1961, Lilian wrote to Charles from Brisbane. 'There is a great need here for personal work among the girls and there are two or three very keen ones, though they themselves are very young in the faith. Apart from the bi-monthly Bible studies to which very few turn up, very little encouragement has been given in the direction of e.g., the Quiet Time and individual Bible study. Please pray that the Lord will give me the wisdom and tact to guide them and encourage them.'³⁷ Charles urged her to 'take something of a spiritual responsibility for the groups you have visited and particular individuals with whom you can keep in touch by correspondence.'³⁸

Judy was a Melbourne nursing graduate who was going to further her studies in Sydney, training to be a midwife. Before starting her midwifery course, she spent time in Adelaide where she stayed with the Stewards. As a travelling staff worker, she visited various local churches, encouraging female overseas students to join AF. Her effectiveness was evident when the AF became known for its strong female leaders a few years later, including people such as Ling Ai Mee, Ivy Goh, Lily Loy, Tan Cheng Seh and Linda Aw.³⁹

On 1 February 1962, Judy wrote to Ian. 'Our Lord continues to be very precious and a help to me. I am enjoying the work very much. To be very frank with you, I do not know how much help I am giving the AF and ANCM [Australian Nurses Christian Movement] and EU. But our Father has taught me a great many things. To listen patiently and come in and at the right time and with the right word to say. I feel His presence so near. I have never been so surprised in my life before. The members seem to have so many things to ask and so many problems. Many of them I have never thought before, or heard of. But He is able and sufficient in all things.'

---

³⁷ Lillian Ho, Letter to Ian Burnard, 2 Feb 1961. MTC/IVF 159-10-11/Staffworkers 1959-61.

³⁸ Charles Troutman, Letter to Lillian Ho, 7 Feb 1961. MTC/IVF 159-10-11/Staffworkers 1959-61.

³⁹ Shen Dah Cheong, Interview with author and Timothy Lim, 2021.

Section 1: Early Days, 1950s to early 1970s

*Judy Ho's graduation in 1958, Melbourne.
From left: Wee Kwong Ming (neé Chong, 1st), Judy Ho (2nd), Theresa Ho(4th).*

For travelling graduates, this brief period between their student days and their eventual professions—scientists, midwives, engineers, architects—was productive and rewarding. It showed them how they could minister effectively to others in the body of Christ. For many, it also gave them a sense of lifelong mission, serving God, wherever they were, with whatever knowledge and skill they had.

The 1960 convention hymn composed by Lilian Ho. She often conducted the OCF choir and wrote many of the early convention hymns.

The Student Christian Movement and OCF

In May 1961, the Australian Council of Churches (ACC) held a consultation on Christian Work Among Students at the University of Melbourne. The ACC supported the Student Christian Movement, rather than the Inter Varsity Fellowship (IVF) or the Evangelical Unions (EU). The IVF saw this as an attempt to force the EU to give up their evangelical position. Despite OCF's affiliation with the IVF, the Australian Council of Churches invited OCF separately and insisted that they should attend. OCF Australia wanted to attend to safeguard their position in the event that the ACC controlled the work in the universities in the future.[40] Charles Troutman believed that the four senior Christian leaders representing the IVF—Bishop Marcus Loane, Professor Malcolm Jeeves, Rev Don Robison and himself—were better equipped to represent OCF. However, he conceded that since OCF Australia had been invited, they were free to attend.[41]

Caught between two Christian groups, each advising a different course of action, the EXCO decided to attend, but as observers only. After informing Charles of this decision, the OCF Australia secretary Edmond confessed to feeling 'extremely inexperienced and totally inadequate' because

---

[40] Edmond Chui, Letter to Charles Troutman, 30 March 1961. MTC/IVF 159-10-11/OCF3.

[41] Charles Troutman, Letter to Edmond Chui, 10 April 1961. MTC/IVF 159-10-11/OCF3.

'there are much more facets involved in this than just the matter of representation.' He asked Charles to advise him in a personal capacity, if Charles felt restricted because of OCF's constitutional autonomy. Charles elaborated on the pressures that the Student Christian Movement were exerting and advised them not to give their answer until they spoke to Ian. Ian flew to Brisbane—foregoing the cheaper rail option—to speak to Edmond in person. On 3 May, the EXCO reversed their decision. OCF Australia did not attend the consultation.[42]

IVF residential staff helped OCF members negotiate situations that were beyond them. Relationships built on mutual respect enabled the IVF staff to contribute without compromising OCF's organisational autonomy. Students took on board counsel because it made sense, and they respected the staff. Residential staff also guided younger travelling staff, provided pastoral care, listened and made suggestions specific to situations they faced.

In 1964, there were four travelling staff workers: Lee Bee Im, Shen Dah Cheong, Phua Seng Min and Guan Chew. Between them they attended the IFES conference in Hong Kong, and local OCF centres in Perth, Adelaide, Brisbane, Melbourne and Sydney. In the late 1960s, Dr Janet Plummer served OCF Australia as a staff worker for around a year. Previously, she had been a missionary in Hong Kong with the Church Missionary Society (CMS). On her return to Australia,

---

[42] Edmond Chui, Letter to Charles Troutman, 3 May 1961. MTC/IVF 159-10-11/OCF3.

the CMS released her to help serve in OCF. As a result, OCF Australia was strengthened. Despite being separated by vast distances, the visits, letters, and prayers of staff workers fostered close fellowship among local centres.

From left: Ian Burnard, Phua Seng Min, Han Ping, an OCF Sydney leader in the 1960s.

As an organisation, OCF Australia was a very simple entity: overseas student groups from several cities that came together annually and took turns to form a national EXCO. Yet, it grew quickly, and had a long-lasting impact on many members. The support of associate members played a crucial role. In all the cities where OCF centres had been established, Australian Christians could contribute to the ministry in many different ways, according to their giftings, from cooking to preaching, from legal advice to counselling. At the same time, the formal leadership remained with full members. This ensured that OCF remained relevant and focused on its ministry to overseas students. And so, OCF Australia quickly became established as a place where overseas students could find help, a place to belong, and friendship with locals and other overseas students.

A further innovation that strengthened the ministry was the creation of honorary travelling staff workers under the banner of the IVF but made up of OCF senior students or graduates. These young men and women, who had themselves been blessed through the ministry of OCF, travelled from centre to centre and served according to what the local committees asked of them. The sacrifice of time, money and maybe comfort, was amply rewarded through seeing God at work through them, a sense of wonder at this, and much joy and friendship.

4. Vision and Leadership

Within five years, the ministry of OCF Australia had established steady organisational rhythms and patterns. It would have seemed so to members, who could look forward to weekly meetings and the highlight of every year—the annual OCF convention, which typically drew 200 to 300 delegates.

Leaders, on the other hand, were thinking about how to improve and what might lie ahead. The Inter Varsity Fellowship (IVF) staff and the OCF Australia leaders imagined different futures for the organisation. In a sense, all our human dreams of the future are presumptuous, and yet leaders must plan. Taking this a step further, spiritual leaders should motivate and rally God's people towards His purposes for them. How does one do this when only God knows the future?

Creation of the OCF Handbook

In July 1960, Ian Burnard wrote to Charles Troutman, 'There are two organisational things in which I think we can help the OCF at the moment. One is the almost redundant OCF Australia Committee.'[43] Three weeks later, Charles replied, 'The more I think about the OCF Australia committee, the

---

[43] Ian Burnard, Letter to Charles Troutman, 25 July 1960. MTC/IVF 159-24/Burnard Ian 1959-60.

more I feel that unless it organises the annual conference, there is not much point in it.'

Perhaps the IVF saw the OCF EXCO as an administrative body only because the Evangelical Unions (EU) did not have a similar committee. The EUs did not need one as the IVF General Committee looked after national administration and leadership. Various local EU, operating out of different universities or teachers' colleges, were affiliates of the IVF. In some places, these affiliates had different names such as Evangelical Students.

In Charles Troutman's view, the Asian Fellowship (AF) had been formed as 'a department or sub-committee of the Adelaide University EU', because the 'grads had been unable to meet the needs of Asian students in Adelaide.' Since then, OCF Australia had affiliated with the IVF. Like other affiliates, it was an autonomous group. The IVF had given encouragement and every support to OCF Australia, and the results had exceeded expectations.[44]

After Ian attended the 1960 AGM at the end of the year, he realised that, unlike other IVF affiliates, OCF did not have the resources of an alumni, such as the Graduate Fellowship, to draw on. Because of this, OCF had developed a drive, spirituality and organisational skills that were 'tremendously impressive'. He went on, 'On this fact alone I am convinced of the rightness of OCF being developed independently of the EUs. Very often I have reservations about too great a

---

[44] Charles Troutman, Letter to Ian Burnard, 16 August 1960. MTC/IVF 159-24/Burnard Ian 1959-60.

separation of EU and OCF (and this concern needs to remain; especially with respect to the EUs) but the value of this must surely be that on their return home the OCFers continue to exercise this drive.'[45]

The word 'drive' was an apt one. It conjures images of cars and travel, momentum and leadership. In the mid-1960s, OCF leaders took the group further than what its founding members and the IVF had envisaged. This had not come about by high-level strategic planning, but by responding to the needs they observed and sought to meet. The 1963 OCF Australia president Shen Dah Cheong realised that the OCF was not just an arm of the IVF or the EU. He saw that OCF needed to articulate its identity and find a way to pass it on.

As noted earlier, the Australian Student Christian Movement (ASCM) was one of the two main interdenominational groups on Australian university campuses prior to the formation of OCF. The ASCM was the Australian branch of the World Student Christian Federation and existed as early as 1896 under different forms.[46] ASCM distinguished itself as a nondenominational movement, concerned with a range of social issues. A 1962 ASCM conference outlined the principle of 'maximum ecumenism', in which Christian groups should work together 'except where deep convictions compel separation'. There was a constant

---

[45] Ian Burnard, Letter to Charles Troutman, 29 December 1960. MTC/IVF 159-24/Burnard Ian 1959-60.

[46] 'Guide to the Records of the Australian Student Christian Movement', https://nla.gov.au/nla.obj-244226401/findingaid#nla-obj-244247683. Accessed 17 Aug 2023.

struggle to free itself from the influence of 'conservative evangelicals' and 'fundamentalists', which led to the split from IVF.[47]

The term ecumenism refers to a Christian commitment to the unity of all believers, in order to witness to and serve all humanity. In this sense, all Christians should be committed to ecumenism. However, biblical truths should not be sacrificed for the sake of enabling more groups to come under a 'Christian' banner.[48]

The Inter Varsity Fellowship of Evangelical Unions (Australia), or IVF, had been formed out of a disagreement with the SCM in three areas: the inspiration and authority of the Bible, the content of the gospel and the doctrine of the church. Charles Troutman wrote that when the ASCM began, it was evangelical because it reflected the theological stance of the day. But because there was nothing in its constitution to affirm the authority of Scriptures, it had lost its original vision and moorings.[49] As a result, the IVF was doctrinally focused. They viewed the SCM as a student movement for ecumenism, while they were a fellowship of believing students for evangelism.[50] However, despite their strengths in Bible teaching and sincere efforts, the gospel had not

---

[47] Renate Howe, *A Century of Influence: A History of the Australian Student Christian Movement 1896-1996* (Sydney: UNSW Press, 2009), 13, 196, 319, 348.

[48] 'Ecumenism', *The Encyclopedia of Protestantism* (New York: Routledge, 2004), 1143, 1144, 1149.

[49] Charles Troutman, 'General Secretary's Report' (IVF, 1958). MTC/IVF 159-27-28/Reports and Committee Papers 1948-68.

[50] *The IVF and SCM in Australia: A Brief History and Background,* Produced by the Inter Varsity Fellowship of Evangelical Unions (Australia), Sydney, August 1958.

gained significant headway among non-Christian overseas students on campus.

In contrast to the IVF, OCF had been formed by Christian overseas students who wanted to help other overseas students. They shared not only the gospel but their lives. Seniors knew how it felt to be bewildered by the strangeness of a new land. Anecdotes abound: dishes washed without rinsing off the suds. Some felt that sleeping between two sheets tucked in tight was very constricting compared to the single bedsheets and loose blankets that they were accustomed to. There was a student who had dry cornflakes for breakfast until he watched Australians pouring milk over their cornflakes the following day.

Mastering English was difficult, especially for those who had attended school in other languages. Even Dah Cheong, who had attended an English-medium secondary school, struggled to understand the Australian accent. Not understanding and not being understood led to all sorts of difficulties. It could make people feel inferior or appear timid and shy. Even if English was not a problem, many missed the sounds of their mother tongue. In Melbourne, Year 12 student Irene Yek tuned in to the radio just to hear Mandarin spoken. Fortunately, she found out about Friday night Mandarin Bible studies in an OCF household in Parkville. For two years, she travelled by train and tram to hear Brother Huang Ee Yuen teach from the epistle of Romans in

Mandarin. As not all OCF members understood Mandarin, Timothy Yung interpreted for Brother Huang.[51]

In the overseas student community, it became known that if you wanted help or friendship, go to OCF. Unlike national clubs, OCF welcomed people of all nationalities. National tensions and rivalries could be overcome in this community centred in Christ. Indonesian and Malayan members enjoyed fellowship despite the Confrontation, a conflict in Borneo from 1962 to 1966. Australian associate members opened their homes and churches to OCF, making local expertise and resources available. Older OCF members carried out this time-consuming work of care, looking out for younger members. OCF was like a big family of brothers and sisters.

This had been Dah Cheong's experience when he had arrived in Melbourne in 1959. He found OCF meetings homely and comfortable because they were put together specifically with overseas students in mind. Soon after, he moved into an OCF household, a narrow Victorian townhouse in Parkville. It was nicknamed the Borneo Longhouse because Dah Cheong and another housemate, Jonathan Lee, were from North Borneo. They learned to cook and clean, and to put up with one another's shortcomings.

Dah Cheong first served on the local OCF Melbourne committee, where he would greet each member at the door with a warm handshake. His memory for names was a great asset. His household hosted monthly OCF fellowship meals.

---

[51] *Pioneering with a Purpose*, (OCF Alumni Network, 2022), 63, 104.

The menu began featuring rabbit curry, passed off as tender chicken (rabbit was much cheaper than chicken at the Queen Victoria Market). Sometimes an observant sister-in-Christ asked why the 'chicken' had so many drumsticks!

Unlike the IVF which focused on university students, OCF was concerned for all overseas students, including high school students and nurses. OCF ministered to those who were outsiders, culturally speaking. By meeting the need for connection, OCF introduced many non-believers to Christ, and many Christians caught a vision of lifelong service to God.

OCF Melbourne committee retreat, April 1963, at Ferntree Gully Station. Shen Dah Cheong is in the front row, second from the right.

OCF Melbourne members singing on trip to Philip Island, 14 December 1963. Photos supplied by David Chong.

In 1963, Dah Cheong and his EXCO team took up a suggestion of Bill Lim, the previous OCF Australia chairperson, to publish an OCF handbook for every member. This would help to capture and pass on the OCF identity. The four EXCO members formed the editorial board. Although this was over and above their other duties, they approached the task with a sense of camaraderie and fun. The handbook took two years to complete. Because of this, EXCO remained under Dah Cheong's leadership in Victoria for a second year. This enabled the EXCO to finish the handbook and to lay strong foundations for the OCF ministry.

In the 1964 preface, Dah Cheong wrote, 'In tracing back to the beginning and the formation of various OCF and Asian Fellowship groups, we are deeply conscious of God's leading hand in this movement and His continual faithfulness in the years that have passed. At the same time, we are reminded of our privilege and responsibility to carry on the task which the Lord has begun.'

The *OCF (Australia) Handbook* contained the history, constitution, and organisational structure of the fellowship. The governing body was the General Committee (GC), comprised of EXCO and leaders of all local centres. Associate members were not allowed to hold a position in the GC. Only full members could do so. Full membership was open 'to all overseas students and graduates on declaration of faith.' Associate membership was open to others on declaration of their faith.[52]

This ensured that the leadership of the group remained with overseas Christians. Founding members such as Edward Cheah, Vincent Chia and Soen Siregar came from churches in Malaysia, Singapore and Indonesia respectively (Chapter 1). Churches in Asia were blessing and influencing OCF Australia indirectly, through their members who came to study in Australia.

Key to true spirituality

In Adelaide, the 1963 Asian Fellowship chairperson was Peter Cheng. His grandmother was one of the first converts in Canton under the ministry of early Pentecostal minister Mok Lai Chi. Peter had grown up in the Kowloon Pentecostal church and had seen his grandmother sitting up in bed,

---

[52] *OCF (Australia) Handbook* (1st ed., 1964), 7.

reading her Bible at dawn by the light of a kerosene lamp. He adopted her habit of Morning and Evening Watch. In Adelaide, Peter sought out Christian fellowship and eventually became an AF leader. He invited Leo Harris from the Christian Revival Crusade (CRC) to speak at a meeting. A younger minister, Barry Chant, came instead. He spoke from John 7:38-39, about how Jesus had promised the Holy Spirit to those who would believe in him: '"Whoever believes in me, as Scripture has said, rivers of living water will flow from within them". By this he meant the Spirit, whom those who believed in him were later to receive. Up to that time the Spirit had not been given, since Jesus had not yet been glorified.'[53]

At that meeting, Sim Hee heard about the baptism of the Holy Spirit and wondered, 'What is this all about? Am I not in faith?' He had recently been baptised in Australia at the Hawthorn Church of Christ where he heard the gospel preached for the first time. Now, with this latest question in his mind, he went home, knelt in private prayer and asked God, 'Is the baptism of the Holy Spirit real?' To his surprise, he started speaking in tongues. With great excitement, he told his AF friends about his experience.[54] Some affirmed his experience as evidence of the baptism of the Holy Spirit, but others insisted, 'No, no, we don't have this in AF'.[55] It angered and hurt Sim Hee to have the validity of his experience

---

[53] Peter Cheng, Interview with author, 2020.
[54] Neoh Sim Hee, Interview with author, 2021.
[55] John and Ivy Tay, Interview with author, 2021.

most university courses were between three to six years, as a ministry to overseas students, OCF Australia would face a 'new era' roughly twice a decade. The *OCF (Australia) Handbook* would prove critical to the continuity and cohesiveness of OCF Australia. It would be especially helpful to new centres, such as OCF Hobart.

Formation of OCF Hobart

In 1962, the Evangelical Union overseas student secretary Andrew Daunton Fear invited Indonesian student Jonathan Parapak for Bible studies. They met at Jonathan's room in Hytten Hall. When friends joined them and the room became too small, they moved to Mrs Reeves' home on View Street. Andrew wrote to the IVF, asking for a senior OCF member to visit and help the new group. In 1963, the OCF Melbourne chairman Leong Kwok Thye visited the group, and some from the Hobart group attended the OCF AGM and convention that year. Close unofficial contact was maintained for several years. In April 1967, the group decided to form an official OCF centre.

Unlike other centres, Jonathan wanted to allow Australians to be full members. He saw that the important thing was the desire to reach overseas students, rather than the status of being one. He observed that not many EU members were interested in reaching overseas students or to come for meetings.⁵⁹ Ian replied that the important thing was not meeting attendance, but friendship between EU and OCF members. Ian also agreed to full membership for Australians but advised that leadership should be held by overseas students, except for 'say one position which could be held by an Australian.' This would safeguard the direction of OCF.⁶⁰ Both the EXCO and Jonathan accepted Ian's suggestion. By maintaining principles while allowing for differences in methods, Ian helped OCF Australia grow in numbers and maturity.

At the 1967 AGM, OCF Hobart was granted affiliation.⁶¹ When Mrs Reeves' home became too small, they moved to the home of Mr and Mrs Alan and Barbara Kilner. The Kilners knew Jonathan from St John's Presbyterian Church.⁶² For the next thirty years, the Kilners opened their home as an OCF meeting place. They had a large sitting room where people would cram in, and after that the Kilners would provide supper.⁶³

Today, the *OCF (Australia) Handbook* is in its eleventh edition and is a resource whereby all the important information about OCF Australia is consolidated. When consulted, it has

---

[59] Jonathan Parapak, Letter to Ian Burnard, 18 June 1967. MTC/IVF 159a-11/OCF 1965-7.

[60] Ian Burnard, Letter to Jonathan Parapak, 27 June 1967. MTC/IVF 159a-11/OCF 1965-7.

[61] 'OCF Hobart', *OCF Australia Newsletter*, 3/2, 1984, 19, 20.

[62] 'Tributes to Alan Kilber and Barbara Kilner', *Pioneering with a Purpose*, (OCF Alumni Network, 2022), 53.

[63] Hwa Yung, Interview with author, 2021.

been useful to new centres and new leaders. However, the vision of OCF is primarily passed on by people who have been called by God and who carry out the work of the ministry faithfully. One limitation of the handbook is that the guidelines it contains are applicable to the situation at the time. As situations change, some guidelines become outdated.

When the handbook was created, Ian Burnard supported Dah Cheong's team even though the IVF might have had a different perception of what OCF was, and therefore what it could be. Because Charles and Ian discerned God's hand at work through OCF, they supported the ministry developing in ways they hadn't considered before. Only God knows the future, but Christians can discern His will by walking through the present prayerfully, watchfully, always asking the question 'What is God doing in our midst?' Humility allows God to use others to speak to us, and unity enables us to function as one body.

5. A Servant of the Church

From the start, OCF Australia declared that it was not a church, but a servant of the church. Yet, each generation of OCF members have had to figure out what this looks like in practice. In the 1960s, OCF centres received many invitations to conduct services, to speak or present items in Australian churches. Many locals were keen to hear testimonies of those who were Christian or who had come to know the Lord in Australia. However, too many of these one-off speaking engagements were not conducive to the faith growth of OCF members as we shall see in this chapter.

Too many invitations

On 31 May 1966, at the Belmore Church of Christ in Sydney, OCF member Miss Kim Yeap gave a wonderful testimony. She might have received prior instruction as per Committee Standing Orders:

'Testimonies should be carefully selected and studied. Avoid any life history or personal glorification.... younger Christians, who do not usually have public speaking experience.... ask them to tell others how they came to know Him...what the Lord has done for them, and NO MORE'.[64]

At the same service, the OCF choir presented a quartet, Miss Guan Chew gave the message on two parables of Jesus,

---

[64] 'Standing Orders for General Committee Members', (OCF Sydney, Circa 1962), 7.IVF 159-10-11/OCF2.

and Tony Chan presented slides on Singapore. Two weeks later, OCF had fellowship tea at the Burwood Baptist Church. Wilfred Chee gave a testimony and more slides were shown. There were so many OCFers present in the congregation that they nearly outnumbered church members. At the end of the service, OCF program cards were distributed. OCF members were like Australian missionaries on furlough and they spoke at many missionary meetings.

Since the mid-1950s, when Dicky Yap occasionally shared his testimony alongside Dr Harrold Steward's preaching, there had been increasing interest in OCF and its members. OCF Melbourne decided to accept no more than two invitations per term. Adelaide leaders also curtailed involvement because they doubted that so many engagements were in the best interest of the fellowship; moving from church to church was not conducive to forming deep relationships.

Nonetheless, OCF Sydney was an energetic group and did their best to meet demand. They used these occasions to encourage Australian Christians to reach overseas students, a mission field at their doorstep. Churches in Sydney responded. In 1964, there were at least five churches with an Asian ministry or interest. When this happened, the relevance of OCF came into question. In 1966, some OCF leaders attributed declining attendance at Bible studies to divided loyalties between church and OCF.

The OCF-church relationship

At the helm of OCF Australia at this time was chairperson John Tay. His best friend was Indran Devadesan. Both were final year medical students on Colombo Plan scholarships. John was from an Anglican church in Melaka and Indran from a Brethren church in Kuala Lumpur. They had great fun debating differing church practices, such as baptism by immersion or sprinkling.

Three years earlier, Indran had been the OCF Sydney chairperson and John the missionary secretary. Indran wrote that OCFers could show that Christianity was not merely a Western religion. They must be careful not to become too Australian so that they could not fit back into home churches. In 1966, John was the OCF Australia chairperson and Indran the missionary secretary. Both leaders 'stressed to members that they should see their stay in Australia as temporary and they should see it as a training period.'[65]

In their six years in Australia, John and Indran had grown in depth of faith and breadth of vision. They completed the Moore Theological Correspondence Course for a Licentiate in Theology. Indran had travelled to Ceylon for his medical electives 'where there is no EU and the Christians are having a hard time from the Buddhist majority.' He wrote two reports about his travels for *Vision*, OCF Sydney's newsletter. After visiting the Vellore Medical Centre in India, he wrote to Ian suggesting that a similar hospital should be established in

---

[65] *OCF Sydney 1957-2007* (OCF Sydney Alumni, Sydney, 2007), 4, 7.

Borneo. Ian advised him to find suitable people to speak to about this, rather than to approach it from an organisational standpoint.

*OCF Sydney bus trip in the 1960s. Indran is in the front, left.
Photo supplied by Yeo Loy Meng via the OCF Alumni Network.*

With these two men on board, EXCO was well-placed to lead OCF Australia to consider how OCF should relate to the church. Prior to the AGM, John Tay and 1962 OCF Australia president Bill Lim wrote papers on the topic. John Tay's paper concluded:

What does this all mean for us in the OCF? It means

1. We should continue to encourage our Australian Christian friends in the partnership of spreading the gospel to overseas students in Australia.

2. We should encourage a firmer church affiliation of OCFers. There should be no 'ecclesiastical gypsies' or 'spiritual butterflies' in the OCF.

3. We should study more closely how all this affects the whole strategy of the OCF.

(From the context of the paper and the times, 'ecclesiastical gypsies' and 'spiritual butterflies' meant people who attended various churches according to programs that interested them, without being committed members of any single local church.)

At the AGM, the GC affirmed the correctness of encouraging Australian Christians in their outreach to overseas students. They stated plainly that OCF was not a church, and OCF members should embrace opportunities to serve in Australian churches, in order to be equipped for future service at home because 'OCF, like the rest of IVF, is a servant of the church'.[66]

Despite long discussions and firm resolve, the question of how best to partner with churches remained. In May 1968, OCF Sydney invited seven churches with significant numbers of overseas students to a meeting. They shared information, rejoiced, prayed for one another and agreed to try not to duplicate efforts. This freed OCF Sydney in one key aspect. As churches were to help members mature in the faith, OCF Sydney did not have to cover every aspect of Christian knowledge in their Bible teaching program. OCF Sydney's annual report stated that what had previously been a problem, was now seen as an opportunity. 'A deep sense of true unity in Christ was felt among all present ... nonetheless,

---

[66] OCF EXCO, 'A New Strategy for the OCF' (1966). MTC/IVF 159-11/OCF Convention 1966-67.

while considering it a privilege, heavier responsibility is expected of us, and the drainage of manpower still remains a problem.'

Across Australia, the relationship between OCF and the local churches varied. The 1968 OCF Australia chairperson Hia Chek Phang called for balance after observing two extremes. One was the Sydney situation where OCF members were so heavily involved in church that they had no time for the OCF ministry on campus and it suffered. The second was in Melbourne whereby OCF seemed to have its own training program that ran independently of churches. As a result, its members had little awareness of how churches function. The danger of this was that members might fall away from the faith when they returned home.

Anglican minister and long-time friend of OCF, Rev Dudley Foord, described this danger in an article he wrote. After returning from a tour of Asia in early 1964, he outlined three reasons why OCF members fall away:

1. difficulties of re-adjustments
2. the temptation to be spiritual butterflies
3. the temptation to covetousness and compromise.

He wrote:

It is possible that OCFers in Australia have not developed disciplined habits in terms of being anchored and committed to one specific church. In fact, many former OCFers maintain they were pampered in Australia and had become spiritual gypsies—attending this or that church only if some special function had been arranged.

This tendency is serious as the New Testament nowhere envisages "lone wolf Christianity". In Christ we are members of one body and we only grow to maturity and avoid instability by being fully committed to a local expression of the body of Christ. In this situation we receive ministry and we give ministry. Any other pattern is foreign to the Bible and is an ensnaring entanglement. Be committed to one church and serve Christ to the fullest out of a heart brimful of unending gratitude for your salvation.[67]

Apart from the reasons Rev Foord outlined, other challenges that OCF returnees faced were family opposition, and an assumption that the Australian way of conducting church and ministry was the only right way. This could be especially true of those who became Christians in Australia. In 1965, OCF Sydney published this (probably) fictional story of Nurse Chin dreading her shift, because of the loneliness she felt at the hospital. She craved Christian fellowship that she had found in OCF:

> 'Hm, that's a problem, isn't it, Chin?' Sue said, eventually breaking the silence. 'You know, could it be that you feel the blessing of Christian fellowship so much, but are afraid to enter the world on your own? Could it be that you are not relying totally on Christ himself? Perhaps you are knowing Christ second-hand and not personally for yourself. Going to all these

---

[67] Dudley Foord, 'So You are Returning Home,' *Vision*, OCF Sydney newsletter, August 1966, 14-16. MTC/IVF 159-11a/OCF 1965-7.

meetings, you share other people's knowledge of Jesus Christ, but you are relying on fellowship to keep up your spiritual life instead of on God himself, who alone is able to be with you everywhere, meetings or hospital wards, and all the time, now, and long after you've left Australia and OCF behind.[68]

In OCF, there was a recognition of the need for members to mature in their faith, to practise spiritual disciplines, to be anchored in Christ himself, and to rely on the Holy Spirit. Although this is true of all Christians, for overseas students who would have to return home and leave the familiarity of OCF and an Australian church, this was even more crucial.

Stanmore Baptist and Kuala Kubu Bahru Chapel

The following account provides a good example of a productive partnership between OCF and a local church. In the mid-1960s, Stanmore Baptist Church in Sydney provided a warm welcome to all. Rev Egerton Long and his wife Betty regularly hosted meals and small group activities at their home. Sometimes, they had overseas students staying with them. Betty was like a spiritual aunt, especially to a group of nursing students at the Royal Prince Hospital in Camperdown.

Church families followed their example and often invited students for a meal after the Sunday service. One such

---

[68] 'Lo, I Am With You Always, Even to the End of the World,' *Vision,* OCF Sydney newsletter, July-August 1965). IVF 159-11a/OCF Australia and states 1964-65.

Stanmore Baptist Church, Sydney, 1967.

couple was Fred and Joyce Lear. They became like parents to Lim Kim Bew and Judy Ho. Kim Bew had been the OCF Sydney chairperson, and Judy an IVF staff worker. When Kim Bew and Judy decided to get married, Joyce sewed Judy's wedding dress. Fred walked her down the aisle because Judy's parents could not be present at the wedding. Rev Long officiated their wedding, and the church ladies organised their wedding reception.

To welcome newcomers, this church of around 250 members, with many OCF members in their midst, organised monthly Student and Nurses Dinners (in those days, dinners were actually lunches). Many students came to know the Lord this way. Through the friendships that developed, mature Australian Christians helped OCF members through life's challenges such as financial problems, exam failure, or relationship breakups.[69] Pastoral care extended to ministry training. For example, Rev Long often brought Kim Bew along with him to home and hospital visitations.

An overseas student by the name of Lim Fong Jwong lived on the same street as the church. Despite his evident disinterest, a church elder used to knock on his door and invite him for service every Sunday. Eventually, Fong Jwong came to church, and then attended an OCF camp where he became a Christian. The change in his character was remarkable. After graduating, he enrolled at the newly established Discipleship Training Centre in Singapore, a small live-in theological college. There, Fong Jwong sought God's will on where he should serve.

By 1970, Indran Devadason had graduated and married Josephine. They moved to Kuala Kubu Bahru where Indran had been posted as a medical officer. They started a church in their spacious home that became the Kuala Kubu Bahru Chapel (KKB). Most speakers at KKB Chapel stayed the weekend at their home. When OCF associate member Jeannette Lin visited them, she was amazed to see about seventy people gather to worship on Sunday afternoon. Indran told her, 'I don't need to visit the people, they visit me, then I invite them to Sunday School and church'. This fruit was a result of many years of faithful and loving service by OMF missionaries in surrounding villages, as well as Indran and Josephine's gracious welcome.

---

[69] Lim Kim Bew, Interview with author, 2021.

Missionary secretaries used to keep in touch with returnees via newsletters. Perhaps it was through this, or through Jeannette that Indran heard that Fong Jwong was training for ministry. Indran persuaded Fong Jwong to go to Kuala Kubu Bahru. In 1972, Indran was transferred elsewhere, but Fong Jwong continued to serve in the church for the rest of his life.

Transient international students enter adulthood in a place other than the one they grew up in. Their time overseas can be a significant period of maturing, character development and acquisition of ministry skills. At the end of their time abroad, they return home. Therefore, in the case of OCF, often one church sows and another church reaps. In these early days, the Australian church sowed and the Asian church reaped.

While in Australia, OCF members were advised to resist the temptation to visit many churches. Instead, they were urged to commit to one church, form friendships and serve God. Learning to be part of a church community was especially important in view of their eventual return to their home countries where there was no OCF.

On its part, OCF has never seen itself as a church, but a servant of the church, even though OCF members had limited time to contribute to church ministry. When the relationship between church and OCF worked well, it was like parents blessed by children who helped out at home although they were tired after school. Even if the children could only wash the dishes, the parents would have appreciated their contribution and attitude. How the OCF members divide their time and contribute in service is best explored in a Christ-like environment where mutual love and submission inform every interaction. In Christ, love and service are never demanded, but freely given. Despite this analogy, many churches that ministered to overseas students were blessed and revitalised, as the students showed great interest in the gospel and a hunger for God's word.

6. Early Bible College students

When OCF was first formed in 1959, its main impact was in equipping overseas students to serve God back home as Christian professionals. After five years, there began a small but steady stream of members who undertook theological training in Australia after graduating in a different field. OCF Australia benefited from the extended time of fellowship and leadership provided by these early Bible College students doing postgraduate studies in theology. They fostered a closer relationship between Australian Bible Colleges and OCF Australia.

Wilfred Chee

In 1965, after graduating from biochemistry in UWA, Wilfred Chee enrolled in theological studies. He served as an ordained Anglican minister in Petaling Jaya, Taipei and Sydney for forty-five years from his graduation until his retirement. In 2016, he wrote, 'I am a Christian today and a preacher today, not because I am a great thinker or a great speaker, but simply because I am a great follower of Christ... I am sensitive to the guidance of the Holy Spirit. When God called me to full-time service, I responded quickly. Just like the apostle Paul, I was not disobedient to the heavenly vision.'

Wilfred Chee had come to know the Lord in 1956 through the Anglican church in Sydney. When he began first-year medicine the following year, his course mate Edmund

Lim invited him to OCF. There, he met other Asian Christians for the first time. He had a hunger for God and grew quickly in his faith.

Wilfred Chee at his graduation at the University of Western Australia, 1965.
Photo supplied by the OCF Alumni Network.

At the time, he lived with several other Malayan boys in a double storey house on Church Street, near Sydney University. After six months, he wanted to move out because his housemates left dirty dishes in the sink, which attracted cockroaches and flies. But the Lord showed him that this was an opportunity to be a Christian witness.

So, Wilfred changed his attitude. He started to think of ways to tell them about Christ. First, he washed all the dishes and swept the floor. He invited his friends to church to hear God's word preached, but they laughed at his suggestion. However, on Sunday afternoons they often had nothing to do except smoke and play cards. At such times, they did not object to Wilfred talking about Christianity and even asked some questions. When his friend Edward fell sick, Wilfred's offer of prayer was accepted.

Opposite the home was a Baptist church. Wilfried befriended the pastor Ken Sweeting and invited him to meet his housemates. Through friendship with Pastor Ken, Wilfred's housemates Philip and Ee began visiting the church. At Wilfred's suggestion, the church started a Youth Fellowship. Australians and overseas students attended. After two years, Philip and Ee became Christians. Unfortunately, despite studying hard, Wilfred failed third year, and transferred to Perth to study biochemistry. One day, he received a letter from his former housemate Edward.

Edward had been admitted to the hospital for hepatitis and given a grim prognosis, but he was not ready to die. He wanted to ask God for help and followed what he remembered of Wilfred's prayers, praying until he fell asleep. In his dream, he heard a voice asking him to get up and wash. At the sink, he was amazed to see healthy pink spots on his face that was sallow from the hepatitis. Edward had spent the past month convalescing and reading the Gideon Bible he found in the drawer by his bedside. No wonder Edward's letter was full of Bible verses. This was a great encouragement to Wilfred.

A few years later, after completing his final biochemistry exams, Wilfred travelled to Victor Harbor for the OCF convention. There he heard Brother Huang Ee Hoe speak on 'Our responsibility today'. Brother Huang read from 1 Timothy 1:12: 'And I thank Christ Jesus our Lord, who hath enabled me, for that He counted me faithful, putting me into the ministry'. The verse leapt out to Wilfred. Paul did not consider the ministry a lowly calling; it was a great privilege! Wilfred felt the Lord say to him, 'Wilfred, you have been faithful in being my witness to your fellow students, I now want to call you to serve me full-time in the ministry and go back to Asia to serve me. Will you obey my call?'[70]

Tears came to his eyes. He went away to pray and asked himself why he preferred to serve Christ in the professions? Was it for worldly acclaim? Finally, he yielded to the Lord.[71] A tremendous sense of peace engulfed him. Later, he gave his testimony to the whole convention. On the advice of his spiritual mentor, Rev Dudley Foord, Wilfred enrolled at Moore College. After two years, he transferred to Trinity Theological College in Singapore to complete his training. Bishop Chiu Ban It, the Anglican Bishop of Singapore and Malaya at the time, ordained him.

Melville Szto

In 1965, Melville arrived to study chemical engineering. Ten years later, he and his wife Salome went to Japan as the first missionaries from Singapore sent by the Overseas Missionary Fellowship (OMF). They served four terms there until 1994. Subsequently, based in Singapore, they trained new missionaries for seven years, before returning to Japan to

---

[70] Wilfred Chee, *His Hand on my Life*, (self-pub., 2016), 10, 43, 44.
[71] *Pioneering with a Purpose*, 150.

serve eight more years until 2010. This is how Melville's change in vocation occurred.

One evening in 1966, during his devotions, Melville read Mark 10:17-25 about the rich young man who could not give up everything to follow Jesus.[72] As he pondered the passage, a small voice said to him, 'What about you? You have prayed to know my will. Are you willing to do what this young man was not willing to do?'

Melville wanted to obey God but his father had sent him to Australia to become an engineer. As the only son, he had family obligations. He could not imagine giving up a prestigious engineering career. He fell to his knees and cried out, 'O Lord, I really want to resolve this matter. Don't let me get up from my knees until this is settled.' He struggled until the early hours of the morning. God graciously enabled him to pray, 'Lord, I am willing, but I know that I cannot do this by myself. Lord, show me the way and give me the courage that I lack.' A great peace came into his heart. He knew that his prayer was accepted.[73] God showed him that he was not required to give up his studies then, but only the willingness to do so.

Meanwhile, with fellow OCF members, he grew in his faith, serving and being served. Most Sundays, Neoh Sim Hee drove him, Tony Loy and Lee Sam Hong to Brownhill Creek to pray. They prayed about their studies and ministry, future career and direction, girls they liked or girlfriends waiting for

---

[72] Melville Szto, *Where Your Treasure Is* (Singapore: Amour Publisher, 2017), 30.
[73] Melville Szto, Interview with author and Daniel Chieng, 2021.

them at home. They brought their inner turmoil, uncertainties, and difficulties to the Lord. Sometimes, they just sat in silence, revelling in His presence.

Melville was the 1968 OCF Adelaide chairperson. He was great friends with the Adelaide University Evangelical Union (EU) president Greg Pearce. (Once, they hitchhiked back to Adelaide from the Woy Woy train station after an interstate conference.) The May camp that year was a joint activity with the Adelaide Uni EU and the Teachers' College EU. Nearly half the OCF contingent (35 people) were non-members. The principal of the Adelaide Bible Institute, Geoffrey Bingham, spoke, on the theme 'The Way'. The host family Rev and Mrs Philip Thomas brought their baby and their dog!

At the end of that year, in Brisbane, Melville heard convention speaker Rev Philip Teng from Hong Kong. 'When you graduate,' said Rev Teng, 'don't limit yourself by thinking that the only way you can serve God is by going back as Christian engineers, doctors, lawyers or whatever you are studying. God may want you to become a pastor, or evangelist, or missionary. Please be open to that, because Asia needs lots of people like that.'

Rev Dudley Foord also spoke at this convention. He asked the students to equip themselves through studying at Bible College after graduating. God spoke to Melville through these two men to ask him to do theological studies as an intermediary step between his engineering studies and whatever it was that God wanted to use him for. After the convention, Melville looked for a job to support himself, and

SPEAKERS

Rev. PHILIP TENG

Rev. Philip Teng, B.A., B.D. (Edinburgh) is a well known Christian minister in S.E. Asia and other countries. As a speaker and Bible expositor, he has been on speaking tours in ten of the S.E. Asian countries, as well as U.S.A. and Canada. At present Mr. Teng is the Chairman of the Church Union of the Christian and Missionary Alliance, Hong Kong; Director of the Alliance Bible Seminary, H.K., and Chairman of the F.E.B.C. Council in H.K. He is also vitally concerned with student work and is the Patron of the Christian Union of H.K. University and Adviser of F.E.S., H.K. Recently Mr. Teng was a main speaker at the second Anzea Regional Conference held in Kuala Lumpur. He will be the Bible expositor at the coming Congress on Evangelism (Asia-South Pacific Region). At the convention Mr. Teng will deliver a series of talks entitled 'Towards Christian Maturity'.

Rev. Dudley Foord, M.Sc., B.D. (London), Th.L., should be familiar to those who have been to the last few conventions. He has long been associated with the O.C.F. as well as the student world. In his student days he was an E.U. president. After the war he gained his M.Sc. at Sydney University, lectured in the School of Physics, and worked as a research executive with the Ford Company. Then he entered the Christian Ministry, and is the part-time Chaplain of the University of Sydney. At present Mr. Foord is the Dean of Moore Theological College. He has made extensive speaking tours to South-East Asian countries and universities, and is familiar with the situation there. At the convention Mr. Foord will be taking a series of studies on the book of Habakkuk, which contains a most relevant message for the Christians of today.

Dr. E. G. GIBSON

Rev. Dr. E. G Gibson is an outstanding person in learning and teaching. He received his ministerial training at N.S.W. Baptist Theological College, and was Pastor of a number of churches for ten years. After that he was the Principal of Perth Bible Institute for eleven years, the Principal of Adelaide Bible Institute for three years (during which he became well acquainted with O.C.F. Adelaide), the Vice-Principal of South Australia Baptist Theological College, and is at present the Principal of the Baptist Theological College of Queensland. Dr. Gibson's interests are wide and varied. After his ordination, he went on with his studies and took B.A. (Hons.) in Philosophy with London University (External), M.A. in Anthropology at Sydney University, B.Sc. (Econ.) majoring in Sociology and Economics, B.D. at Melbourne College of Divinity, Th.D. at Berkeley in California, and B.Ed. in Western Australia.
In 1964 he visited Singapore, Borneo and Malaya, and was a main speaker at the Singapore Keswick Convention. At the coming convention Dr. Gibson will be delivering four studies on the topic 'Christ in all the Scriptures'.

Rev. D. FOORD

1968 Brisbane convention speaker profiles from a convention pamphlet.

Melville and Salome at Melville's graduation at Adelaide University.

to save up money for his theological studies. With trepidation he sent off a letter to his parents. To his surprise, they wrote back to say that they would support his decision, even if they didn't think it was the right one.

As a result of this, Melville was able to serve as the OCF Australia president in 1969. He worked for one year as an engineer to save up money. During this time, a nursing student Salome from Indonesia started attending OCF. A deep friendship developed between them. Melville chaired the 1969 AGM in Clarendon, South Australia, and returned to Adelaide to get engaged. Melville and Salome had a long

The 1968 OCF Australia convention at Victor Harbor where Melville was the convention chairperson. Second row (seated), from far right: Melville (1st), Salome (2nd), Sim Hee (7th), Geoff Bingham (9th), Dudley Foord (10th adult) with children at his knee.

engagement in Adelaide and returned to Singapore for their wedding. They did this to honour the wishes of Melville's parents, as he was their only son. By this time, Melville had completed three years of theological studies at the Adelaide Bible Institute (ABI). As an external student with the Melbourne College of Divinity, he also obtained a Bachelor of Divinity, by completing subjects such as Hebrew and Systematic Theology that were not offered at the ABI.

The year that Melville had arrived in Australia, 1965, was the year that OMF began accepting people from Asian countries as missionaries. (OMF had previously been called the China Inland Mission and had been founded by Hudson Taylor.) Home Councils had been set up in several Asian countries including Malaysia and Singapore. Melville and Salome were the first of many OCF alumni who became OMF missionaries.

Yong Chen Fah

In 1967, Yong Chen Fah heard God call him to serve him back in Kota Kinabalu, Malaysia. After graduating and working for a year, Chen Fah studied at Moore Theological College. In 1974, Yong Chen Fah returned home and eventually became a Bishop in East Malaysia. In his long years of service, he had a significant ministry among the Chinese, Indonesians, and indigenous people of Sabah. In 2007, he ministered to the

Chinese in Sydney for three years at the invitation of Archbishop Peter Jensen.

In 1966, Chen Fah had arrived in Sydney to do a Bachelor of Arts. He joined Andrew Lu's Bible study group. Chen Fah thought Andrew looked very intellectual with his thick glasses. The group members enjoyed long debates late into the night and became firm friends. Chen Fah also attended St Barnabas Church in Broadway.

Soon, Chen Fah was active in EU and OCF. Midway through his studies, he joined other OCF Sydney members to meet new students at the airport. After this initial contact, he spent a week with each new student to help them settle in. At the end of the week, OCF members would invite them to an evangelistic barbecue. (They used to serve chicken wings because that was the cheapest cut of meat.) Through generosity and hospitality, OCF demonstrated God's love in a practical way that others could experience.

During his second year, while doing geography homework in his small room at the Anglican's Men's College opposite Sydney University, he heard an audible voice. 'Chen Fah! Why don't you give up your ambition? I want you to do my will in Kota Kinabalu.' It was a curious encounter and a difficult question, for Chen Fah wanted to become a teacher, to dedicate his life to teaching young people, while his father wanted him to go into business. Chen Fah pondered and prayed about how he should respond.

Six months before his final exams in 1969, the May 13 racial riots tore through Malaysia. He wondered if this might be the end of Malaysia as a nation. But the Spirit of God led him to think deeply otherwise. He wanted to test out if the voice he had heard in his second year, was the Lord. So, he spent a year teaching economics and geography at St Andrew's Cathedral School. At the end of that time, he was convinced of God's call.[74]

From 1970 to 1972, Chen Fah studied at Moore Theological College. He got to know other students and staff very well. Many students board at Moore College and there is a vibrant student life. The first year was spent in dialogue

OCF Sydney members with Hwa Yung at the 1971 convention in Perth. From left: Hwa Yung, Barnabas and Lorraine Koo, Yong Chen Fah and his wife Mida, Jennette Lin and her fiancé Jimmy Kuswadi, Joseph Santino. Hwa Yung and Chen Fah were the 1971 and 1972 OCF Australia chairpersons respectively.

---

[74] Yong Chen Fah, 'Building a Church with God's Vision' (Self-pub, 2022).

with his lecturer, also the principal, tearing down his understanding of God, before building it up in the second and third year. In those final years, he had to preach at St Barnabas Church. After his sermon, his lecturers asked him how he had felt. 'Very scary,' he replied half-joking, 'with you people sitting there.' 'You did well,' they laughed with him.

Chen Fah realised that barriers to friendship between Asians and Australians existed because of the 'Yellow Peril'. The phrase had been coined during the Western imperialist expansion era of the 19th century and depicted East Asians as an existential threat to the West. The Japanese attack in the Pacific and on Australian soil during World War II had exacerbated this fear. Many Australians could not tell Japanese and Chinese apart. However, Chen Fah knew that Australians were very friendly once you got to know them. He wanted to bring Australians and Asians together.

Chen Fah's view of the importance of friendship was echoed by Ian Burnard. In a letter to IVF affiliates, Ian wrote:

> Overseas students have become so much part of the fabric of Australian society that we tend to take them for granted. When this happens, we tend to feel 'integration' has been achieved. But in practice isolation increases. The opposite, special attention to overseas students, breeds a false dichotomy —'overseas' verses 'Australian' as if basically the two differ in essential respects. But this too is not true to biblical and practical considerations. What is true is that <u>every</u> relationship we have with anyone at all needs working on; and getting to know those whose

cultural background differs in degree a little more than between say 'independent school' and 'state school' educated, requires more work still.

Ian urged all members—overseas and Australian students—towards a vision of friendship and evangelism.[75] Both Ian and Chen Fah saw friendship as the key to working together and realised that not everything had to be carried out at an organisational official level. When Chen Fah observed that OCF was good at organising meetings and hospitality, but weak in theology, he invited Moore College lecturers to OCF, hoping that they might see the potential of overseas students. Out of this, esteemed Anglican churchmen Peter Jensen and Paul Barnett began nighttime lectures specially for OCF members. Around six students, mostly postgraduates, gathered regularly and learned from some of the best Bible teachers in Sydney. These were very lively sessions of dialogue and discussions.[76]

In 1972, Chen Fah became the OCF Australia chairperson. Recognising the challenges of leading OCF Australia on a national scale, Chen Fah focused his personal efforts on a small group of overseas students at the University of New England Armidale and conducted regular Bible Studies with them. They were like informal OCF members and came for some activities and camps. Although the group was not very large, members grew in faith. Several

---

[75] Ian Burnard, Letter to IVF affiliates in universities and in RMIT, SAIT, WAIT, NSWIT, QIT, copied to Yong Chen Fah and OCF centres, 28 June 1972. MTC/IVF 159-11/Overseas Students (OCF) 1967-72.

[76] Yong Chen Fah, Interview with author, 2021. Transcript pp. 21, 22.

became Chen Fah's lifelong friends and gospel partners in East Malaysia. (OCF Armidale was affiliated in 1984 but dissolved in 2000.)

OCF members in this early period grew up during a time of global political upheaval. Many were born during or just after World War II. Many came of age as their countries agitated for self-governance. Even when all the outside world is on fire, the internal battle between self-determination or God's rule is no less keenly felt. God called some early members to surrender their professional aspirations, and to change the course of their lives to serve him. After earnest wrestling, they surrendered to their Lord and went on to long and fruitful ministries, testifying to God's faithfulness in every season and situation.

7. The Wider World

Sometimes, the battles we see as critical fade into insignificance when we gain a broader perspective of the struggle. For example, in 1959, Asian Fellowship wanted the name Austral-Asian Christian Fellowship instead of OCF Australia. At the Cowes Convention, they eventually compromised on their preferred name, and the other OCF centres also allowed them to keep their name Asian Fellowship. In 1965, after a few African brothers joined them, they voluntarily changed their name to OCF Adelaide.

Differences of opinion are bound to exist. When we cannot agree, we can trust God to reveal his guidance in good time. When we see clearly what is important to God, then we can work more effectively in the good works that he has prepared for us. One such question arose around ten years after its formation. OCF Australia had to decide if it should cooperate with secular bodies in order to welcome new overseas students to Australia.

From Many Nations

In Adelaide, Hia Chek Phang had sought out Christian fellowship and found OCF. He thought they were a little conservative. The men would sit on one side and the ladies on the other side of the Pirie Street Methodist Church meeting hall. After the meeting, they ate fish and chips together and walked over to the Anglican Church. He found their order of service very interesting—the congregation kneeling and getting up and repeating prayers from the Book of Common Prayer. His Presbyterian church in Singapore only read directly from the Scriptures.

Hia Chek Phang came from a Christian home and grew up in a Teochew Presbyterian Church in Singapore. Later, he and his parents moved to an English congregation where he met the Youth for Christ (YFC) national director Liew Kee Kok, who mentored Chek Phang. They set up Christian school fellowship groups across Singapore. When the Catholic schools forbade such clubs, they set up meetings in nearby churches or at the Inter School Christian Fellowship office. Chek Phang led the singing while Kee Kok preached. Later Chek Phang led the whole service.

The Australian government awarded Chek Phang a Colombo Plan scholarship. He arrived in Adelaide on a blustery summer's day in 1965. He was dropped off at his temporary accommodation at the Flinders Street YMCA with no further help. After settling down, he and two other new student arrivals went out to try to find Chinese food late in the afternoon, but found the streets deserted. How this exacerbated the feeling of homesickness! They had left Singapore a week ago for Sydney on Chinese New Year's Eve when large extended families got together for a huge celebratory meal. Chek Phang asked a stranger for directions. 'I'm sorry I can't help you. I am a stranger here myself,' he replied. Chek Phang thought how helpful it would be if people familiar with the needs of overseas students could meet new arrivals and even better if they were Christians!

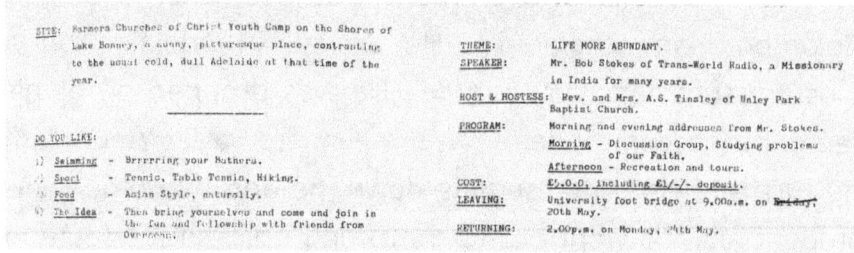

1965 OCF Adelaide May Camps registration form. MTC/1VF 159-11a/OCF Australia & States 1964-5.

At this time, OCF Adelaide used to have May camps to the north of Adelaide. In 1965, members went door-to-door in the rural town of Barmera, inviting all the towns' people to attend an evangelistic meeting. Mr Bob Stokes of Trans-World Radio, who had been a missionary to India for many years, delivered a gospel message. About fifteen people gave their hearts to the Lord.[77] The following year, the May Camp was held in Melrose, near the Flinders Rangers. The camp organising committee got to know the Methodist and Anglican ministers at Melrose. They publicised the evangelistic meeting at the Melrose Town Hall in every available medium—TV, radio, newspaper and personal invitations—and also sent out prayer letters to Christian friends. Two hundred people came from as far as 60 miles away. The AF members presented a musical arrangement and gave testimonies, and Mr Graeme Smith preached. Twelve locals and six Asian Fellowship members went forward into the counselling room to learn more about Jesus Christ. Student leaders, and the Methodist and Anglican ministers all helped with the counselling work. In 2021, Chek Phang recalled what happened:

> We would normally go to the northern part of South Australia, away from the city and so on. So that was very interesting, because what we did also was to meet with one of the churches there. And of course, many of them in the 1960s have never seen an Asian before. You can imagine what it's like when suddenly fifty of us or so showed up in their small rural church where their normal Sunday congregation was thirty to forty! We shared with them what countries we came from, what we were studying etcetera. Hopefully, we helped them to see that the Church of Jesus Christ consists of people from many nations![78]

---

[77] Neoh Sim Hee, Oral History Interview, 2021.
[78] Hia Chek Phang, Oral history interview, 9 April 2021, Transcript p. 11.

Operation Welcome

By this stage, usual efforts to welcome freshers continued, but it was becoming more difficult to contact new students, especially those who did not live at the university colleges. All this while, Chek Phang kept thinking about how to help new overseas students. More and more of them were coming, and it would be sad if they had the same forlorn feeling that he had experienced upon arrival.

Then a series of events presented Chek Phang with an opportunity. First, the Commonwealth Office of Education asked Chek Phang if he could welcome other Colombo Plan scholars like himself. Chek Phang agreed. Through this, he established good relations with various government and voluntary organisations. An official from the Department of External Affairs then gave OCF Adelaide names and contact details so that they could welcome new students. When a Coordination Committee for the Welfare of Overseas Students in South Australia was formed, OCF Adelaide became involved.

State-wide efforts became formalised at a national level through the establishment of the Australian Organisational Coordinating Committee for Overseas Students (AOCCOS). It was a voluntary body of government and non-government groups interested in overseas students. Some OCF groups had already seen this as a wonderful opportunity and were already helping out locally. Other OCF groups were more cautious and wanted a theological basis before they acted.

Any reticence likely stemmed from Clause V of the OCF Australia constitution stated that, 'No joint activities shall be arranged with any secular body which would undermine the Aims and Objectives and the Doctrinal Basis of OCF (Aust)'.[79] The 1966 AGM minutes recorded the following: 'Mr Ian Burnard comments that we ought not to co-operate with non-Christians unless our aim is achieved and doctrinal basis is retained. <u>Melbourne</u>: Did not accept a proposal of organising a snow trip with a non-Christian society; instead had invited members of this society to come [to an OCF activity]'.[80]

In 1968, Hia Chek Phang served as the OCF Australia chairperson. In this capacity, he presented OCF Australia with a theological basis for working with secular bodies. He wrote, 'It is not possible for OCF to share with others the love of Christ without being involved in the physical, emotional, mental and social needs of overseas students. In fact, we should be the people most concerned with these needs.' To be aware of these needs and try to meet them, OCF would need to consider working together with some non-Christian bodies, if their aim is the interest of all students. In encouraging OCF to be open to the opportunities presented by AOCCOS, Chek Phang observed that all matters approved by the AOCCOS were recommendations only and not directives. Each invitation to work with a non-Christian organisation had to be examined individually, with prayer for

---

[79] *OCF (Australia) Handbook*, (1st ed., 1964), 7.
[80] OCF Australia AGM Minutes (Sydney, 1966), 12.

direction from God. Chek Phang helped OCF broaden the way it saw itself and how it related to others.

After Chek Phang presented a sound Scriptural basis to justify cooperation, OCF Australia could mobilise all local centres to respond effectively as one united national body. Through Chek Phang's leadership, OCF Australia became very involved in Operation Welcome, at an organisational and individual level, leading to many new contacts and members.

The success of Operation Welcome in these years is evident from a 1972 letter Ian Burnard sent to a church minister who was thinking of installing a chaplain in Canberra to reach the increasing number of Indonesian students. Ian replied, 'Rather than a chaplain to overseas students, one really needs a prophet and a pastor among one's church who can challenge and help members to simply keep their eyes open, and their homes, inviting to your home the foreign students you meet in the community on different occasions. Also, all students have some contact with overseas students and they should be encouraged to bring people to their homes.'[81]

Taking Operation Welcome a step further, Chek Phang encouraged church families to participate in the 'Host Family Scheme' run by the External Affairs welfare department.[82] Previously, it had been largely OCF, IVF and Graduate Fellowship working together to welcome new students. As far

---

[81] Ian Burnard, Letter to Rev Gerald Hanscamp, 27 July 1972. MTC/1VF 159-11/Overseas Students OCF. 1967-72.

[82] Chow Tat Kong, "Freshers Welcome Activities of the Various OCF Groups (Adelaide)", *News Magazine of OCF (Australia)*, 1969.

as we know, this was the first time that church families were involved in a formal way across different denominations. This led OCF centres around Australia to oversee the formal welcome of new overseas students and for many church families to open their homes to overseas students. Hospitality extended to hosting students before and after conventions. From across the Tasman, invitations were extended to students in Australia, offering board in Christian homes if they wished to vacation in New Zealand.

Chek Phang's prior training in Singapore, for example through Youth for Christ, which was a broad youth organisation, had given him maturity and skills. Using these, he helped OCF work more closely with many Christian churches and bodies, even paving the way for new directions and initiatives such as the Host Family scheme. Through united Christian efforts, the diversity of OCF members grew, and it became a vital and vibrant Christian witness in several cities. Chek Phang also helped OCF progress to a higher level of societal engagement without compromising Christian character. The fruit of these years is evident in the diversity of OCF Australia membership as seen in the table following, diversity in full and associate members, places of study, and countries of origin.

The attraction of OCF was not primarily in its programs, important as those were. Rather, its nature and strength was as a home away from home for overseas students. Yet, it was not an enclave of foreigners. Through the support of

Australians in churches and IVF, OCF welcomed overseas students to a big family of Asians, Africans, Australians and others. All shared the same 'family name' as all had the same Heavenly Father.

Coming back to the question of whom OCF should work with, perhaps it is helpful to take a step back and view our work on earth from a larger perspective. The apostle Paul did so when he wrote 'For our struggle is not against flesh and blood, but against the rulers, against the authorities, against the powers of this dark world and against the spiritual forces of evil in the heavenly realms.' (Ephesians 6:12). From this vantage point, we can live more easily with differences of opinion within Christian communities, such what name should a group be called, and take a less defensive position with regard to working with secular bodies.

For our fight is not against any group of people, organisation or entity in this world. It is against the spiritual forces of evil that affect life on earth through injustice, oppression, and isolation. Our weapons are not guns, but love, grace and a willingness to serve others, for example, through welcoming newcomers and the foreigners. In communities where God is honoured, His character finds expression through His children relating to one another as spiritual brothers and sisters, in genuine friendship. Together, they demonstrate the essential nature of their Heavenly Father.

Section 1: Early Days, 1950s to early 1970s

- 2.

Membership statistics of OCF groups in Brisbane, Sydney, Melbourne, Hobart, Adelaide, Perth. August 1968.

	Brisbane	Sydney	Melb.	Hobart	Adel.	Perth	Total
Total members	24	84	81	26	46	44	305
Full members	19	70	61	15 - o/s	35	34	234
Asso. members	5	14	20	11 - Aust.	11	10	71
F. Membs. saved in Aust'a.	7	16	17	5	10 approx.	6	61
Average attend'e.	25	60/110	110	23	40	45	328 aver'e

Notes
1. in the membership of OCF Hobart, there is no distinction between full and associate members.
2. among the 10, only 4 assoc. members of Perth Ocf are in Perth at present.
3. 'average attend'e' = per public meeting in 1968.
4. total overseas students, fuul-time and part-time, in Australia is roughly estimated to be in the order of 13,000.

	Brisb.	Sydney	Melb.	Hobart	Adel.	Perth	Total
Univ'ty	18	28	29	24	23	18	140
High sch. & colleges	-	12	18	--	5	10	45
Nursing		8		1			9
Other courses	3		14			6	23
Working	3				7		10

Notes
1. ' - ' = nil, blank space = not given, may/maynot be 'nil'.
2. Adel.: '5' include Bible College
'7' other courses & working, mainly latter.

ORIGIN/	Brisb.	Sydney	Melb.	Hobart	Adel.	Perth	Total
Malaysia	5	29	28	7	19	19	107
Singapore	3	16	13	3	11	10	56
Hongkong	3	20	13	1	4	4	45
Indonesia	7	2	5	4	-	-	18
Brunei	-	-	2	-	-	-	2
SthVietnam	1	1	-	-	-	-	2
Philipines	-	1	-	-	-	-	1
New Guinea	-	1	-	-	-	-	1
Africa	-	-	-	-	1 -Uganda	1	2
							234

- 2.

Taken from the December 1968 OCF Australia AGM minutes. Demographics of OCF members, showing a diversity of country of origin and the institutions in which they were studying or working. Note how OCF Hobart made no distinction between full and associate members (Chapter 4 Formation of OCF Hobart).

8. Returnee Missionaries

When OCF Australia was formed, many Australian Christians saw overseas students as potential gospel bearers to their home countries. This was at a time when foreign missionaries were being expelled from countries such as China. In Australia, OCF members also wanted to be equipped to serve God at home because they realised that the churches in many of their countries were weak in comparison to the wealth of Christian resources in Australia.

At the 1968 OCF Australia convention, Ian Burnard taught on 'Spiritual Leadership Training'. He noted that 'the current division between missionary and other evangelistic enterprise might not adequately allow for the full impact of the Old Testament and New Testament teaching.'[83] Disciples of Jesus Christ are called to live out their faith wherever they go, some in cultures they grew up in, others in cross-cultural settings.

Since then, OCF members have spread out all across the world. Most returned home, some went to foreign countries, and others remained in or returned to Australia. The impact of OCF returnees, especially as global population mobility increases, is not only about travelling to places where witness is scarce, but also about the quality of the light they bear, as it passes through the lens of their lives.

---

[83] Ian Burnard, *Notes on Spiritual Leadership Training*, 1968 Convention. MTC/1VF 159-11/OCF AGM (Dec 1968).

Continued Exposure

First issue of The Way magazine.

In June 1961, from their Hong Kong office, the IVF produced the first edition of *The Way: Witnessing to Asian Youth*. It was a quarterly magazine 'linking English-speaking Christian students in Asia'. It contained articles on Christian living, testimonies and news on efforts to reach students in the Far East. OCF ordered 500 copies for sale in the mid-1960s (110 each for Melbourne and Sydney). Several OCF members held editorial positions.

Finance for the magazine came from the Overseas University Fund, which was a centralised means for IVF affiliates to support missionary work among students in other countries. OCF centres contributed to this fund. For example, just under half of OCF Melbourne's budget was allocated to it, with their other expenses being for hall hire and the purchase of Christian literature.

Many returned missionaries became associate members, spoke at OCF, or invited OCF to their special meetings. Sometimes, this was possible because the IVF arranged itineraries of visiting speakers with the OCF conventions in mind. Dr William Lees, who had been mainly working with the indigenous people of Borneo, spoke at the 1964 convention. He said that he had been praying for the Chinese of that island for ten years. He praised God for hearing his prayers, for on the platform with him, were two Chinese young men from Borneo, the outgoing and incoming chairpersons of OCF Australia, Shen Dah Cheong from Sabah and Wong Toh Sing from Sarawak.

Thus, OCF developed a global concern, and sense of calling. This is evident in the convention themes: Preparing now in Australia to serve Jesus Christ overseas (1959), Christ the only answer for Asia (1960), Ambassadors for Christ (1961), and Servants of the Most High God (1966).

The connections made in OCF often continued outside Australia. When Dah Cheong returned to Kota Kinabalu for holidays, he sometimes accompanied Borneo Evangelical Mission (BEM) pilot Bruce Morton to visit Chinese villages. Dah Cheong could speak Chinese, which the BEM missionaries couldn't (many learned languages of the indigenous people, rather than Chinese). On one occasion, after disembarking from the light plane, Dah Cheong and Bruce saw a Chinese Christian farmer praying under the hot sun. The farmer invited them to his house. He only owned one cup, so they had to take turns to drink.

OCF Melbourne at a one-day conference at the China Inland Mission office in Melbourne, 31 August 1963. Photo supplied by David Chong.

However, interest in *The Way* declined in the late 1960s. Phua Seng Min lamented that there had been no article contributions by OCFers for the past two editions, except a cartoon strip by Dr Bill Lim of OCF Sydney. Sustaining missionary interest among members was challenging. The OCF Perth president lamented that only twelve members turned up at a missionary meeting, despite it being term holidays. In 1965, the OCF Australia missionary secretary Stephen Chang report noted:

> Are we not tackling the almost impossible in seeking to interest all OCFers in the total world-wide missionary task of the Church? How many of us here at the AGM are genuinely interested? ... peculiar to OCF is the work of God in those areas which the

"Western" church considers the missionary field of its endeavours, but which is the work of God in our home country and in our local church.[84]

Stephen suggested that the primary focus of missionary secretaries should be to encourage members to keep abreast with news from home and to pray for needs in their home countries and local churches there. In this natural way of keeping in touch with news from home, OCF would be cultivating mission-mindedness and preparing members for future service. Where there were members also interested in missions further afield, then the missionary secretary could provide more information to those individuals.

For OCF members who had been preparing in Australia to serve Jesus Christ back home, returnees were missionaries. In fact, missionary news and returnee news was sometimes printed on the same page of OCF newsletters. In 1968, the OCF Melbourne Newsletter had a missionary news section, with news of returned OCFers Mrs Richard and Veronica Lee, and their involvement in their church. On the same page was a newsflash about Indira Gandhi restricting foreign missionaries because of allegations of 'anti-national activities of foreign missionaries'. There was also a need for doctors in Tanzania. Where were the Christian doctors?[85]

---

[84] Stephen Chang, 'OCF Australia Missionary Secretary's Report', 1965 AGM Minutes. MTC/IVF 159-11a/OCF AGM and convention 19656-66.

[85] 'Missionary News,' *OCF Melbourne Newsletter*, 1968. MTC/IVF 159-11a/OCF AGM 1968.

Newsletters

After close fellowship in Australia, keeping in touch with past members was a priority for many OCF leaders and centres. In response to a call for returnee news, associate member Jeannette Lin wrote a letter after travelling to Singapore, Kuala Lumpur, Kota Kinabalu, and Hong Kong. Her letter mentioned an astonishing twenty-three individuals or couples. In 1970, OCF Sydney published this letter. Excerpts follow.

Lawrence Chia who is honorary general secretary for SU [Scripture Union] finds that his commitments at the university as lecturer are very time-consuming. He is also candidates' secretary for the Overseas Missionary Fellowship in Singapore. He and his wife, *Pek Choo* are involved in their church where Lawrence is sessions clerk. I was privileged to enjoy their hospitality for a few days and met their little girl, Marion.

Many of you will still remember *Guan Chew* who recently returned to Australia to do a B. Ed (Hons). Last year, Guan was very ill, but is thankful to be much improved in health. Her love and desire to serve the Lord was wonderful to witness. If you are a girl and would like to stay with Guan for a few days, I am sure you will find her fellowship very enriching.

In *Kuala Lumpur*, Rev Wilfred Chee and his wife Lily are also blessed with a little girl. Wilfred is one of the three ministers serving the Anglican circuit in KL and is the main preacher of sermons in Chinese. I found his service and faithfulness very challenging. He came to pick me up in a Volkswagen which I *thought was his. He said it wasn't, nor was it a church car. Later he admitted that one of the doctors from his church, on leave in England, had asked him to look after and drive this car and after the doctor returns, another was going home for the rest of the year and had also asked Wilfred to look after his car. The church cannot afford to buy him a car but, I rejoiced to see how wonderfully God provided as his work would be much more difficult without transport. Pray for them, they may not have much by worldly standards, but I believe they are rich in God's love.*

...

Lim Kim Bew and Judy left Australia when **Kenny** was a baby, but now he is an active young boy of four. Their contributions in Sabah have been richly blessed but now they face a crossroad as Kim has finished his present contract. Pray for them to know God's will for the future. They also have another baby, Colin.

...

Moving on to **Sabah**, the OCFers are mainly from Melbourne. **Shen Dah Cheong** and his wife **Annie** serve in the Chinese section of their church amongst people who are not so highly educated yet still need Christ's love. Shen is also a Bible Society secretary and Moody Films Representative. I was humbled by their faithfulness and willingness to serve Christ. Their little boy is also called Eric.

...

One thing which impressed me greatly—how effective our Christian living depends on our individual relationship to Jesus Christ and how willing and available we are for his use. It does not matter what country we are in or how many OCF committee positions we hold but the crux of it all, whether we stand or fall— how real is your personal relationship to Jesus Christ? How obedient am I to his will?

It is sad but true I did meet and hear of OCFers who are not continuing with their Christian lives, but again, how real is your commitment to Jesus Christ because when all our Christian friends are gone and all the props taken away, only Christ remains. Is he enough?

As Bishop Dain said at an IVF missionary conference in 1965, 'AS NOW—SO THEN'.[86]

In December 1969, Ian Burnard wrote that the overseas student situation in Australia had changed since the Colombo Plan was inaugurated in 1952. Not all overseas students intend to return to their home countries and some come 'with the quite definite intention of remaining here … many even of the Colombo Plan students do not end up serving in their countries of origin'. Therefore, the vision of OCF had partially been annulled and should be rephrased:

> We in the OCFs and the EUs are anxious to present to every student the claims of the Lord Jesus Christ, and to prepare to serve him in missionary service in our vocation wherever God calls us to serve him; we

---

[86] Jeanette Lin, Letter to OCF Sydney Newsletter editor, *Vision*, OCF Sydney Newsletter, 1970. MTC/IVF 159-11a/OCF states 1969-71.

recognise that the missionary attitude is an evidence of discipleship of Jesus Christ, and it calls for death to ourselves, possibly physical and certainly a willingness to accept the consequences of standing for Jesus Christ wherever we are, and however difficult the circumstances will be; we recognise too the call of God for some to serve him in communities outside our own and we ask each others' prayers that we shall all uphold one another in serving him in such communities, specially praying that we shall be saved from escapist motives, from selfishness, and willing always to serve the poor and weak, and to exercise personal and collective justice in all our affairs.

Ian added this footnote to his report: 'It was exciting (and a bit terrifying) to see the attitude of OCFers at OCF Conf Jan 1970 as generally one of willingness to go home and serve Christ whatever the cost. There was a real missionary theme—missionary in a very good sense.'[87]

Around this time, four young graduates founded Perkantas, a Christian student fellowship group in Indonesia. Three of them had been OCF leaders. This is how it came about.

Perkantas

In 1969, after the OCF convention in Brisbane, Jimmy Koo (Kuswadi as he is now known) took the train to Sydney. He

---

[87] Ian Burnard, *Overseas Students in Australia*, [Handwritten report] December 1969. MTC/ IVF 159-11/Overseas Students (OCF) 1967-72.

thought about the challenge put to him by Chua Wee Hian, the IVF General Secretary to return to Indonesia to start a work among local students.[88] Two years prior, at the AGM, Ian Burnard had raised the need for more manpower in Indonesia and had said that the best way was to release one or two graduates to do the work of travelling around.[89] In 1968, Jimmy Kuswadi had given a presentation on the need in Indonesia at the OCF AGM.[90] OCF Australia had also sent several small monetary gifts (often from OCF convention surplus) to Soen Siregar, the second chairperson of OCF Australia. While working as an engineer, he was trying to reach Indonesian tertiary students.

As the train sped on, Jimmy thought about giving up his career as an electronics engineer. It was a Colombo Plan scholarship that enabled him to gain this qualification from the University of Tasmania. He had taken over the leadership of OCF Hobart from founder Jonathan Parapak. Jimmy was working happily in electronics and involved in OCF Sydney. As a Colombo Plan scholar, he was bonded for several years to the Indonesian government. After six months, the Colombo Plan officer tracked him down to Sydney and told him that he had to return to Indonesia. With Wee Hian's challenge in mind, he readily agreed and returned to Jakarta in mid-1970. Officials in Jakarta told him that there were no job vacancies for him and released him from his bond.

---

[88] Jimmy Kuswadi, Interview with Joshua Sim and Bob Rick Looi, 20 October 2021, Transcript p. 20.

[89] OCF Australia AGM minutes (Sydney, 1966), 15.

[90] OCF Australia AGM minutes (Brisbane, 1968), 13.

Taking this as God's providence, Jimmy agreed to serve students in Indonesia for three years. OCF Australia paid half his salary, and the other half was raised in Indonesia. To begin with, Jimmy contacted his former high school classmate, who was studying at a private university. Through this connection, he began Bible Studies with interested students. Jimmy reconnected with Jonathan Parapak, who was lecturing at the prestigious University of Indonesia. He helped Jimmy secure a part-time lecturer's position there. This was a huge blessing; the volatile situation after the failed 1965 Communist coup meant suspicion was cast on anyone not studying or working on campus in a formal capacity.

On 29 June 1971, Perkantas was formally registered by four Indonesian professionals. David Wang had just graduated from the United States. The other three were former OCF members: Soen Siregar (OCF Australia's second chairperson), Jonathan Parapak (OCF Hobart's founder), Jimmy Kuswadi (OCF Hobart's past chairperson). They chose Soen to be the first Perkantas president, and appointed Jimmy as their first staff worker.

Around this time, Wee Hian visited Jimmy, who was still living with his parents. Although they were not Christian, they were supportive of his work.

'Jimmy,' said Wee Hian, 'it would be better for you to be married and have your own home as a base from which to work. Is there anyone you're interested in?'

'Well, there's Jeannette,' replied Jimmy, 'but she is in Sydney.'

Jimmy and Jeannette had never dated but had attended the same meetings about four nights a week: Moore College lectures, media classes for Christian communications, and a Bible study that Jimmy started in the Eastern suburbs. Jeannette had also visited Jimmy for three weeks in Jakarta when she volunteered with the World Council of Churches. Jimmy had arranged for Jeannette to be billeted at his parents' home. Their friendship clearly had potential, but Jimmy had no money to return to Australia. Wee Hian arranged for Jimmy to speak at the 1971 OCF convention in Perth, after which he travelled to Sydney to marry Jeannette. After the wedding, Jimmy and Jeannette moved into their own house in Jakarta. With Jeannette onboard, the ministry among female students grew. In August 1974, Jimmy and Jeannette returned to Australia.

Today, Perkantas is a widespread and thriving ministry that has spread out from Jakarta. They have hundreds of campus branches and thousands of members throughout the provinces of Indonesia.

After a decade and a half of consistent growth, across many institutes of education, Christian denominations, and nationalities, OCF Australia started to have a positive impact on Christian ministries beyond Australia. This impact was felt in churches in Australia and beyond, and in other Christian ministries such as Scripture Union and Perkantas.

This early period was the height of affection and cooperation between the IVF and OCF. Much of it can be attributed to the love that Ian Burnard had for overseas students and his wise counsel. Ian retired from the IVF in the early 1970s and joined the police force. The constant travel to minister across Australia was taxing and ill-suited to family life. Ian's gift to OCF was in the Christ-like manner in which he related to the students, wise yet humble, demonstrating the importance of personal relationships in the work of ministry.

OCF Australia was established as a fellowship around Jesus Christ. Week after week, the Holy Spirit brought the life of Christ to members as they spurred one another on through Bible studies, encouraging words and corporate prayer. Unencumbered by expectations and tradition, new and innovative ideas were trialled, often to good effect as there was a plurality of godly men and women to guide the students. OCF Australia flourished as a spiritual family away from home. In this family, all who were willing were used by God and contributed according to their giftings and skills. As they served one another, they found a place to belong.

Section 1: Early Days, 1950s to early 1970s

OCF AUSTRALIA IN THE EARLY 1970S

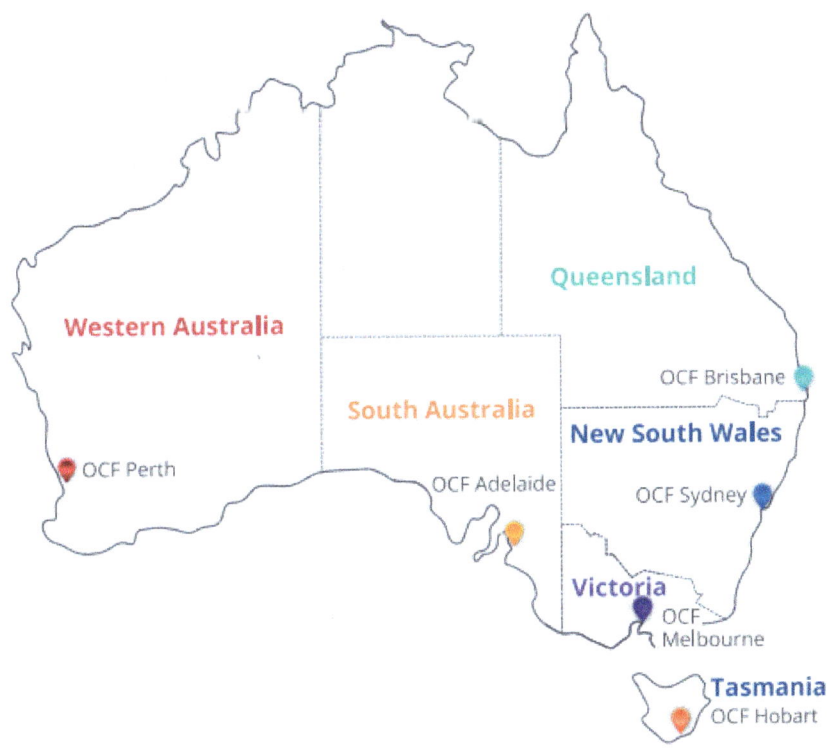

Section 2: Middle years, mid 1970s–late 1990s

By 1970, there were six cities with one OCF centre each. OCFs Perth and Hobart had been added to the four founding centres of Brisbane, Sydney, Melbourne and Adelaide.

After a period of steady growth, most of these centres faced the question of how to manage growth. Centres had more members, and they lived further apart. Should there be more than one OCF centre per city? If so, how should these groups relate to one another? If a new university already had Christian groups on-campus, was there any need or reason to form an OCF group there? How could OCF minister to overseas students in far-flung towns or cities?

As centres found their own solutions to these questions, they developed local distinctives to a greater degree. Yet, since formation, the rhythm of OCF had continued unchanged—weekly local meetings and an annual convention and General Meeting. AGM discussions took on a more urgent tone because of the complexity of responding to huge changes of this period such as the abolishment of the White Australia Policy. AGMs became a place where leaders had to wrestle with the challenges of their times and engage with their fellow brothers and sisters in Christ, some with opinions very different from their own. This ongoing process shaped and reshaped the OCF identity, making it sharper on certain fronts due to conclusions reached by student leaders after corporate deliberations.

At the local level, strong friendships, a love of God's word and a concern for overseas students continued to energise the fellowship. By the end of this period, signs of strain were beginning to appear, possibly due to expansion without a commensurate addition to resources.

9. Melbourne

Since 1959, OCF Melbourne had been meeting on Sunday afternoons at the Chinese Church of Christ on Queensbury Street in the city. In addition, many members also gathered on Friday nights for informal Bible studies in several locations. Over the years, this included rented houses in Parkville, Hawthorn, Carlton and Clayton. These Bible study groups were formed spontaneously by students, who found it convenient to meet near where they lived.

All the Friday meetings were held near the city centre, except for the Clayton Bible study group. Not many Clayton members wanted to make the long trip into the city for public OCF meetings. Disinterest and then disunity crept in. In some ways, these were natural by-products of growth in numbers and diversity. Fortunately, after a brief break in fellowship, OCF centres in Victoria regrouped, closer than before.

At a national level, OCF Australia faced its first major challenge since formation: the possibility of immigration to Australia challenged the assumption that all overseas students would return to their home countries to serve God there.

Three co-chairs: Parkville, Clayton, La Trobe

Parkville

By the mid-1970s, the Parkville Bible study group had grown to occupy two adjacent double-storey townhouses on Gatehouse Street on Friday nights. An audio cable and speaker connected both houses, so that both groups could sing together, from the songbook *Songs of Glory* and also some in-house compositions. Most members attended

Pastor Allan and Val Webb singing at a gathering at their home in Melbourne, circa mid-1970s. Photos of missionaries overseas adorn the wall. Photo supplied by the OCF Alumni Network.

Swanston Street Church of Christ (COC) on Sundays, and one of the ministers there, Pastor Bruce Morton and his wife Ruth, supported the Parkville group. At Swanston Street COC, both Pastor Morton and Senior Pastor Allan Webb had a great love for overseas students.

In 1971, the Swanston Street COC Senior Pastor Dr Lloyd Jones had fallen gravely ill. When the congregation approached Associate Pastor Allan Webb to take his place, he and his wife Val reiterated their primary aim of working with overseas students. The Webbs were Queenslanders who viewed their time in Melbourne as a season of preparation before missionary service in Asia. When the congregation affirmed that he should focus on overseas students, Pastor

From left: Bruce and Ruth Morton, Dora, Geoffrey and David Chong, 1973. Photo supplied by the OCF Alumni Network.

Webb accepted the role of senior pastor. The student ministry, that had begun during Dr Lloyd Jones' tenure, grew to the point whereby Pastor Webb told the board that he needed help. Not long thereafter, there was a knock on the door at Pastor Webb's home in Kew.

The man introduced himself as Bruce Morton (See the section *Continued Exposure* in Chapter 8*)*. He said, 'You might think this is very, very strange, but I know about your ministry at Swanston Street. My wife and I have been missionaries in East Malaysia for twenty years. We just miss so much our involvement with Asian people, and with students. Would you mind if we started to worship at your church?'

'Not at all,' said Pastor Webb. 'We would love to have you come.'

Pastor Webb shared this with the church board. He explained that Bruce and his wife Ruth attended Wattle Park Gospel Chapel and had previously been missionaries with the Borneo Evangelical Mission.

'This seems to be God, His intervention and leading,' they said. 'Why don't you ask him whether he would be willing to consider the possibility of not just attending, but becoming part of the ministry team?'

Bruce agreed. Allan and Bruce became firm friends and colleagues. Tuesday morning pastor meetings, supposed to be for half an hour, sometimes extend to three or four hours, as they prayed together, and shared their vision, hopes and dreams. Bruce and Ruth Morton became an integral part of the Parkville Bible study group, and even relocated from their Box Hill home to Parkville.

La Trobe

In August 1976, a group of La Trobe students went away for their first Bible Camp. Their Bundoora campus was about an hour's drive northeast of the city. They had been doing Friday afternoon Bible studies at Chisholm College, a residential college, with Pastor Allan Webb.

At the camp, Pastor Webb led a series of four studies on the Sermon on the Mount. He had written questions that were probing and practical:

> 'Could you rank, in order of importance, how the Christian community should be a force in society: individual purity, radical lifestyle of love, involvement in the needs of society, separation from society?'

> 'In my opinion the reason why our group is not a vital force within the Uni is because we don't intimately know: a) God, b) each other, c) the Scriptures, 4) the needs of our fellow students."[91]

After the camp, the students decided to form OCF La Trobe to be a light on campus.

---

[91] Allan Webb, 'Study 1, Evaluating My Attitudes,' in *Latrobe Bible Study Camp* (Melbourne, 1976), 3.

Section 2: Middle years, mid 1970s-late 1990s

OCF Clayton, mid-1970s, with Pastor Pat Kavanagh. Photo supplied by OCF Alumni Network.

Clayton

In the early 1970s, a large influx of Malaysian and Singaporean students began arriving to study at Monash University. Some of them were Christian and attended the Clayton Bible study group on Friday nights. Christian students invited their friends from the residential halls and surrounding apartments. There were few social opportunities in Clayton and students came on Friday nights—whether from boredom or interest, it didn't really matter. Together, they studied the Navigator series on Christianity, a widely used Bible study series. Some argued their way through the study, others were open to the message. All contributed to lively and engaging Bible discussions and enjoyed a simple supper of hot drinks and biscuits afterwards.

From 1972 to 1976, Phua Kwee Sin was a postgraduate student at Monash University. He had become a Christian at the end of 1968, when he was a first-year student at Melbourne University. Subsequently, he served in OCF Melbourne, in various roles of increasing responsibility, until he became the OCF Australia chairperson in 1973. On weekdays at the Monash university campus, he would often meet new students to encourage them in their studies and faith journey.

In 1973, Pastor Pat Kavanagh took up the role of pastor at the Clayton Church of Christ, located near Monash University. He was a faithful and gifted Bible teacher, always keen to share the gospel message. He had been a butcher before his conversion and joked that he lost half of his vocabulary when he became a Christian. He saw the needs of overseas students and made every effort to welcome them to church. Church members brought students home for meals and learned how to cook basic Chinese food. The students' interest in the gospel revitalised the church. Through the witness of the church and students at the Clayton Bible study group, many overseas students came to know the Lord.

By 1974, there were more people attending Clayton Bible studies than OCF Melbourne public meetings. In one year, attendance at OCF meetings in the city halved to only 35 members. In 1975, OCF Melbourne public meetings ceased altogether. The following year, a restructuring committee proposed that all Bible study groups function autonomously with their own leadership. Each group would send representatives to the annual OCF Australia AGM. Parkville voted 'yes', but Clayton voted 'no'. Yue Chee Yoon was a first-year student when the vote in Clayton was taken. His impression was that Clayton did not want to be the little brother of OCF Melbourne. As a result, OCF Melbourne dissolved and wound up on 30 May 1977. The ministry in Clayton continued as the Clayton Overseas Christian Group.[92]

Victorian Centres Regroup

In 1977, the Clayton Overseas Christian Group elected Yue Chee Yoon as their leader. To Chee Yoon, it did not make sense for Clayton to exist as an independent group. He saw benefits of being part of a larger Australia-wide group to share resources. Chee Yoon initiated the move of Clayton to re-join OCF Australia. Even though the La Trobe Bible study group was smaller than Parkville and Clayton, all had the sense of being equal partners. Hence, in 1978, OCF Australia was co-chaired by leaders of these three groups.

In 1979, the new student leaders of the three groups formalised what their predecessors had initiated. Calvin Ma, Daniel Wong and Freddy Boey were leaders of Parkville, La Trobe and Clayton respectively. With the help of a former member of OCF Melbourne, Pastor Chia Chek Kwang, they wrote a new constitution for OCF Melbourne. Each leader brought this proposal and constitution to their members. All

---

[92] Yue Chee Yoon and Tracy Yue, Interview with author, 2021. Transcript p. 3.

members voted in favour of the constitution. And so, OCF in Victoria reformed as OCFs Parkville, La Trobe and Clayton.

OCF Geelong

As a result, the chairpersons of the three groups took turns to host quarterly meetings where they could support one another and plan joint events such as combined May camps. With renewed unity, the Victorian centres were able to help overseas students in Geelong. Freddy would drive his beat-up Volkswagen to minister to the small group there. Calvin often went along. They used to belt out their favourite songs on these long road trips. OCF Geelong was re-affiliated in 1980. (It had first been affiliated in 1961, but low student numbers and high leadership turnover led to its dissolution in 1964.)

Declaration of the Priority to Serve Our Own People

While the Victorian centres were regrouping, the Fraser government wanted to introduce an Overseas Student Charge in 1978. (Tertiary education had been free for domestic and international students under the previous Whitlam government.) Australian students opposed the overseas student fees because they feared that domestic students would eventually also be charged tertiary education fees. Calvin heard that some OCF members had been caught up in these protests.

In this confused state, the OCF Australia EXCO, hosted by Victoria, considered what they should do. It happened that Hwa Yung, a former OCF Australia chairperson, was visiting Australia to marry Bee Teik, a member of Clayton OCF. Hwa Yung was completing his theological training in the United Kingdom. He was passionate about OCF members returning to Asia where the needs were urgent and immeasurably great. Hwa Yung's message resonated with the EXCO. At their invitation, Hwa Yung addressed the General Council (GC) at the 1978 AGM in Sydney.

There, OCF leaders wrestled with how to lead OCF in the turmoil of a changing education and immigration landscape. OCF Australia's founding vision had been for its members to prepare in Australia to return home to serve their respective countries.[93] The GC unanimously agreed that God had a unique purpose for OCF members, and that their time in Australia was not by chance. Rather, God wanted to make them his instruments to bring the gospel to those who had not yet heard. Furthermore, they saw that Asians could reach other Asians more easily than Anglo-Celtic Australians. They reasoned that OCF was a training school to equip God's labourers, in Asia and beyond. As such, all OCF members should carefully consider God's purpose for their lives, and not to seek migration simply because the option was available.

Thus, at the 1978 AGM, to signal their firm commitment and to communicate all this, the EXCO and leaders from each

---

[93] Calvin and Joyce Ma. Interview with author, 2021. Transcript pp. 24, 26 – 28.

of the seven centres (Adelaide, Hobart, Newcastle, Sydney, Brisbane, Melbourne, Perth) signed the 'Declaration of the priority to serve our own people':

In seeking to please God, I _____ pledge to affirm this declaration with God being my witness and helper.'

After the AGM, OCF Sydney hosted the convention with 260 members and an exuberance of having recaptured God's vision for OCF.[94] A united OCF Australia leadership went back with the message to their centres, 'Unless God speaks to you clearly otherwise, return to your home country to serve Him and His church' along with a renewed focus on prayer and fasting, being discipled and equipped to return home. In Victoria, Calvin, Freddy and Daniel organised the first ever Returnees Camp to give students nearing the end of their courses an opportunity to spend a few weeks in a Bible College, an opportunity likely unavailable after they returned home.[95]

Through serving together, the three leaders grew very close. The demands of ministry had been great due to growth in all Victorian centres, but also full of joy. (OCF Clayton had moved to the religious centre on campus that seated 400 people by this stage.) Freddy was the first of the three to graduate. Before he left, the trio met for dinner in a small and noisy Chinese restaurant. After the meal, they walked to Swanston Street Church, to the little nook in front of Knox Hall, and sat on the dustbins in the carpark. As Daniel

---

[94] *OCF Sydney 1957-2007*, 12.
[95] Calvin Ma, Email to author, 21 August 2023.

remembered it, 'The Lord just prompted us to pray at this spot. It proves God can make any place holy and sanctified as long as his servants are willing and faithful to obey him.'[96]

The change of Australian government policy allowed graduates who had found employment to remain as permanent residents. Many overseas students, including OCF members, decided to stay on. OCF Sydney saw that permanent residents could help OCF fulfil its vision of equipping its members to return home. As a result, the 1979 AGM minutes record a statement acknowledging the role of Australian permanent residents in their support for OCF.

> 'Some of the OCF members interpreted the manifesto as a way of telling them to go home; this created a sense of "second class" Christians insofar as the permanent residents were concerned. It was felt that the problem laid in interpretation. Subsequently, a motion was passed at the 21st AGM, 1979 (Melbourne) that read: "AGM recognises the role the permanent resident can play towards achieving the aims and objectives of OCF (Australia)." At that AGM, the issue on the Government Policy Change was discussed. Many members had decided to go home prior to the change in policy. It was agreed that "regardless of any policies, OCFers should have the aim of equipping themselves well to return home." It was proposed that OCF "should encourage church involvement, as there is no OCF back home, but Church. OCF is NOT a church."[97]

---

[96] Daniel Wong, WhatsApp to author, 27 July 2023.
[97] *OCF (Australia) Handbook* (5th ed., 1992), p. 12, quoting minutes of the 21st AGM in 1979.

By this time, Kwee Sin had decided to remain in Australia. Sometime later, he bumped into a former OCF member. After their short conversation, Kwee Sin realised that this person had kept quiet about their desire to remain in Australia because the push to go home had been so intense. Personally, Kwee Sin felt that this should be a matter for each individual to decide before God. This episode shows the difficulty of trying to capture, in a two-page document, a sentiment for all of OCF Australia, which came from good intentions and real conviction.

Carlton

Meanwhile, OCF Parkville continued to grow, to the point of overcrowding so much so that some members stopped attending. Those who remained found it hard to integrate into such a large fellowship. Prayer meetings and training programs were poorly attended. Leaders concluded that some degree of quality had been sacrificed because of numerical growth.

The OCF Parkville leadership considered whether they should start a new centre, especially as nursing students and those from the Royal Melbourne Institute of Technology (RMIT) could not attend outreach and lunchtime events at Melbourne Uni. They prayed and discussed alternatives at special meetings where all members were given an opportunity to speak. They could divide according to where people lived, or where they studied. OCF Parkville members studied at Melbourne Uni, RMIT, Pharmacy College, Swinburne, and high schools. Some were working graduates. Most members lived in the suburbs of Carlton, Parkville and North Melbourne.

Eventually, the group decided that OCF Parkville would cater for Melbourne University and returning students, whereas a new group—OCF Carlton—would comprise of RMIT students, other colleges and the working graduates, and they would meet at the Lygon Street Church of Christ. Pastor Bruce and Mrs Ruth Morton remained OCF Parkville advisors, while Pastor Pat and Mrs Kavanagh became OCF Carlton advisors. The Kavanaghs had moved from Clayton Church of Christ back to Lygon Street Chapel.

By the end of 1982, an OCF Carlton committee was appointed, with Vincent Lo the first president. Henry and Juliana Kong, and Wayne Gurney were among the working graduates who pioneered OCF Carlton. The affiliation of OCF Carlton was warmly received at the 1982 AGM.

As a result of commissioning key people to start up a new group, both OCF Parkville and OCF Carlton had to find more leaders to take care of cell groups, which were small groups for Bible study discussions and often where pastoral care took place. Through this, they discovered hidden talent among their members. Within three months, God blessed their step of faith when both OCF Parkville and OCF Carlton grew further. Vincent was very conscious that it was the Lord's work. He wrote an article on 'OCF Carlton, vision for growth: a perinatal perspective' for the OCF Australia newsletter. He concluded by quoting Psalm 127:1, 'Unless the Lord builds the house, the builders labor in vain.'[98]

The decentralisation of OCF centres in Victoria gave students in various educational institutes the freedom to seek God, while enjoying the benefits of fellowship as one body. In Victoria, the number of OCF centres increased, spreading out over a larger area. This made it easier for students to attend meetings, as some Australian cities span huge distances. The problem and solution of urban sprawl played out over the greater part of a decade. This meant that successive generations of OCF leaders met the challenges to the best of their ability, according to what they discerned as God's will, before handing the ministry on for the next generation to adjust and reshape. The question of migration was a larger and more complex issue that OCF Australia is still wrestling with to this day. Perhaps to wrestle, as we seek the mind of God, is a good thing. In so doing, we recognise that none of us have all the answers. This recognition in itself is a hallmark of humility, a precursor to true fellowship.

---

[98] Vincent Lo, 'OCF Carlton Vision for Growth: A Perinatal Perspective,' *OCF Australia Newsletter* 1/1, 1983, 20, 21.

10. Sydney

In 1974, OCF Sydney implemented a Priority Year to help members prioritise their busy lives. Of particular concern was that OCF Sydney no longer seemed to be effective in reaching out. Personal Evangelism Groups (PEG) were formed to rectify this. Both Priority Year and Operation PEG 'flopped', which led OCF Sydney part-time staff worker Peter Tow to remark, 'failure lies in each one of us, for in the final reckoning, organisation cannot substitute for real spiritual concern for those without Christ.'[99] However, change was just around the corner.

Sydney's District Bible Study Groups

In 1976, Chris Chua was the OCF Australia chairperson, and Koo Tuk Su the OCF Sydney president. Together, they led OCF Sydney through a period of growth and restructuring. By this time, Sydney was a huge city with thousands of overseas students. Advisors encouraged OCF Sydney to go to where the people were. Evangelism could be done locally, while public meetings would become teaching sessions. The OCF Sydney leadership saw District Bible Study Groups (DBSG) as the means to achieve this. The seed of the solution had already been planted some years prior.

Back in 1962, OCF Sydney had started two Bible study groups that were autonomous and decided on their own

---

[99] *OCF Sydney 1957-2007,* 10.

programs. They met fortnightly, alternating with public meetings which had lost their homely feel because of size—90 attendees on average, but it could reach 200 on special occasions. From 1962 to 1976, OCF Sydney ran between two to five such groups. As group leaders and members were all students, and meeting places were rented properties, membership composition and meeting locations kept changing. The health of the groups depended on a number of factors such as the calibre of the leader and the suitability of Bible study material. Furthermore, if churches in the area were running similar activities, interest in OCF Bible study groups waned. Church engagement was positive, as the needs of students were being met. In contrast, inadequately trained OCF leaders or unsuitable materials were problems that should be resolved. So, in the mid-1970s, when the OCF Sydney leadership saw DBSGs as key to outreach, they turned their attention to these groups to organise and resource them properly.

In 1976, Koo Tuk Su became the OCF Sydney chairperson. In October of the same year, an OCF Program Planning Committee was formed, led by Chris Chua. They sought to fulfil the OCF vision by training Bible study leaders well, so that when they went home, they could continue to serve the Lord in their churches. To do this, the committee developed a three-year Bible study series, suited to the average time students remained in OCF. The series systematically covered important topics through book studies, such as Mark (the ministry of Jesus), Acts (the birth of the church), and Romans (Christian doctrine). Bible study leaders were trained in sound principles of Bible interpretation, and practical skills of facilitating small groups. This huge structural, training and resourcing change was accomplished through many leaders at OCF Sydney working together. Furthermore, at least five OCF Sydney members were studying at Moore Theological College at the time, including Tuk Su and Chris Chua. These two young men worked closely together. They led OCF Sydney with a macro view across many District Bible Study Groups. Tuk Su concentrated on counselling, pastoral care, and troubleshooting; while Chris focused on Bible study and training.

From left: Bruce Winter (7th, wearing a tie), Chris Chua (8th), Koo Tuk Su (9th). Circa 1978.

The venue of CDG1 in the suburb of Lewisham.
Many OCF members attending Sydney University in the 1970s attended CDG1.

The DBSGs became known as the Northern, Central and Eastern District Bible Study Groups, or NDG, CDG and EDG respectively. They were located where the students lived, mostly close to universities they attended. NDG was close to Macquarie University, CDG to Sydney University, and EDG to the University of New South Wales (UNSW). There was no university in the southwest, but there were high school overseas students who lived there. Ho May Leng opened her home in the suburb of Campsie to these students, who were mostly from Hong Kong and Malaysia. Hence, there was a South West District Group for a time. Chris Chua helped lead Bible studies there, until those students went to universities, almost all of them to UNSW. By this time, there were already four EDGs, so they became EDG5.

All these Bible study groups met at the rented houses of OCF members. The homely atmosphere of the Bible study groups attracted many overseas students. Soon, hosts were not only tidying up the lounge, but also their bedrooms and sometimes even the laundry! After Bible studies, they ate supper from mismatching plates and cups. This humble just-as-I-am hospitality became an oasis of genuine friendship for poor overseas students, unable to afford glitzy entertainment or fancy restaurants.

South West District Group, late 1970s.

From 1974 to 1979, attendance at DBSGs quadrupled to 275. Much of the growth was in the east, near UNSW, where many overseas students were enrolled. The overseas student quota in Australia varied for different courses in different universities. Newer universities such as Monash in

Melbourne and UNSW—tended to have more places for overseas students, compared to more well-established universities such as Sydney and Melbourne University.[100]

In 1979, Tuk Su passed on the OCF Sydney leadership to Colin Lee. (At this time, the term of the OCF Sydney leadership was three years.) OCF Sydney also appointed Chris Chua as Honorary General Secretary and employed Melanie Moana two days a week to minister to female OCF members. Melanie's salary was supplied by offerings from the students at OCF Sydney meetings. Chris declined payment as he had started work in a Chinese church.[101] For state level planning, Tuk Su, Chris and several other leaders formed an early

EDG3 in 1982.

---

[100] Stewart E Fraser, 'Overseas Students in Australia: Governmental Policies and Institutional Programs,' *The University of Chicago Press* 28, no. 2 (1984): 286.

[101] Chris Chua, Interview with author, 2021.

Bible study group in Glebe, late 1970s

version of the Executive Board, with Colin Lee focusing on administration and strategic growth. The Executive Board would invite students to form new groups when existing groups became too large, or when a new ministry opportunity presented itself.

For some years, there had been a Bible study group in a rented house in the suburb of Glebe. It catered to Sydney University students and overseas student nurses who worked at the Prince Alfred Hospital next to Sydney University. In the late 1970s, OCF members moved out of the Glebe home. To replace it, CDG1 started in Petersham, also near Sydney University. When CDG1 became overcrowded, Indonesian student Rostina Tioniwar was sent to lead a new group that started in Moore College to cater for the Sydney University students who stayed at Deaconess House.¹⁰² The Executive Board also initiated a Nurses' Fellowship for nursing students whose roster made it difficult for them to attend OCF regularly. Regular lunchtime on-campus meetings at UNSW were also started as a means of outreach.

Sometimes, the initiative to reach out to a particular group came from the District Group leaders themselves. In mid-1981, EDG1 re-evaluated the vision of their group and were reminded of the OCF's aim to reach out. They realised that many Indonesian students were arriving, but few came to OCF. After several months of prayer, the Lord brought four new Indonesian high school students to join them. The group eventually grew to 25 people, with special provisions, such as Indonesian Bible Studies to remove the language barrier as far as possible. They also had fortnightly prayer meetings, with a fellowship dinner.¹⁰³ OCF Sydney leadership approached AFES to help them look for a staff worker to support its ministry. AFES recommended and appointed Graham Cocks, who spoke Indonesian fluently, to be the AFES link staff worker for OCF, with special attention for EDG1. A call for donations towards Graham's salary was published in the 1983 OCF Sydney magazine.¹⁰⁴

As OCF Sydney grew larger, administration and communication became a challenge. In response, a Steering Committee was formed in 1980 comprising of the Executive

---

[102] Chris Chua, WhatsApp to author, 1 August 2023.
[103] Ratna Chong, 'The Indonesian Ministry,' *The Mustard Seed*, 1983, 30, 31.
[104] 'Staff Worker Support Scheme', *The Mustard Seed*, 1983, 10.

Board and leaders of all District Groups, the UNSW campus outreach and Workers' Fellowship leaders.

In 1982, OCF Sydney celebrated its 25th anniversary. The ministry had grown to 11 District Groups, an outreach arm at UNSW, and one Workers' Fellowship.[105] With the exception of the Workers' Fellowship leader, all '21 frontline workers' were full-time non-theological students. Colin Lee observed that OCF Sydney had become isolated from other Christian groups, the AFES in particular. Compared to the founding years, OCF Sydney lacked the input from local Australian Christians, staff workers and permanent residents.

'The average [OCF Sydney] leader is a second- or third-year University student with little experience in Christian leadership. He is caught up with fulfilling his responsibilities in OCF and often in church as well'.[106] However, at a church popular with OCF members, one of the pastors started to see OCF as a distraction. There was disappointment when OCF members did not participate in the life of the church. Sometimes students stayed up so late on a Saturday night for their DBSGs that they couldn't wake up for church the next day.[107] This situation led to much discussion around the responsibilities of an OCF member, and the OCFer and the church. Topics such as these led Colin Lee's EXCO to update the *OCF (Australia) Handbook*, a transitional copy in 1982, and then a fuller update published in 1984.

---
[105] Vincent Chin, 'Chairman's Report OCF Sydney', *The Mustard Seed*, 1983, 6, 7.
[106] *OCF Sydney 1957-2007*, 5, 10, 18.
[107] Vincent and Mary Chin, and Peter Chin, Interview with author, 2022.

Adding to the Handbook

This comprehensive revision of the *OCF (Australia) Handbook* was carried out almost twenty years after it was first published. From this point on, the Handbook would be updated with greater regularity, highlighting a need to constantly articulate the vision and aims of OCF Australia, and adapt its structures and processes in a changing context. Articles added to the Handbook in the early 1980s include:

- 'Evangelical position of OCF', by Chris Chua. It gives a broad view of what it is to be an evangelical. At its core, it is someone who believes in Jesus Christ, and is motivated and captured by the good news of Jesus Christ for all people.

- 'Visions and Aims of OCF', which emphasised the two-fold aspect: present (to reach out and build up), and future (to send home). In this article, the 1978 Declaration was published. (See the section *Declaration of the Priority to Serve our Own People* in Chapter 9).

- 'The Local Church and OCFer', and 'Responsibilities of an OCFer'. Both urged OCF members to actively serve in OCF and their local churches. However, some items outlined as minimal church involvement come across today as rather prescriptive, such as, 'Regular attendance at <u>all</u> Sunday services—morning and evening.' Other points have shaped OCF practice to this day. For example, 'Committee meetings and OCF activities should never clash with Sunday worship times.'

Taken together, these articles helped to define some important areas for OCF Australia, which student leaders saw as crucial to its life.[108]

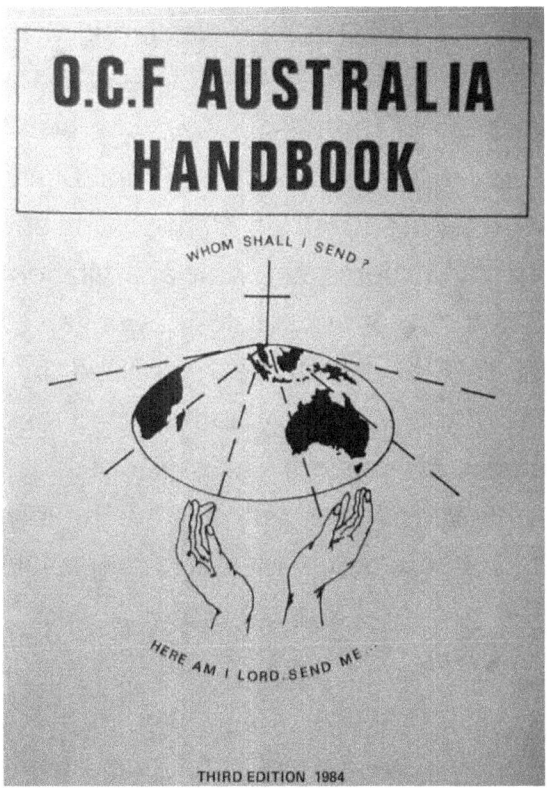

Cover of the OCF (Australia) Handbook, third edition, 1984.

In summary, to encourage and sustain growth, OCF Sydney centralised pastoral care, training and administration. At the same time, District Groups had the freedom to exercise

---

[108] Calvin Ma, Email to author, 'Question about [why the] 'Declaration to Serve our own People' [was] inserted into the Handbook', 21 August 2023.

leadership and set direction. The overall effect was to strengthen the whole group, while it grew in diversity and in its capacity to meet local needs. This method worked well due to the number of mature Christian student leaders available in the late 1970s to disciple and encourage young members in the faith.

By this stage, OCF Australia was larger than it had been in the 1960s. Back then, the response of leaders to issues arising were shaped through interactions with one another and with the IVF General Secretary Ian Burnard. Ian was relational in his approach to problem-solving and raising new leaders. After Ian's retirement, official affiliation with the IVF was maintained but, pragmatically, ties began to loosen. The reasons for this have not been studied by the author, although one of the IVF history books noted the following, 'To begin with OCF was regarded as part of the IVF though the affiliation was very loose. As it grew rapidly, the mixed tertiary/non-tertiary members raised difficulties within IVF and over the years OCF has become a large organisation standing on its own feet.'[109]

By the 1980s, OCF Australia was led by a whole new generation of student leaders, who had close relationships with various mentors and pastors in their cities. However, on a national level, they did not have any one individual or organisation to guide them, or to carry their institutional memory. Therefore, student leaders grappled with and responded to challenges as best they could. Leaders started

---

[109] John and Moyra Prince, *Out of the Tower*, (Sydney: ANZEA Publishers, 1987), 40.

using the *OCF (Australia) Handbook* to pass on their decisions, even though the message did not always filter down to local centres, or to subsequent generations. Furthermore, the message sometimes became more pointed over time than had been intended. Without original writers to demonstrate that service flowed out of deep and dynamic faith in Christ, or to explain their intent and provide nuanced interpretation, guidelines could become prescriptive and prevent innovative solutions to new challenges.

11. Adelaide

In 1977, a new diaspora church, the Austral-Asian Christian Church (AACC) in Adelaide, employed a part-time staff worker for OCF Adelaide. As OCF had been so formative in their spiritual journey, the church founders wanted to give back to the group that seemed to be in a rut.

A Diaspora Church Funds a Staff Worker

In 1974, OCF Adelaide comprised of four Bible study groups that met in different locations. Through their study of Hebrews, the group for college and nursing students saw the need to reach Asian migrants in Adelaide. At their encouragement, former Asian Fellowship member Neoh Sim Hee started a Bible study group in his home. This became a place where Asian Christians in Adelaide, including former OCF members, could bring their friends and tell them about the Lord. Over the next two years, more people joined them, including former Asian Fellowship chairperson Peter Cheng.[110]

In 1976, evangelist Andrew Gih from China travelled around Southeast Asia and Australia. He encouraged the Chinese diaspora to set up churches to reach other Chinese. Peter and his wife Amy hosted a dinner for him. Andrew urged the group to pool their resources to begin the first

---

[110] Neoh Sim Hee, 'The Austral-Asian Christian Church and OCF,' *OCF [Adelaide] 25 Years: to him be the glory 1956-1981*, 1981, 18.

Asian church in Adelaide. Thus, they formed the Austral-Asian Christian Church (AACC).

Unexpected opposition came from OCF, which maintained that OCF members should return to their home countries. Some local ministers also objected because they felt that it would be better for migrants to become part of existing churches. However, when Sim Hee, Peter and others explained that Asians were best placed to reach other Asians, these ministers gave their support to the new church. As the new church had no pastor, three respected preachers shared the preaching rota. They were Rev Geoff Bingham, an Anglican minister and principal of the Adelaide Bible Institute; Dr Barry Chant a Pentecostal minister; and Dr Victor Pfitzner, principal of the Lutheran seminary.

Meanwhile, OCF Adelaide seemed to be lacking direction. So, in 1977, AACC employed Geoff Sunstrom as OCF Adelaide's part-time staff worker. The church set aside more than half her offering to do so. Geoff recalled the conversation.

'We're looking to appoint a staff worker, something like twenty hours a week,' said Sim Hee. 'We would really like that person to be Chinese, but you're doing the job, so we're inviting you.'

'Cool,' said Geoff. 'I'm in for it'.

Geoff had been converted through the ministry of the Adelaide University Evangelical Students in July 1966. Having no church background, he joined OCF where he was nurtured as a young Christian. It was perfect for him. One and a half years later, after completing his science degree and teaching diploma, he enrolled at the Adelaide Bible Institute. From 1977 to 1982, Geoff served as a part-time staff worker in OCF Adelaide.[111]

Mid-way through Geoff's ministry to OCF Adelaide, there came a turning point for the group. In 1979, several new students from overseas joined them. By this stage many OCF members attended AACC. There was a relationship of mutual love between the students and the church, which was like a spiritual home. Asian lunches provided a weekly opportunity to connect with many uncles, aunties and church families. Some students also helped in work among refugees at the Pennington Resettlement Housing area for Vietnamese. In time, Cambodian refugees started arriving. On occasions, AACC services were conducted in English, Chinese and Cambodian!

Merrilyn Teague, a returned missionary from Papua New Guinea, started attending OCF Adelaide in 1981. She also ministered to the Cambodians. Unknown to both groups, Merrilyn had just recovered from cerebral malaria, and was still trying to recover from a broken heart. It became evident that she had a gift of connecting with people across cultures. Not long after, AACC employed her as their missions pastor and released her to serve OCF as needed, as Geoff Sunstrom was no longer in their employ.

In 1986, EXCO moved from Victoria to South Australia. Due to the high turnover of students, the OCF Australia

---

[111] Geoff Sunstrom, Interview with author and Joshua Chan, 2020.

president Mark Goh saw the need for a resource person who could provide stability and continuity to centres around Australia. By this time, Merrilyn had already made several interstate trips upon the invitation of OCF centres there. Thus, EXCO recommended that Rev Merrilyn Teague be appointed as the national resource person for OCF Australia. The General Council unanimously accepted her nomination. As it turned out, she served in OCF for the next three and a half decades, and became known as Aunty Merrilyn, signifying affection and respect on account of her age.

Guidelines on the Charismatic Movement

In 1983, OCF Adelaide hosted the 25th annual convention in Victor Harbor. The convention theme was *Faith in Action*. The camp booklet foreword read: 'the theme of this Convention, developed in our minds at a time of spiritual renewal in OCF Adelaide. The importance of the power of prayer has been the hallmark of a year evidenced by the working of the Holy Spirit.'

Anglican minister Rev Geoff Bingham delivered the main messages. Originally from Sydney and educated at Moore College, he had spent many years in Pakistan as a missionary. In one of the sermons, he taught from Romans 3:19-31and said, 'Faith is the response of man to the revelation of God. Faith constitutes trust, union with and dependence in Him.' He explained how the cross of Christ draws people together, forming a community around the death and resurrection of

Christ. One afternoon of the convention was set aside for the 350 convention delegates to invite the townspeople to a Good News concert. That night, several Australians came and joined the students in the packed Mount Brecken Hall. Rev Geoff Bingham delivered a powerful message, and some responded to the Lord.

At worship sessions, OCF Adelaide sang wholeheartedly. A few raised hands while singing. Some OCF centres objected to the style of worship because they felt it was pushing a Pentecostal agenda. Student leaders discussed and argued about this late into the night. The next morning, the Rev Bingham brought them all together. Peter Teo was the incoming OCF Australia chairperson from Melbourne. In a 2022 interview, he recalled what happened.

> *Peter Teo:* overnight [he] came up with two pages of teaching and he brought all the leaders together and he taught us. I tell you what impact that made on me because 'wow'. I was thinking, 'wow, he is so good theologically'. He saw the division and he is able to come up with some solution that would help us bridge together our differences. ... And so, while we can allow for certain practices that may differ from other churches, we will have to find a common ground to allow everyone to express their faith.

In 1984, EXCO led by Peter Teo published a *Statement of the OCF's position regarding the Charismatic Movement* in the third edition of the *OCF (Australia) Handbook*. OCF leaders had the foresight, maturity, and respect for one another to formulate

Peter Teo, in front of the Swanston Street Church of Christ in Melbourne, circa 1980. Photo supplied by Peter Teo.

a statement endorsed by all. It began with a recognition that no one in OCF should feel cramped or restricted in seeking all of God's blessing, but we also need to strive to maintain the unity of the Spirit. We must never emphasise any one interpretation to the extent that it causes division.

The view of the fellowship was that the gift of tongues was but one of the gifts of the Holy Spirit. Members were free to hold other views on this, and on the baptism of the Holy Spirit, as long as they did not press their personal view on others. When teaching about spiritual gifts, members were asked *'not to teach as the only admissible view dogmatic interpretations which may be capable of a different biblical understanding and thus offending fellow members.'*[112]

This document was removed from the Handbook in 2003 because it was no longer useful. Various centres had settled into ways of worshipping and exercising the gifts of the Holy Spirit with which they were comfortable. However, at national conventions, more care and consideration were required, especially on how speakers were selected and briefed. Once, a convention committee had invited a speaker to give his testimony. Unfortunately, the speaker went beyond this and called for students to come forward for prayer. His pushy manner did not respect the interdenominational character of OCF. Pastor Allan Webb, a long-time supporter of OCF, implored Aunty Merrilyn to take control of the meeting as the OCF Australia resource person. She walked down the lecture hall steps to the stage and asked the speaker to stop. From the front, she apologised to any students who might have been offended or confused and invited them to speak further to her or to Pastor Allan Webb. The 1983 *Statement of OCF's position regarding the Charismatic Movement* was a good starting point, but OCF Australia also relied on the wise counsel of godly men and women as the group wrestled with the practical outworking of the principles described.

---

[112] *OCF (Australia) Handbook* (3rd ed., 1984), 25-27.

OCF Adelaide circa 1984 rehearsing for a musical. From left: Yap Chong Hua, Andrew Wong, Tan Lor Lee, Wendy Hoare, Wong Lye Kheng, Wong Kong Seng, Chew Kim Yong. Photo supplied by Yap Chong Hua.

In 1987, Chew Kim Yong served as the OCF Australia chairperson and chaired the AGM in December. On the whole, OCF membership was on the increase and there had been six new centres affiliated in the decade so far: OCF Geelong 1980, Carlton 1982, Canberra 1983, Armidale 1984, Flinders 1986 and Wollongong 1987. A love for the Lord fuelled the expansion. However, growth increased ministry workload. Whether small or large, each centre had their own struggles. Some leaders were discouraged or spiritually dry. It did not help when they received unsolicited advice or were questioned over their methods.[113]

To add to this, tensions over the Charismatic Movement were simmering. Leaders felt compelled to guard the institution of OCF—some wanted to guard it from being too charismatic, others wanted to guard against quenching the fire of the Spirit. Many of the smaller centres and less-

---

[113] Chew Kim Yong, Interview by author and Benita Loh, 2021. Transcript p. 13.

1987 OCF Australia AGM in Adelaide. Photo supplied by Nar Chin Keow.

experienced leaders felt out of their depth and bewildered by the undercurrent of tension.

'Can I say something?' asked Jason Wong, the president from Perth. 'I sense that Jesus does not feel welcome here. We are doing our own thing and ignoring Him. He is not included in our discussions—He is grieved. We desire to serve Jesus in our respective countries, but how can we unite together to serve if we cannot even get along as students in Australia? How can leaders in disharmony lead members towards the OCF vision?'[114]

'Let us pray,' said Kim Yong. Tears and prayers of repentance flowed. By the end of that session, leaders were reconciled to one another in Christ. After the AGM, the 29th annual convention began. On the final day, Dr Grahame Blanchard led the delegates in communion. Aunty Merrilyn sat among the students. The beauty and preciousness of the Lord Jesus Christ overwhelmed her. Tears rolled down her

---

[114] Jason Wong, *Trash of Society*, (self-pub., 2017), 66.

cheek into the communion cup she was holding. In the hushed reverence, she saw in her mind's eye, an outline of the map of Australia, and students rising here, there and everywhere. She saw their backs only, not their faces. She saw flaming arrows going to the north end, to the east end and to the west. The students were holding these arrows which became a banner. There were multitudes going out. She realised that they were graduates going back and going out, thrust into a ripened harvest field.

'Lord, will you confirm if this is a vision from you?' she prayed. Bible verses flooded her mind, quicker than she could speak them or write them down, 'now is the time for harvest', 'I am not ashamed of the gospel of Jesus Christ', 'how will they hear without a preacher' and many more. She knew that within the hour, the students would be scattered. Silently, she prayed, 'If you want me to share this, it has got to be now. Will you make a way?'

'Merrilyn, would you come up and close in prayer?' she heard Dr Blanchard calling her up from the front. Taking this unexpected invitation as permission to speak to the whole of OCF before they dispersed, she told them about the vision and then closed in prayer.

Like Melbourne and Sydney, OCF Adelaide grew and developed its own distinctiveness: a deep concern for those outside Christ, and an openness to the work of the Holy Spirit. Sound Biblical teaching and mature Christian mentors helped them exercise their faith in an environment where there were diverse views about the Charismatic Movment. This approach was documented in the *OCF (Australia) Handbook*, but its effectiveness was dependent on the willingness of members to submit to its counsel.

In 1986, the appointment of Aunty Merrilyn as EXCO Resource Person was the first organisational change since the formation of OCF Australia. She provided continuity to the ministry and became a spiritual mother to many. Her input was made possible by a diaspora church, whose founding members found a way to give back to the ministry of OCF that had been so instrumental in their own spiritual journey.

1987 OCF Australia convention delegates in Adelaide. Photo supplied by Nar Chin Keow.

12. Perth

Since 1959, there had been only one centre in Perth. In 1987, they met fortnightly at the Claremont Baptist Church near the University of Western Australia and started discussing the possibility of establishing two more OCF centres in the city.[115] By 1990, OCF Murdoch and OCF Curtin had been established. What or who gave the students such impetus and energy to form two centres in quick succession?

Jarrahdale Leadership Camp

In 1987, OCF Perth chairperson Jason Wong opened the Leadership Training Camp to all members. He believed that God could use anyone to do great things. The question was not whether they exhibited leadership potential, but if they had encountered Jesus. On the recommendation of two of his committee members, Jason invited the OCF Australia resource person Aunty Merrilyn to be the camp speaker. As the camp drew closer, concerns surfaced: they had never had a female speaker before, and she was known to exercise the gifts of the Spirit. Would this cause division? The group looked to Jason for a decision.

Jason had only become a Christian three years earlier during his first year in Australia. He felt ill-equipped to deal with doctrinal differences. After praying over the matter, he fell asleep and dreamt that he was at the leadership camp.

---

[115] Jason Wong, *Trash of Society*, (self-pub., 2017), 34.

OCF Perth local committee 1986-87. From left: Jason Wong (1st), Yvonne Choo (3rd), Jerry Siran Langan (4th with raised arm), Ho Yin Meng (5th in black T-shirt), Goh Siao Yen (6th in white skirt), Then Chee Tat (7th). Photo supplied by Goh Siao Yen.

There was a disturbance. In the commotion, the speaker was looking at him. Jason recognised Aunty Merrilyn from a photo he had seen. She was waiting for him to decide whether to grant her permission to speak. In the dream, Jason knew that he could stop her or let her continue. He heard the Holy Spirit say, 'It's okay Jason, it's okay. Everything will be okay.' Jason woke up, breathing quickly. After recalling details of his dream, he knew that all he needed to do was to allow the Holy Spirit free rein to move at the camp.[116]

On the first day of the camp, around fifty students met outside Currie Hall. Excited chatter filled the air. Aunty Merrilyn met many of the students for the first time. Lim Jit Cheng was a second-year business student at the Western

---

[116] Jason Wong, *Trash of Society*, (self-pub., 2017), 54-56.

Australian Institute of Technology (now called Curtin University). On the bus to Jarrahdale, Jit Cheng sat next to Aunty Merrilyn. Concrete buildings soon gave way to farmlands and yellow wattle in full bloom.

At the camp, Aunty Merrilyn delivered messages on the role of Christian leaders as servants and shepherds of God's people. Everyone shared in good fellowship, precious worship and magnificent singing—even duets to 2 am! Jason saw female members open up to Aunty Merrilyn as a spiritual mother. Jason shared from Joshua 23:1-2, about Joshua's burden and concern that God's vision be passed on to all Israelites, and he drew parallels to the OCF vision.

'A vision is a motivating force,' said Jason. 'A vision is the revelation of God's plan for you. It is not what you want to do for God, but what He wants to do through you.' Meanwhile, God had laid a burden on Jit Cheng's heart, which he shared with the Perth committee. The vision was for three OCF centres in Perth—OCF Perth, OCF Murdoch and OCF Curtin.[117] Unknown to everyone, things would move very quickly from there.

When worship began on the final day of the camp, Jason felt God's love embracing the whole group. Tears of joy flowed down his face. After worship, Aunty Merrilyn began preaching. 'In the Old Testament, slaves were allowed to go free, but if they wished to stay because they loved their master, they could do so. The Lord has many servants but he wants bondslaves. Will you be his bondslaves?'

---

[117] Lim Jit Cheng, Interview with author, 2022.

The Holy Spirit had just impressed upon her this question for the group moments before. He also brought to her remembrance Psalm 40:6-8, which she now read.

Sacrifice and offering you did not desire—

but my ears you have opened—

burnt offerings and sin offerings you did not require.

Then I said, "Here I am, I have come—

it is written about me in the scroll.

I desire to do your will, my God;

your law is within my heart."[118]

She also explained the context of the Psalm, referring the students to Exodus 21:1-6, whereby Hebrew slaves who did not want to leave their masters, despite being free to do so, would have their ears pierced, signifying their choice to become servants for life. Jason felt God speaking to him. He was ready to run forward, kneel before God and let God pierce him and mark him for life. He knew that he was under no obligation to surrender his life. Yet, he was willing to lay all at the feet of Jesus—titles, achievements, accolades, assets. He heard Aunty Merrilyn ask, 'Is anyone ready to be a bondslave to be marked for life?'

Many students moved forward. Chairs were moved away to free up space for many more who were responding. Jason was on his knees sobbing. The floor felt as if it was on

---

[118] Merrilyn Teague, 'Revival in Perth', a report written in 1987.

fire. With burning hearts and bended knees, many sobbed quietly. Aunty Merrilyn prayed for each one who came forward. As she did so, the Holy Spirit gave her some words of prophecy for individuals. She prayed for Jason last and told him that she saw him with uniformed people in high places. It was a strange vision because although Jason was to complete his national service in Singapore after university, he had not passed the medical test to qualify for Officer Cadet School. He would never become an officer.

As many of the students had not heard of words of prophecy before, Aunty Merrilyn taught them that all words of prophecy must be tested to ensure that they are consistent with Scriptures. If you receive a word of prophecy and are unsure of it, just put it on the shelf. If it is from the Lord, it will come to pass.[119]

By this time, the group had been praying, worshipping and waiting on the Lord for a few hours. The bus trip had to be pushed back till much later in the afternoon. Later, some voiced concerns over the exercise of the gift of prophecy that had not been seen in OCF Perth before. However, this did not divide the group. Instead, there was a great sense of unity in wanting to be obedient to the Lord, to serve him wholeheartedly.

In his 2017 autobiography, Jason wrote, 'The words God spoke to me through Aunty Merrilyn are no longer on the shelf; they have already come to pass. I did wear a uniform and become a career officer in the uniformed service. I also

---

[119] Jason Wong, *Trash of Society*, (self-pub., 2017), 54-58.

received several promotions and attained the position of second-in-command, except that I wore a blue uniform, not a green one.'

The Formation of OCFs Murdoch and Curtin

The Swan River bisects the city of Perth with four tertiary institutions, two on either side of the river. On the north side, stood the University of Western Australia (UWA) and the Western Australian College of Advanced Education, which has since become the Edith Cowan University. On the south side, stood Murdoch University and the Western Australian Institute of Technology (WAIT), which later became Curtin University.

Friday night OCF Perth public meetings were held in Claremont, north of the river and students from both Murdoch and Curtin had to travel some distance to attend these meetings. With so many new overseas students, there were clear advantages of forming groups in the south for more effective outreach. In 1988, a year after the Jarrahdale leadership camp, several Singaporean students started OCF Murdoch. By 1989, OCF Perth had around 80 members, and OCF Murdoch 52 members.[120] Most OCF Perth members studied at UWA, but a few studied at Curtin.

From 1988 to 1989, Jit Cheng served as the OCF Perth chairperson. During this time, the plan to start OCF at Curtin

---

[120] 'Distribution of OCFers in Australia', *OCF Australia Newsletter* 89/4 and 90/1, 1990,16.

New OCF Perth chairperson Lim Jit Cheng welcoming the local incoming committee of 1987/88. From left: Then Chee Tat, Ho Yin Meng, Alfred Wong, Kenneth Chin, Goh Siao Yen, Louis Ho. Photo supplied by Goh Siao Yen.

was discussed. As the only Curtin student on the OCF Perth committee, Jit Cheng was tasked to see it through. Postgraduate student Lionel Chin had been approached in November 1987 to start OCF Curtin but declined as he was still new to Australia and to OCF. He felt that other students such as Jit Cheng were better placed to lead such a venture. By 1989, Lionel had spent two years in OCF Perth and he agreed to lead a new group.[121] The EXCO in Victoria—chairperson Tan Loke Mun and member Ho Yew Kee—also strongly encouraged Jit Cheng to set up OCF Curtin in view of the burgeoning number of overseas students there.

---

[121] Lionel Chin, Interview with author, 2022.

In 1986, WAIT had been the first institution to admit full fee-paying students as well as the first to have student intakes in July (up until then student intakes into Australian tertiary institution were in February). In December 1986, WAIT became Australia's first institute of technology to be awarded university status and was renamed Curtin University of Technology.[122] Overseas student numbers in Perth, particularly from Malaysia and Singapore, shot up significantly from 1986 onwards.

Against this backdrop, the OCF Perth committee decided to seek affiliation with the Curtin Student Guild to start a new outreach work at Curtin. However, their application was not slated for any guild affiliation meeting in 1989 and was instead pushed to early 1990 into the new academic year. Although Jit Cheng was completing his studies and due to return to Malaysia in December 1989, he was resolute to see through the setting up of OCF Curtin and decided to extend his stay in Perth for another two months for this.

At that time, the Curtin Student Guild was run by the students themselves. With funds to disburse as they saw fit, wild Friday night parties were common at the Guild House, one of the residential colleges. Staying in Guild House, Jit Cheng would lead some unpopular pushback measures on the way monies from foreign student guild fees were being spent. Prior to the Student Guild meeting in early 1990, Jit

---

[122] 'Curtin University of Technology,' Curtin University, accessed 24 August 2023, https://www.curtin.edu.au/about/history-facts/history/curtin-university-of-technology/.

Cheng had been informed through the grapevine that there would be strong opposition from the present guild members on the admission of OCF Curtin. A vote was unlikely to pull through. This was not unexpected and a small group of OCF members at Guild House began gathering to pray over this.

As Jit Cheng was leaving Australia soon, he asked fellow student Ben Lee to attend the guild meeting with him, both for support, as well as follow up when OCF Curtin was set up. Ben was part of a small Bible study group led by Jit Cheng among the Curtin students at that time. On the morning of the guild meeting, both young men walked together from Guild House quietly across the cricket pitch, each silently committing to the Lord what lay ahead. Upon reaching the guild office room, Jit Cheng said to Ben, 'This is it.'

The tables had been arranged in a square, with student representatives from all the other clubs. It was an eclectic group, including representatives of the Curtin Christian Fellowship, made up mainly of local Australian students.[123] When the OCF Curtin proposal came up, there was a huge debate: Why do we need another Christian organisation when we already have one?

'This is different,' said Jit Cheng. 'OCF has been around for a while. There is OCF Perth which caters more for the UWA students. Since Curtin is seeing an increase of many foreign students with two intake admissions per year, it's time for Curtin to have its own OCF centre to cater for the students here.'

---

[123] Ben Lee, Interview with author, 2022.

Yet, the prevailing sentiment was pure opposition: If we admit one more club, there will be less money for the rest to share.

As debate became heated, a very quiet Australian Christian girl stood up and spoke. 'These people have come all the way here to study in Australia. We should have the decency to welcome them warmly to multi-religious, multi-faceted Australia. Australians are better than this.'

When she stopped speaking, the room fell silent. Jit Cheng had known her since the joint CF-OCF convention in 1989 in Sydney, but he had never seen her speak like that before. 'I was utterly shocked,' remembers Jit Cheng, 'God was clearly at work. It was as if He had come into the room and tied everyone's tongues up.' Then, without any hint of protest, the Student Guild proceeded to vote for the birth of OCF Curtin. After the meeting, Jit Cheng and Ben walked back across the same cricket pitch. In silence again, but this time in awe at what God had accomplished. As they reached Guild House, Jit Cheng turned to Ben and said, 'My job is done—I can now return home. Over to you guys now'.

Jit Cheng passed the leadership baton of OCF Curtin to Ben Lee and Lionel Chin. A small group of OCF Curtin students began praying every Monday morning before lectures on campus. Eventually, they also met on Friday nights at Curtin. As Lionel was graduating soon, he nurtured the younger Curtin students in their faith and encouraged them towards leadership. When Lionel left in mid-1990, he handed over the reins to Peter Chen, the first president of

OCF Curtin. The centre was officially affiliated to OCF Australia at the 1990 AGM.[124]

1990 OCF Curtin Committee. From left: Dinah Phua, Peter Chen, Lionel Chin, Ben Lee, Leong Tat Chee, Anne George. Photo supplied by Ben Lee.

Bullsbrook Camp

In June 1990, OCF Australia chairperson Tan Loke Mun visited the OCF Perth camp in Bullsbrook, a forty-minute drive northeast of Perth.

The speaker, Archdeacon Yong Chen Fah, had served as the 1972 OCF Australia chairperson and had since become a key Anglican leader in Sabah, Malaysia. Although tall and imposing on first impression, the students soon found Archdeacon Yong to be a fun-loving person, game for any opportunity or challenge.

---

[124] Lim Jit Cheng, Interview with author, 2022.

During the camp, the organising committee gathered in a room behind the Mess Hall to take stock. Most of the campers were having a really good time. Collectively, the committee sensed that the Holy Spirit wanted to do a significant work, but there was a barrier in the way. They spent time in confession and prayer. One of the camp committee members Lionel Yap recalled it as a time of openness and vulnerability before the Lord. They had prayed for longer than expected till there were knocks on the door, their friends asking if everything was alright. Eventually, they left the room with a great sense of expectation that God was going to move. Over dinner, they had an hilarious time, as usual.

When Archdeacon Yong took the pulpit after dinner, he smiled and said, 'I prepared a message for this evening, but I feel that we should instead spend this time praying for one another. Let me start by sharing my life with you. My career started in OCF. When I went home in 1972, I went through a dark patch. All Sabahan church leaders will remember the dark ages in the mid-1970s when the church in Sabah was too comfortable and people said, 'Oh, don't worry. We have our pastors, our friends—' all expatriates. 'They will look after us and take care of us.' But the government did not renew the visas of foreign missionaries and pastors. How many leaders were there in Sabah at that time? How many local leaders were there at the time? How many Anglican churches were there across Sabah? A lot more than the number of leaders available. A small group of us met and prayed. We asked God

—every year, just give us one more leader for every one of us here. Just give us one more. Today the church in Sabah is led by national leaders, completely localised.'

After Archdeacon Yong's sharing, campers went up to the microphone to talk about what God had done in their lives at the camp. The first person to share was OCF leader Louis Ho. 'As one of the older ones, I am supposed to be a senior, not supposed to come up and share about how God has really touched me during the camp.' After him, other campers spoke candidly about their lives, even opening up about taboo topics, personal shortcomings, rocky relationships, or family involved vice-related business. Yet it was not a depressing time. There was a great sense of freedom, a release from hiding and shame. Tears of joy flowed. One of the first-year students, Dominic Voon, experienced deep inner healing. The committee was elated. It was as if their openness in private with one another had spilled out into the whole camp.

In between the sharing, they sang worship songs.[125] In the crowd, Loke Mun noticed one of the campers looking confused and bewildered. When Loke Mun asked if he could say the words Jesus Christ is Lord, the young man replied, 'I am fine to say it but my mouth won't say it. My brain can hear it, but my mouth won't say it.' Loke Mun led him outside the hall so that they could talk in private.[126] A moment later, those in the hall heard shrieks. Bishop Yong walked slowly to

---

[125] Lionel Yap, Interview with author, 2022.
[126] Tan Loke Mun, Interview with author, 2021.

the back of the hall, went outside and closed the door behind him. The worship leader stepped forward and encouraged all to focus on God. The pianist played the song *Majesty* again and the campers sang out in worship.

The majesty of God's presence filled the hall and seemed to grow in intensity. They continued singing for quite some time until Rev Yong returned, took his place at the pulpit and said, 'No need to be afraid. We were involved in some ministry outside.' Several people had prayed for the young man, and an evil spirit had left him. Subsequently, all who knew the young man were struck by a dramatic change in his personality. From a quiet reserved person, he became joyous and outgoing. Many campers who had been lukewarm in their faith experienced a personal spiritual awakening. Some put their faith in Jesus Christ for the first time. Rev Yong Chen Fah had a sense of deep gratitude. This camp was like an affirmation that God alone had called him into full-time ordained ministry back in 1969, when he was in OCF.

After the camp, OCF Perth approached Pastor Bob Gregory from the Thornlie Church of Christ, which many of them attended. At their request, Pastor Gregory taught them on spiritual warfare, to stand on the authority of God's word and to deal with any demonic activity by using Scripture.

OCF Perth went through a season of spiritual growth, which enabled them to host the 1993 OCF annual convention. Because Perth was so far from the rest of the states, this had only happened twice before. Lionel Yap and Dominic Voon co-chaired the convention.[127] As a result of working together to organise the convention, the three WA centre leaders recognised the benefit of forging closer ties. They formed the OCF WA Steering Committee. In subsequent years, OCF WA held three joint statewide OCF meetings every year, one hosted by each centre. In addition, centre leaders met regularly. This reinforced the notion that the WA centres were members of one body, even though each centre had its own identity. It also enabled active and tangible support whenever a centre experienced decline. This increased the resilience of WA centres, so that they were better able to serve God's purposes.

---

[127] Lawrence Peh and Dominic Voon, Interview with Joshua Sim, 2020.

13. Streams of Living Water

Imagery of living water is woven throughout the Bible. For example, in Jeremiah 2:13, Yahweh calls himself the source of living water. In John 4:10, Jesus likened true worship to drinking from springs of living water. In John 7:38, Jesus said that rivers of living water will flow out of the belly of the one who believes in him.

The entire ministry of OCF is predicated on the premise that OCF members were wandering in a spiritual desert until they found the source of living water. A concern for others motivated them to organise themselves, to persuade their friends to drink from the wellspring, so that they would thirst no longer. The organisational framework of OCF Australia helped members to fulfil the primary task of introducing others to this living water. In the late 1980s, a season of spiritual fulfilment resulted in a period of significant growth in several OCF centres.

Promises for Parkville

In 1986, OCF Parkville in Melbourne had around sixty members. The leaders were adept at organising meetings and facilitating Bible studies. Yet, they felt spiritually dry. The OCF Parkville committee went away on a prayer and fasting retreat. Early one morning, their chairperson Hon Hoh sensed that God wanted him to go to a quiet place to pray. At 4 am, he drove to Sandringham Beach. There, he opened his

Bible. He continued reading from where he had left off in his daily devotions, from 2 Corinthians 6:1, 2: 'As God's co-workers we urge you not to receive God's grace in vain. For he says, "In the time of my favor I heard you, and in the day of salvation I helped you." I tell you, now is the time of God's favor, now is the day of salvation.'

The word *now* made Hon consider how Paul was referring to the present as God's time of favour. Surely it applied equally to the ministry of OCF Parkville. It quickened in Hon a sense of immediacy regarding what the Holy Spirit wanted to do in Parkville. Verse two was a reference to Isaiah 49:8. So, Hon turned to Isaiah 49, and read from verses 8–23. As he read, the Lord gave him five promises for the ministry of OCF Parkville:

1. evangelism (v. 9)
2. spiritual fulfilment (v. 10)
3. restoration of praise and worship (v. 13)
4. increase in numbers (v. 20)
5. favour and honour before authority (v. 23).

Hon returned to the retreat and shared this with the committee. They continued praying, holding on to these promises. A few days after the retreat, during Hon's private prayer time, a vivid picture came unbidden into his mind. He saw Price Hall in Swanston Street Church of Christ, the regular meeting place of OCF Parkville, with people tightly packed together, overflowing from the hall to the kitchen at

OCF Parkville circa 1991 at the Lower Hall of Swanston Street Church of Christ, Melbourne.
Photos supplied by Tan Loke Mun.

the back. The following year, OCF Parkville experienced spiritual renewal. Membership doubled from 60 to 120. People were filled with joy at the evidence that God was working in their midst.

The OCF Parkville leadership began thinking of a new OCF centre at Melbourne University. As Hon was about to graduate, he realised the importance of passing on the baton of leadership to some who would run with the vision. Melbourne University building undergraduate, Hii Howe Shing from Sibu, Malaysia, was the prayer secretary at the time. His gentleness belied his strong faith. Howe Shing agreed to take over the role of OCF Parkville chairperson.

After Hon graduated, he worked in a secular field for three years, before taking up a position at the South Yarra Church of Christ. Hon had received a call to the ministry through the preaching of Dr James Hudson Taylor III at a missions conference organised by the Swanston Street Church of Christ. Hon and his wife Voon Ling served as advisors to OCF Parkville and OCF Clayton for many years up to the early 2000s.[128]

Geelong Blessed by Barrabool Hills Baptist

At this time, Geelong OCF found a spiritual home church at Barrabool Hills Baptist Church. The pastor there, Pastor

---

[128] Hon Hoh, Interview with author, 2022.

Stewart Rae, had been a missionary to Japan, and his wife Gwen had been born in China to missionary parents.

Under Pastor Stewart's leadership, the church welcomed overseas students studying at Deakin University's Geelong campus. Families and couples were asked to take a student under their wing and be spiritual parents to them. Sue Tonkin was a very shy nurse, but said to her husband, Graeme Tonkin, 'We must volunteer to host a student.' He was surprised as it was totally out of character for her. They volunteered to become host parents. Through this, they formed a close friendship with a Malaysian architectural student from Sabah, Chang Chiew Bong, and his girlfriend Dora Ngui. In 1987, the church had a week-long seminar on the Holy Spirit. It sparked off a spiritual revival in the church and in members' personal lives. It was joy unspeakable and the church and OCF Geelong grew in numbers.

In 1986, Tan Loke Mun became the OCF Geelong chairperson. Pastor Stewart Rae mentored him in the role, even if Loke Mun was too radical for some. The Lord Jesus had rescued Loke Mun from the gangs in Petaling Jaya. He considered himself a child of the Pentecostal movement in Kuala Lumpur. When he arrived in Australia with $750 in his pocket, OCF members met him at the Geelong train station and he stayed with them for a week while he searched for a place to rent. There were around seven other overseas students in the same situation. He later recalled the experience of staying temporarily at the home of OCF members:

So, we sat, we slept in the living room of the house. And we ate [sitting] on the floor. We ate a lot of fish and chips because it was the easiest thing to buy. And there were apples in the garden and we ate apples. We were poor. … I got to know some people who were also staying in the OCF house. And we chose who were going to be our housemates. And they [the OCFers] actually were very kind. They drove us around. Every morning you have to wake up, look at the newspapers, and you look for the cheapest house for rent. And then the OCFers were very kind, because there is no public transport in Geelong. So, they drove us around to go look at the houses, and we quickly decided which we wanted. We saw quite a few, some were like haunted, [chuckles] really run-down places. … everyone who stayed and ate [sitting] on the floor there [at the home of OCF members] were in some way or other touched by Christ and they used to attend OCF, some more than others, but they had great respect for what OCF did for them.[129]

As Loke Mun became more involved in OCF and attended OCF Victoria Easter Camps, he started to understand the struggles of OCF Geelong more deeply. Many were quiet and less confident than students at larger and more prestigious universities in Melbourne. Exam results usually brought bad news to several members. He was convinced that God, through the Holy Spirit and Scripture, could turn things around. At OCF Geelong, they began memorising Scripture together, and used a sheet of 32 commands titled 'The one

---

[129] Tan Loke Mun, Interview with author, 2021.

From left: Graeme Tonkin, Tan Loke Mun, Pastor Stewart Rae, at the 40th OCF Australia convention in Melaka, Malaysia, 1999. Photos supplied by Tan Loke Mun.

anothers'. Through this, they learned to admonish one another (Rom. 15:14, Col. 3:16), bear one another's burdens (Gal. 6:2), confess faults one to another (Jam. 5:16) and so on.

The ministry grew to the point whereby about half of the overseas students at Deakin University were OCF Geelong members. There was a close relationship between the Australian families at Barrabool Hills Baptist and the students. It was an exciting time, and there was a great willingness to serve God. When Loke Mun went on to study Masters in Architecture at Melbourne University, he moved in with Pastor Hon Hoh and Hii Howe Shing. Loke Mun then became part of OCF Parkville.

Formation of OCF Flinders

In 1988, Peter Ting took over from Kim Yong as the OCF Australia president. This would be South Australia's last year as EXCO. Peter felt so much younger than his seniors, Mark Goh and Kim Yong. So much had already been done that he wondered what more he could do in only one year?

After enquiring of the Lord, Peter decided to visit every OCF centre across Australia that year, to create a working relationship at the national level. He wrote a series of articles on vision for the OCF Australia newsletter, explaining that to have a vision for the world, you must start with a vision for one person. Whenever he visited a centre, he would speak at great length, exhorting them not to let anyone look down on them because they were young, not to rely solely on guest speakers, but learn to preach from the Word of God, and to make disciples.

Peter was from Sibu in Malaysia and had arrived in Adelaide in 1982, as a high school student at Sacred Heart College. His favourite pop song was *Do You Know Where You're Going To?* by Diana Ross. It resonated with him because at the time, he was directionless. He was a nominal Christian, but Christianity seemed to be no more than a boring ritual.

In December 1983, at an Austral-Asian Christian Church youth camp, he prayed and asked Jesus to come into his life. Although he had previously been a churchgoer, the Bible now became alive. He read it till it fell apart, after which, he stapled different books of the Bible together. After finishing high school the following year, he accepted a place at Monash University in Victoria to do engineering. In 1985, he moved to Melbourne where he stayed in a household of OCF Clayton members. Despite his best efforts, he failed the year. Through his failure at Monash, he learned that it was not enough to study hard, but to study effectively and strategically. He transferred to Flinders University to study computer science and returned to Adelaide. There, he resumed contact with Pastor Barry Chant and Dr Grahame Blanchard. These two older men—one a pastor, the other a dentist—mentored the young firebrand. Peter discussed Scripture with Pastor Barry and spent time at the Blanchard family home during holidays.

At Flinders University, a group of students had been meeting at the Religious Centre at lunchtime. They also met as a cell group of OCF Adelaide. In late 1983, Saw Kim Chun had started a group with eight people. By 1985, the group had grown to twenty. They considered if they should be part of Students for Christ, a Pentecostal student group, or whether they should join the OCF. After prayer and seeking the Lord, they decided to join OCF. But still, they did not have the numbers or confidence to start a new campus group.

When Peter returned from Melbourne, he provided enthusiasm and confidence to officially form Flinders OCF. Peter chaired the first AGM of Flinders University OCF. They had Friday lunchtime meetings, Monday prayer meetings, and met fortnightly at Peter's home on Saturdays. On a regular basis, Peter mobilised OCF Flinders to do outreach at the Flinders Medical Centre chapel, as well as to visit aged care facilities during the Christmas season. They were encouraged to find people receptive to their singing. Aunty Merrilyn was instrumental as a spiritual mother and helped to establish the group. At the 1986 OCF Australia AGM, OCF Flinders was officially affiliated.

At the 1988 AGM, Peter Ting presented a session on International OCF, where he encouraged members to be trained to lead small groups. This would enable them to serve God when they returned to Asia, or wherever God called them. Peter was not content with the survival mentality of trying to prevent returnees from backsliding because of the pressures of work. Instead, he urged them to see their workplaces—where they would spend the most time—as ideal opportunities to witness. Peter Ting's message was well-received in most centres, but some OCF Sydney leaders were wary of his emphasis on students preaching the Word.

After graduating from Flinders University, Peter and Abby were married. Peter went on to study theology at Tabor College under the leadership of Pastor Barry Chant. In 1990, Peter attended one last AGM in Melbourne before leaving Australia. At the AGM, there were long discussions over whether permanent residents and citizens could be leaders, and whether OCF was too charismatic. He was given one minute to speak, and too soon the bell rang 'ding, ding, ding' but still he pressed on. Peter recalled the event.

> I had holy anger at that time; holy anger in the sense that I'm concerned with my brethren who debate and [spend] too much time on the doctrine and too much time on the constitution. Because I've been to quite a few OCF meetings, why not talk about how to reach out to more people? How to make more disciples? How to better prepare ourselves for home? Because many of us will be going home. You know, the few may stay behind, but [the] majority will still be going home. I was thinking [that] we should be thinking about all these, like how to work with GCF Graduate Christian [Fellowship], the receiving end. Make sure there is a receiving end, your own church receiving us, so that we won't disappear into the wilderness.[130]

At the halfway mark of this story, thirty years after the formation of OCF Australia, the fellowship had grown larger, and its leaders had inherited a growing body of documents around how it should function. Yet, some matters seemed to be discussed at each AGM without resolution. This was partly because of a changing context. For example, there were a growing number of second-generation migrants, who contributed a great deal to the ministry as permanent residents and citizens, but the constitution forbade them from being in the GC.

Furthermore, student leaders had to see the wisdom and validity of guidelines handed down before they submitted to its recommendations. The *Statement of the OCF's*

---

[130] Peter and Abby Ting, Interview with author, 2021.

position regarding the Charismatic Movement had been published in 1984, which helped to explain the position of the fellowship and guide guest speakers. However, at the personal level, being mutually respectful and not dogmatic depended on character and maturity, matters of the heart not enforceable by guidelines. As a result, a sense of frustration and unease around certain topics crept in at national-level discussions.

Despite these organisational complexities, OCF Australia continued to be a place where young people encountered God and were transformed by the gospel. They drank from springs of living water. Out of their spiritual fulfilment, they served God wholeheartedly. Some OCF centres became more conscious of the leading of the Holy Spirit in various ways. Where godly Christian ministers and local churches supplied good guidance and sound Biblical teaching, OCF members exercised spiritual gifts effectively in a loving community of faith. As a result, they grew in their concern for others, hunger for the Word of God, and effectiveness in ministry.

14. Vision for Expansion

EXCO members Tan Loke Mun and Ho Yew Kee standing far left and right respectively. Merrilyn Teague in the centre. Circa 1990 in Melbourne. Photo supplied by Tan Loke Mun.

In 1989, EXCO member Ho Yew Kee from OCF Clayton presented a paper on the *Expansion of OCF Australia* at the AGM. He focused the attention of OCF leaders around Australia to consider growth in a systematic and strategic way. Although OCF Australia had been growing since its inception, such a united nationwide approach had not been articulated before.

Yew Kee noted that OCF Australia had just over 900 members, only 2% of the 45,000 overseas students in Australia. He exhorted the OCF leadership to form an OCF centre on every campus with a sizeable overseas student population. He suggested three means of achieving this:

1. register as university clubs wherever possible
2. identify homogeneous groups (students from the same country or who spoke the same language) and minister to them in a culturally relevant way
3. set achievable targets.

He suggested a target of twelve new centres by the mid-1990s. There were pros and cons of establishing new centres; for example, the difficulty of replacing student leaders in small centres with high student turnover. However, on balance, he believed this was offset by the benefit of each campus having its own OCF centre that could focus on reaching that campus.

In the late 1980s, there were several large OCF centres around Australia, each with students who had been touched by God and wanted to serve Him. These larger centres had the potential to commission its members to start new centres. In the first half of the 1990s, five new centres were affiliated: OCF Kew and Queensland University of Technology (QUT) in 1989, and OCFs Caulfield, Curtin and Melbourne Uni in 1990.

Formation of OCF Kew (Swinburne)

In Melbourne, Koh Swee Ann was training for the ministry and wanted to reach international students in the eastern suburbs of Melbourne. He decided that OCF would be a good group to affiliate with because he believed in the OCF vision. He approached OCF Carlton student, Ho Wey Jing, whom he knew from the Chinese Gospel Hall Wesley Uniting Church. Together with Chris Gibson, the chaplain of the Eastern Suburbs Technical College, they started OCF Kew, whereby Kew was the suburb where they met. OCF Kew attracted students from Swinburne and the nearby Methodist Ladies' College. (Some of the college students had older siblings or relatives in OCF Parkville.) A Malaysian couple Wong Chin Wong and his wife Hoon Bee from the nearby Northcote Presbyterian Church often cooked for the students.

At its largest, OCF Kew was a group of around twenty people, from various churches, including Catholic, Richmond Assemblies of God, Uniting Church, and some who did not go to church. Despite being a small group, they embarked on various projects—printing and selling T-shirts, producing OCF-embroidered badges, and staging a Christian musical *Friends Forever* at RMIT. Although they had to bear some financial risk by hiring the RMIT hall at commercial rates, they not only shared the gospel, but also made some profit! There was a great sense of enthusiasm and joy in the group.

Over the years, OCF Kew moved to various churches that had a heart for international students: St Columbus Anglican Church, Habitat Uniting Church (previously a different name), and Hawthorn Chinese Christian Church. OCF Kew had to move now and again, because church boards and church visions also change over time. When having overseas student ministry was no longer part of the church's vision, they would start to charge rent and OCF would have to find a new place. After his ordination, Rev Koh left Melbourne in 1991, but Rev Chris Gibson continued to minister to OCF Kew.

After his graduation, Wey Jing received an Equity and Merit Scholarship to do his postgraduate science degree at the Chisolm Institute of Technology. The Victorian chairpersons asked if he would organise the 1990 Victorian Easter camp, and he agreed. He led an organising committee with members from OCF centres Carlton, La Trobe, Clayton, Geelong, and Parkville.

The camp theme was 'Desire, Discipline, Dedication'. For four days and three nights, students shared meals, slept in dorms, and heard from Pastor Scott Wilson from Harvest Bible College (a college of the Assemblies of God) challenging them to desire God wholeheartedly and dedicate themselves to him. Pastor Scott was a good teacher who respected the interdenominational character of OCF. From Joshua 6:8-14, he taught them three keys to bringing down walls—obedience to God; discipline; patience. Many camp delegates became serious in their faith. OCF Kew and new centres soon to be formed—Melbourne Uni, Caulfield, and Frankston—provided them opportunities to serve God. In this way, OCF Victoria entered a period of growth.

After the camp, some of the OCF Victoria chairpersons chided Wey Jing for organising a camp that was 'too charismatic'. In fact, Wey Jing himself was amazed to see that some campers received the gift of speaking in tongues, while others fell to the floor and appeared to be asleep. Later these ones said that the Lord had been ministering to them. One young lady was delivered from an evil spirit. Wey Jing belonged to a traditional and conservative church. Organising a 'charismatic camp' had not been his intention. However, he thought that if God wanted to move this way, and the majority of campers seemed to have benefited from it, so let it be.

In 1992, the Eastern Suburbs Technical College became Swinburne University of Technology in 1992 by an Act of the Victorian Parliament. Eventually, OCF Kew was renamed OCF Swinburne.

OCF Kew with Chris Gibson, 1998.

OCF Kew celebrating Chris Gibson's birthday, 2001. Photo supplied by Tan Kim Ki.

Formation of OCF Melbourne Uni

The 1990 OCF Parkville chairperson Howe Shing was a soft-spoken man of prayer. He had been in an accountability group with Loke Mun and Pastor Hon Hoh where they shared personal struggles and joys and prayed for one another. Under Howe Shing's leadership, OCF Parkville grew to the point where they had enough members to start a new OCF centre on the grounds of Melbourne University itself. Although most OCF Parkville members studied at Melbourne Uni, OCF had never met on Melbourne University grounds. (At its formation in 1958, OCF Melbourne met at the CMS Hostel. It then changed location several times. Since its dissolution and rebirth as OCF Parkville in the 1970s, it had met at Swanston Street Church of Christ.)

From left: Pastor Hon Hoh, Tan Loke Mun, Melbourne, 1990.

In 1990, OCF Parkville commissioned a small group of twenty Melbourne Uni students, led by commerce student Tai Lee Nah, to start a new group. Several OCF Carlton members also joined them. Initially, they met in a tutorial room for weekly lunchtime prayer meetings. Soon after, they started meeting on Friday nights.

Lee Nah and four other girls lived in a grey townhouse with a red door on Haines Street, North Melbourne. The shabby exterior belied the wonderful things happening on the inside, much fun and laughter, meals shared with visitors, committee meetings and music practices. For several years, it was a hub for OCF Melbourne Uni (MU), and many other similar places sprung up as members started renting flats and houses together.

In July 1990, Lee Nah wrote this in her journal: 'Praise God for our first OCF MU meeting yesterday night. Pastor John de Smit spoke on our theme 'Here I am'. Prophecy by Graeme Tonkin: OCF will receive many people who are broken and hurt. We need to allow God to heal them.' Graeme Tonkin had had a long association with OCF Geelong, and regularly travelled from Geelong to Melbourne to support the young group.

Friday night OCF meetings soon become the highlight of the week for members. After a long week of lectures, they felt excitement build as they walked towards Union Hall. In that hall of terrible acoustics, they sang and worshipped wholeheartedly. Many nights people gave their lives to the Lord, sometimes through a visiting speaker, other times through Discovery Groups, which were Bible studies for non-Christians. Amazingly, some became Christians even though Discovery Group leaders were unable to provide satisfactory answers. In all this, there was a sense of expectation: what will God do next?

As committee members were inexperienced, they often prayed for God's leading and direction as they had not been this way before. Seeking the mind of the Lord for Melbourne Uni campus was exciting. After praying together, the committee often shared what they thought the Lord might want them to do. They tried many things. Some worked better than others. Two initiatives that took off were a six-week program called Workers' Training to train up new leaders annually, and the other was a follow-up system of older members discipling younger ones. The benefit of this could be seen in one of the converts, Raymond Leong, who became a Christian during the 1991 OCF Melbourne Uni July camp at Anglesea.

Ng Kui Jen and Michael Fu were assigned to follow up Raymond, and the three of them met each week. Raymond looked forward to the opportunity to open up about struggles, pray together, and search Scriptures. Kui Jen and Michael were engineering students. Raymond, being a law student, used his legal training to examine the Word. He would question everything and try to present both sides of the argument. There were times he disagreed with Kui Jen and Michael. On occasions when satisfactory answers eluded them, they said, 'Look, if we knew everything, we would be God.' Raymond learned to remain humble, to always go back to the Word, and to trust that God would unpack it eventually. Thus, Raymond grew in his faith by being part of a community of dedicated, committed Christians.

Pastor Hon Hoh sometimes spoke at OCF MU camps (see the Parkville section in Chapter 13). By this time, he was one of the pastors at Clayton Church of Christ. He told OCF MU about the promises which he received in 1986. The students were encouraged and continued to pray for the Lord's will to be done at Melbourne University. The longing for spiritual fulfilment that Hon desired at the beginning of his term as OCF Parkville president was fulfilled again. Hon saw it as a multi-stage fulfilment of the promise he had received.

OCF Melbourne Uni Returnees Night 1995. From left: Raymond Leong (4th, behind the guitar).

Most OCF MU members attended Swanston St COC and Richmond AOG. Committee members asked pastors of their churches or other more matured Christians to disciple them, and they in turn discipled younger members. Bruce Hill, the youth pastor at AOG, met up with three of the guys on the committee together every month. Pastor Stewart Rae spoke occasionally and became Raymond's spiritual father and would visit him even after Raymond had graduated and returned to Malaysia. OCF MU students would also attend special functions in each other's churches; for example, Missions Fest at Swanston COC, summer teaching schools at Waverley Christian Fellowship by Kevin Connor, or Wycliffe Bible Translation camps. There was a strong sense of unity and fellowship in the Lord Jesus Christ. On doctrinal differences, the motto was: in essentials unity, in non-essentials liberty, in all things, charity.

Raymond had become a Christian in his first year. In 1995, his fourth and final year, he took up the role of OCF Australia president. The previous year, an Emergency General Meeting had been held. Raymond sought to move beyond tensions about local churches and parachurch organisations that will be described in the next chapter. These tensions were diverting the attention of OCF from its core mission. Through OCF, Raymond had befriended students who did not have the freedom to choose their religion in their home countries. He realised how opportune the time in Australia could be for such people. He also saw how OCF members could be a witness to Jesus Christ in their home countries. To reach out, to build up and to send home; this was OCF's core mission.

OCF Melbourne Uni at the Victorian Easter Camp 1996, Rawson Village. Photos supplied by Tan Kim Ki.

Formation of OCF Caulfield and Frankston

In the late 1980s, there was news of an imminent merger between Monash University and the Chisholm Institute of Technology, comprising both its Caulfield and Frankston campuses. Foreseeing a surge in overseas students, OCF Clayton thought it would be good to start a Christian fellowship group at the Caulfield campus.[131]

The 1989 OCF Clayton chairperson Michael Tam approached Simon Sie, a student enrolled at Chisholm Institute, to discuss the proposed idea. Michael spearheaded the formation of OCF Caulfield.[132] With a sense of adventure, Simon, Michael and a few other overseas students began praying together every week at the Caulfield campus. Meanwhile, another OCF Clayton leader, Leong Seng Keat, was cell group leader to Leong Sea Heng, a Year 12 Monash High School student. On Sundays, Seng Keat would drive Sea Heng to the Mulgrave Chapel, a Brethren Assembly. In 1990, Sea Heng began his studies at Monash University's Caulfield campus, along with many other Christian students who started their tertiary education that same year. Accounting and business courses were especially popular among international students. The inaugural committee, headed by Simon, decided to meet at the Caulfield campus.

By mid-1990, a group of about fifteen Caulfield students began meeting for worship and Bible studies on campus on

---

[131] Moses Khor, Interview with author, 2020.
[132] Tan Loke Mun, Interview with author, 2021.

OCF Caulfield. Sea Heng is standing, second from the left

Friday afternoons. As they hoped to attract students going about their usual study routine, they chose a meeting room that many students passed by on their way to the library, lectures, or tutorials. Some individuals joined OCF, partly because of its convenience and strategic location, and later put their trust and faith in the Lord Jesus Christ.

In 1991, OCF Caulfield officially registered with the Student Union, and moved their meetings to Friday nights. As a result of the student union affiliation, OCF Caulfield secured an annual grant of $1000 to support its activities and enhance its impact on campus. The group used the money to buy a keyboard so they could worship God through music. They made concerted outreach efforts, such as operating an orientation booth to raise awareness about OCF among new students. Regular attendance grew to about fifty members.[133]

OCF Caulfield was blessed by supportive and nurturing advisors. Some of them came from Clayton Church of Christ. Some people who contributed greatly to their growth in the formative years were Max and Irene Williams, Ming Fook, and Dr Phua Kwee Sin and his wife Dorothy (See the section on Clayton in Chapter 8).

First outing of OCF Caulfield. Back row from left: Advisor Ming Fook (1st), advisors Dorothy (2nd) and Phua Kwee Sin (3rd), advisors Irene (4th) and Max Williams (6th). Middle row from left: Daniel Ang (3rd) and Simon Sie (7th). Photos supplied by Leong Sea Heng.

In 1995, PhD student Daniel Ang initiated OCF Frankston. The Frankston campus was further away from the city and had fewer international students. Nonetheless, OCF Frankston blessed and served students at the campus until the OCF centre closed in 2009.

In the 1990 OCF Australia newsletter, Tan Loke Mun wrote, 'If OCF is going to see the mighty works of God, we need to let

---

[133] Leong Sea Heng, Ricky Lee, Simon Sie, and Yeoh Seng Hock. Interview with author, 2022.

God be GOD.'[134] For Loke Mun, Yew Kee's targets were not impossible, but leaders needed the empowering of the Holy Spirit to serve God effectively. EXCO commissioned a series of four articles on Spiritual Warfare by Aunty Merrilyn. In the first of these articles, she wrote, 'There is a mighty spiritual battle raging now, unseen to the naked eye but seen by those Christians who had their eyes 'opened' to SPIRITUAL WARFARE.' Despite the reality of evil, Christians could stand firm in their faith by making room for Jesus in daily living, by reading the Word and in prayer.

As OCF members regularly practised these spiritual disciplines, they gained a truer perspective of the greatness of God and love. He enlarged their vision of what he could do and wanted to do in their midst. The expansion of OCF did not rely on one or two outstanding visionary leaders, but on spiritual eyes of faith being opened, and the Holy Spirit equipping and empowering many members, so that everyone had something to contribute, everyone had a part to play. Those with the gift of leadership became committee members; those with the gift of teaching became Bible study facilitators; the musically gifted joined the worship team; not to mention those with the gift of hospitality, pastoral care, administration, graphic design and so on. The result was a growth in the capacity of OCF Australia to minister to the increasing number of overseas students in small and large centres around the country.

---

[134] Tan Loke Mun, 'OCF in 1990,' *OCF Australia Newsletter*, 89/4 and 90/1, 1990, 3.

15. Pressing Internal and External Concerns

After three decades of growth, many overseas churches knew of OCF, especially those in Malaysia and Singapore. However, a new church planting movement put OCF Australia in the difficult position of having to defend its right to exist as a ministry. Furthermore, a greater number of theologically trained pastors and staff workers resourcing other on-campus student ministries caused the suitability of OCF's student leaders to be questioned.

The La Trobe convention

In 1990, Pastor Barry Chant, Dr Victor Koh and Dr Kriengsak Chareonwongsak spoke at the 31st OCF Annual Convention at La Trobe University. The first two speakers had been approved much earlier, while Dr Kriengsak was a last-minute addition.[135] (Later, as a result of this episode, new guidelines stipulated that potential convention speakers had to be presented to the GC one year in advance, and the GC would select convention speakers together.)

Nine years prior, Dr Kriengsak had founded Hope of Bangkok, which became known as 'the largest Pentecostal and Charismatic church in the country, and the only significant church founded by a Thai'.[136] At the time of the

---

[135] Tan Loke Mun. Interview with author, 2021.
[136] Allan Anderson, *An Introduction to Pentecostalism* (Cambridge, UK: Cambridge University Press, 2004), 129.

convention, he was planting Hope of God churches internationally. His vision for world evangelisation through church planting resonated with some OCF members.

Not too long beforehand, the 1988 OCF Australia chairperson Peter Ting had proposed an International OCF, encouraging OCF returnees to equip themselves to serve God in their home countries. Instead of relying on western missionaries, OCF members should make an impact in Asia and beyond. At that time, it was a concept with no vehicle, because the OCF vision was to go back to serve God in local churches. OCF has never had a vision for church planting because it has never seen itself as a church. However, as Peter had not outlined any specifics, what form International OCF could take was open to interpretation and imagination. Peter's ideas, coupled with Dr Kriengsak's personal example of returning to Thailand although he had been converted in Australia, inspired some OCF members to join the Hope of God (HOG) movement. Dr Kriengsak is no longer with the movement today.

In early 1991, Hope Singapore was founded by a team that included four couples who had been active in OCF: Andrew and Soo Feng Cheang (OCF La Trobe), Chiew Bong and Dora Chang (OCF Geelong), Peter and Abby Ting (OCF Flinders), and Ben and Dinah Lee (OCF Curtin).[137] The team pooled their resources, living and working together in

---

[137] In the second year of Hope Singapore, Charmaine Chee and Lawrence Ong, both from OCF Perth, served as church leaders also.

establishing the new church. They had little connection with events unfolding in OCF Australia subsequently.

In the early 1990s, the view of the HOG movement was that a church that is functioning as it should need not rely on parachurch organisations to help it fulfil its role. The HOG is, or aims to be, a fully-functioning church. Therefore, if a HOG church is in a particular location, parachurch organisations are not needed there.[138] This HOG view was communicated to some OCF members. The implication was that OCF was no longer needed in the several Australian cities where new HOG churches had been established.

Deeply concerned, the EXCO commissioned a fact-finding exercise on the movement.[139] As a result of this exercise, the EXCO proposed to distance OCF Australia from the HOG movement through two motions that they presented to the General Council (GC) at the 1993 AGM. Founding OCF Australia member Professor Lawrence Chia flew in from Singapore to speak in support of this move. One of the main concerns was the fervour with which members encouraged others to join the movement, causing Christians to leave their own churches and student fellowship groups. In Singapore, some concerned pastors and parents were asking if OCF was a channel for HOG, seeing that many former OCF leaders were leaders of the movement.

---

[138] 'Explanation of the Motions carried at the Extraordinary General Meeting of the Overseas Christian Fellowship Australia on 9 April 1994, concerning the Hope of God Movement', a paper written as a result of the 1994 EGM.

[139] Samuel Wong, Interview with author, 2022.

At the AGM, many of the GC members felt ill-equipped to handle a matter that spanned several countries and Christian organisations. Some found it hard to understand how Christian leaders could hold such opposing views. Was the movement a dangerous fringe group, or were they a growing church movement passionate for world evangelisation? Most centre leaders had no trusted local advisors at the AGM to turn to. Aunty Merrilyn was present as the EXCO resource person, but EXCO that year did not have a close relationship with her and they did not avail themselves of her counsel. These young leaders felt the burden of responsibility to safeguard the ministry of OCF and their members.

Under pressure to act, the GC voted to carry the two proposed motions a few hours before the end of the AGM.[140] I was at this AGM as the outgoing chairperson for OCF Melbourne Uni. For many years, I regarded it as a personal failing that I had supported this vote for it necessitated an Extraordinary General Meeting (EGM) just six months later. At this EGM, these motions were reworded to remove specific mention of the church. Instead, it highlighted the importance of operating respectfully of other Christian churches and groups, respecting the principles of working interdenominationally. In retrospect, I realise now that the situation had developed to the point that neither a yes nor no

---

[140] 'Summary of evidences presented to the 35th OCF (Aust) AGM (1993) regarding the Hope of God movement', a report written as a result of the 1993 OCF Australia AGM.

vote at the AGM would have resolved the matter satisfactorily or with finality.

This topic remained on the AGM agenda until 1997, causing distress to the people involved. Perhaps OCF Australia could have found a less painful way to handle the matter if there had been a plurality of mature Christians guiding OCF Australia through the issue as it unfolded. Today, we appreciate members of the Hope church as gospel partners and thank God for their witness that makes the light of Christ shine more brightly.

In retrospect, the main issue for OCF Australia was the mischaracterisation of its ministry as a temporary solution, useful only when the church is not functioning well. Many healthy and thriving churches have affirmed and supported the ministry of OCF. In later years, OCF Australia would drop the word 'parachurch' as a descriptor in view of the negative connotation it carried in some circles. Various other descriptors have since been used, such as a missionary arm or a specialised ministry. While both of these carry some truth, the words 'missionary' and 'specialised' suggest a level of training and organisation that can be misleading.

In fact, OCF is a fellowship. It comprises Christian students coming together regularly to bless one another, and to reach out to their friends. As such, it is often made up of Christian students from several local churches who want to reach fellow students at their universities. OCF Australia is driven not by grand strategies, but by friendship, the simple but powerful connection that Christians have with God and one another. Local centres often take on the appearance of a family because its members are overseas students far from home, and in OCF they find a place to belong.

A Question of Hermeneutics

From 1991 to 1993, OCF Sydney hosted EXCO. As part of his duties, the 1993 OCF Australia chairperson Samuel Wong visited Perth. At the time, ninety OCF Perth members were using the *2:7 Series* by the Navigators, a discipleship curriculum designed for small groups, to be led by trained facilitators. The OCF Perth discipleship program participants outnumbered their public meeting attendees of 50 people. Memorisation of Bible verses was part of the discipleship training program.

At an OCF Perth meeting, Samuel asked the group if they knew a particular verse, and the whole group recited it together with great gusto. The OCF Perth leader, Lawrence Peh recalled Samuel's visit.

> He brought over this inductive Bible study thing from EXCO ... I remember the Bible studies that we had at that time. We always start at 7.30, which is the usual OCF time. I don't think that we even did singspiration [worship] and other things. We just went straight into the Bible. We learned about this inductive Bible study, which means study the Bible for itself without using any Bible guide, but just look at the text, learn from it, apply it in our lives. [We] went all the way through past midnight, and to have the group

stay in that sort of a situation, not because you have to do it or else—that wasn't how it was. People were interested in it. I really feel that was the time of revival.[141]

Samuel was heartened by OCF Perth's embrace of Inductive Bible study methods, but dismayed by what he saw as poor hermeneutics when he visited some centres. Once, an OCF leader said to him, 'I have been afraid of the dark for a while. But I read 1 John 4:18, "There is no fear in love". I realised then that I need not fear the dark, because there is no fear in love.' Samuel replied:

> Brother, let's read this verse in context. This passage is talking about how we are to love one another. The context clearly says that if we do not love others, we do not know God, for God is love. The consequences of not knowing God is judgement. However, if we love our brother, we demonstrate that we know God and therefore have no fear of judgement. 'Perfect love' is when we love others the way God loves us. It is wrong to pick out promises from the Bible that spring out to you. You are using God's word to meet your own needs and fears, misunderstanding and mishandling Scripture. If you do this, you will never understand God's purposes for you, that is, to save you from your sins through Jesus Christ.

Samuel wrote about this in a 1993 article for the OCF Australia newsletter. He expressed his concern that although

---

[141] Lawrence Peh, Interview by Joshua Sim, 2020.

many claimed to believe in the sufficiency of the Scriptures, their improper use of the Bible denied that claim. In the same article, Samuel wrote 'Since God's word is eternal, its truth is unchangeable regardless who reads it. There is no place for relativism. Thus, there is only one way in which we are **expected** to read the Bible... There is one truth and therefore one interpretation. Do not confuse interpretation with application which can be many.'[142]

Even in evangelical circles, however, not many would state it in such black and white terms. Although God is unchanging and all-knowing, none of us are. Correspondingly, the idea that there was only one correct interpretation of Scripture and any one group guarded that interpretation was bound to be challenged. Thus, Samuel did not always have an easy time when he travelled around Australia visiting OCF centres with his message. Once, Samuel had to leave his hosts' home in the wee hours of the morning to avoid further disagreements.[143]

As the outgoing OCF Melbourne University chairperson, I was at the 1993 AGM in Perth. I remember that EXCO organised a session on OCF Australia's doctrinal statement. The speaker dismissed any subjective experience of God. He said that God does not speak to anyone in any special way, through visions, impressions, feelings, or Scripture out of its historical setting and context. The response of OCF members

---

[142] Samuel Wong, 'Perfect Love Casts Out Fear,' *OCF Australia Newsletter*, July-August 1993, 4, 5.

[143] Samuel Wong, Interview by author, 2022.

was varied. Some agreed with him, but others who sought to faithfully read Scriptures in context, believed that this didn't preclude the possibility of God speaking in other ways. The speaker's position divided the audience by virtue of their responses, genuine questions and hesitations, whether or not these were voiced. At AGMs, there was no time to wrestle with these questions. Instead, in our private thoughts or in the estimation of others, there were charismatics, non-charismatics and anti-charismatics, all labels that did not encourage honest conversation, stimulate Christian growth or promote unity.

Meanwhile, OCF Sydney was facing its own challenges. The once popular horse-riding camp was discontinued in 1990 due to low numbers. Although over 200 people attended orientation night, there were not enough members to follow up new contacts.[144] Attendance at the Sydney-wide public meetings on Fridays dwindled to about ten people, while the life of OCF seemed localised to District Groups. The OCF Sydney chairperson Peter Chin saw decentralisation as one of the factors contributing to decline, and added three resource persons, each one looking after three to four District Groups or campus groups. Peter Chin was the last OCF Sydney chairperson to hold the position for three years. After him, the term was shortened to two years. A number of Sydney OCF members attended the 1990 La Trobe convention, but

---

[144] *OCF Sydney 1957-2007*, 34, 35.

Reach Out, Build Up, Send Back

OCF SYDNEY STRUCTURE 1990

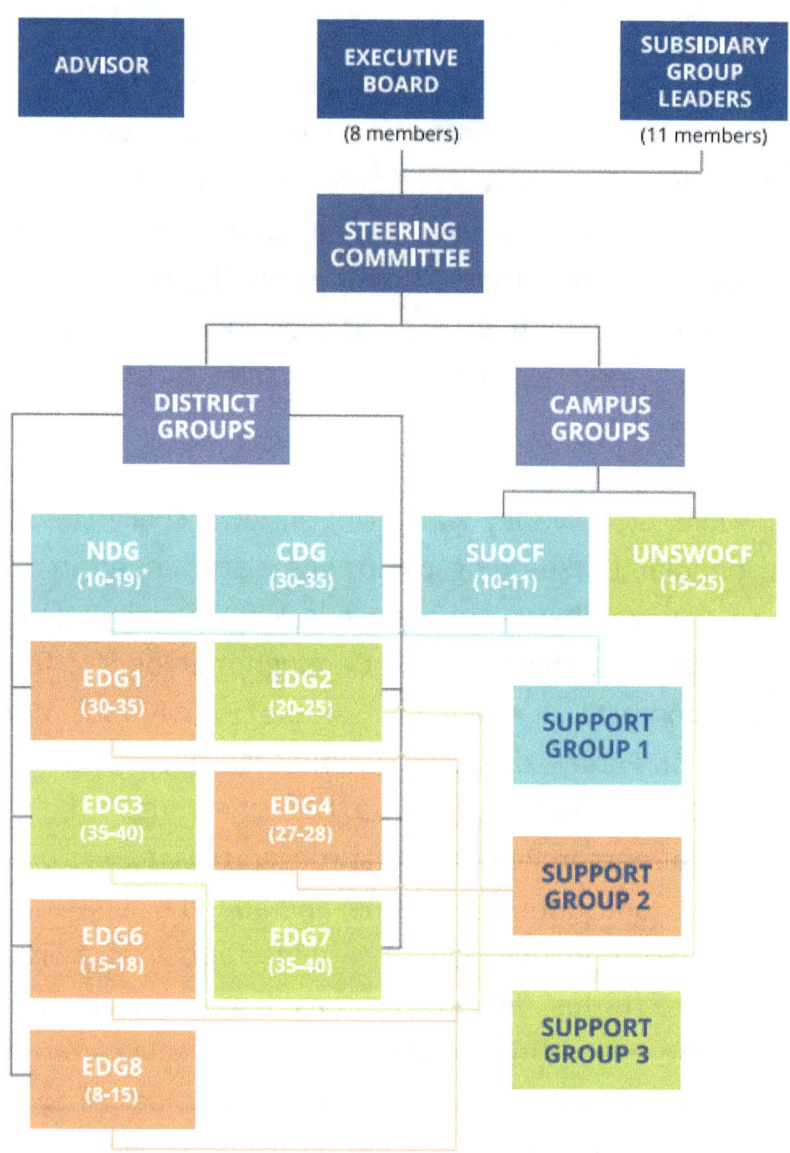

* Weekly Attendance

Redrawn from diagram published in OCF Sydney 1957–2007.

they were uncomfortable with the exercise of the prophetic ministry from the pulpit.

In 1991 alone, the OCF Sydney membership declined from 230 to 167. Three District Groups either closed or merged. A taskforce revamped the Bible study program to suit shorter student stays in OCF. In 1995, OCF Sydney employed former OCF leader and medical doctor Errol Smith as the General Secretary. Shen Dah Cheong, the 1963 and 1964 OCF Australia chairperson, headed a fundraising committee. Seventeen percent of the salary came from OCF members, the rest from ex-OCFers, with the deficit covered by the committee themselves. Esther Lukabyo later joined OCF Sydney as a staff worker. Staff workers stabilised OCF Sydney, but generally failed to reverse the downward trend over the years. Esther attributes the declining OCF membership to more options for Christian fellowship on campus, such as the Fellowship of Christian University Students (FOCUS), the campus arm of the St Matthias Anglican Church.

In 1996, a break-in at an OCF ministry house in Lewisham resulted in the move of OCF Sydney to St Barnabas Church in Broadway, walking distance from the University of Sydney and from Moore Theological College. It was thought that its proximity to Sydney Uni would be helpful. However, by 1998, 'It became clearer that the move to St Barnabas had caused the quality of the fellowship during the Saturday meeting to deteriorate. Easier access to the meeting place also meant that it was easier to make a quick exit home or otherwise. The previous practice of staying on, for up to an hour after the formal meeting was over, to fellowship over tea and biscuits was no longer the norm.'[145] Some Sydney OCF members were boarders at Moore College. They invited the Bible College students to speak at OCF on each of the AFES doctrinal points weekly.

Faced with challenges, OCF Sydney turned to its strengths of administration and sound Biblical teaching. However, other Sydney churches and campus groups were also providing good Bible teaching, often by ordained ministers or full-time theologically-trained staff. The 1998 Sydney University OCF president Ong Chong Wei observed that such ministries were attractive to time-poor Sydney students.[146] Although genuine friendship and good fellowship continued at OCF Sydney, it seemed that fewer and fewer were finding their way there.

Pushback Against Experiential Emphasis

In 1996, Lee Chee Keat took on the role of OCF Australia chairperson. He had served as the OCF Clayton chairperson and was at the 1993 OCF Australia AGM in Perth. The teaching that Scripture must have supreme authority over reason, experience and tradition caused him to re-examine his doctrinal beliefs and Christian walk thus far.

---

[145] *OCF Sydney 1957-2007*, 51.
[146] Ong Chong Wei, Interview with author, 2022.

Chee Keat had arrived in Melbourne in 1989. Kenneth Liew, an OCF Parkville leader who was from the same church in Ipoh, discipled him. Kenneth persuaded Chee Keat to organise gospel meetings at the Anglican boarding house in Bendigo where he lodged. Kenneth wanted to encourage other Christians there, but Chee Keat was hesitant and afraid. Quoting from Romans 1:16, Kenneth reminded him not to be ashamed of the gospel. Chee Keat sought permission from his school and organised several weekend gospel meetings. OCF Parkville members drove up to run those meetings. Although the return drive took three and a half hours, the OCF members were encouraged to see up to fifty boarders attend the meetings, and some come to accept Christ as their Lord and Saviour.

Praying in tongues used to give Chee Keat the courage to witness at boarding school. However, by 1996, Chee Keat had begun questioning if the gift of tongues he practised was the same experience that the early church had at Pentecost. Reading 1 Cor 13, he concluded that love is the greater gift. He decided not to dwell on whether or not the gift of tongues that he had was real. He also came to the conclusion that he had placed experience over Scripture in the past and sought to correct this.

By this stage, OCF Carlton had been uncomfortable with OCF Victorian Easter camps for some years due to what they perceived to be a growing expectation or reliance on outward signs. Accentuating these concerns was a charismatic movement that began in North America in the mid-1990s called the Toronto Blessing. Unusual phenomena such as people 'falling under the power' or 'slain in the Spirit' were becoming common place in some churches and Christian fellowship groups around the world.[147] When a similar incident happened at an OCF Victoria Easter camp ministry night, OCF Carlton members and leaders were confused and concerned. They did not understand what had happened, and some felt afraid. As a result, OCF Carlton took decisive action and stopped attending OCF Victoria Easter camps as a group. Instead, they went to the Belgrave Heights Easter camps. However, they still sent a few committee members to OCF Victoria Easter camps, because the committee members were more senior, more mature, and more able to process differences in practice. OCF Carlton still attended OCF Australia conventions and saw itself as very much a part of OCF Australia, but gradually drifted apart from the rest of OCF Victoria.[148]

In his role as the 1996 OCF Australia president, Chee Keat and his EXCO travelled to other states and also interacted with other Christian student groups on campus. Two staff workers of other groups impressed upon him the need for OCF Australia to employ a staff worker. The first reason was because of concerns that some OCF members were putting experience ahead of Scriptural authority, potentially becoming vulnerable to false doctrines. The

---

[147] Allan Anderson, *An Introduction to Pentecostalism* (Cambridge, UK: Cambridge University Press, 2004), 162.

[148] Sources from former OCF Carlton members with a good understanding of this period.

Delegates at the 1995 OCF Australia AGM in Melbourne. Lee Chee Keat was the incoming OCF Australia chairperson. In the photo below, he is the only one facing the camera

second reason was to improve Biblical literacy among members. It was noted that some OCF members could not explain the gospel clearly. Improving Biblical literacy in an entire organisation was time-consuming and would require the dedicated attention of a staff worker to remedy.

Aunty Merrilyn was still the national resource person of OCF Australia, as she had been for the past ten years, but not all centres availed themselves of her input. In the vast continent of Australia, it has been difficult for any one person to have a close relationship with all centres, especially with the high turnover of student leaders. With the worldwide church divided over the question of how the Holy Spirit works, student leaders felt wary of consulting pastors whose views on the matter were different from their own.

For Chee Keat, the combined effect of these issues was that he felt ill-equipped to lead a national student organisation. Yet, looking at the local leaders gathered around the table at the AGM, he was amazed that God had brought all the local centre leaders through another year, despite personal inadequacies, criticisms from outside OCF, and tensions within.

Across OCF Australia, some centres were open to the charismatic influence, others opposed it. Still others were ambivalent or confused by undercurrents at AGMs that they did not understand. The inability to resolve this issue definitively chipped away at the effectiveness of the fellowship. However, local centres remained tight-knit and OCF Australia continued to be effective at the local level, and largely at the state level as well.

At the national level, OCF Australia found it hard to articulate or justify its existence when challenged. Although many pastors were supportive of OCF Australia, they could not defend it to other churches, because OCF Australia was not the ministry of any one church, nor did it have a governing board of senior and well-respected members of the community as is the case with many larger organisations such as the Australia Fellowship of Evangelical Students. There has been no documentation or evidence that OCF Australia has ever considered forming such a governing board. The desire to maintain student leadership was most likely the reason for this.

OCF Australia was not created to be a force for world evangelisation, although many members went on to be missionaries, serve on missions boards, or bear witness in places that were a mission field. Neither was it created to be a theological training centre, although many members gained a lifelong love for God's word that led to sound hermeneutic skills, and skills in leading small group Bible studies. From the start, OCF Australia was built on friendship and thrived by being a family away from home for many overseas students. As such, it was ill-equipped to engage with churches that did not see the need for its ministry, or groups that criticised OCF's student leaders on account of their lack of theological training.

16. Catalyst and Safeguard: A Board Envisaged

Between 1997 and 2000, OCF Australia had 24 affiliates, the highest number of centres since its formation. Student leaders at the helm of this larger and more diverse organisation saw value in consolidating the input of their advisors scattered in local centres around Australia. If they could create a way for these advisors to work together, OCF Australia would benefit from the counsel of people from different backgrounds, with different strengths, ministering in different locations. In response to this, the 1997 EXCO chairperson Yong Tuck Yean initiated steps to form a board of advisors. He envisaged that it would function both as a catalyst for growth or new initiatives, and a safeguard to protect the ministry and its members.

The Help of Resource Persons and Local Advisors

In 1997, EXCO created a framework to multiply the number of resource persons supporting the GC. They did this by publishing two documents:
1. *The OCF (Australia) Standing Order for the Selection and the Conduct of Resource Persons for the EXCO.*
2. *The OCF (Australia) Guideline and Criteria for the Selection of Local Centre Advisors.*

After publishing these documents, EXCO started a process with the GC to appoint resource persons in order to form a Board of Advisors (BOA) as soon as possible.

Resource persons would advise the GC and influence the ministry at a national level. Therefore, the more binding standing orders applied to them, compared to the guidelines applied to local centre advisors. Reflecting this difference, resource persons had to be theologically trained, a criterion not applied to local centre advisors. All resource persons and advisors had to be spiritually mature, and committed to the doctrinal basis, vision and aims of OCF Australia. They had to be members of a local church, and not be in any financial difficulties. They were not to impose their advice on the committee, while the committee had to give due consideration to any advice regarding the benefit of OCF as a whole.[149] The tenure for local advisors would be one year, after which both parties could re-evaluate the partnership. This would provide a way out if there were serious doctrinal differences, or if advisors' circumstances had changed and OCF was no longer a suitable ministry for them.

Preferably, the advisors would be from different denominations, and they would maintain good work relationships among themselves, and be accountable to one another. As a student-run body, OCF Australia needed a way to hold resource persons and advisors accountable, and they chose to rely on the collective wisdom of the adults they trusted. While the EXCO was drafting up these documents, a situation in Tasmania highlighted the inadequacies of OCF Australia's existing structure.

---

[149] *OCF (Australia) Handbook* (6th ed., 1998), 21-28.

Crisis and Opportunity in Hobart

In 1996, Tuck Yean had visited OCF Hobart to promote the end-of-year convention. Some OCF Hobart members attended the convention and were blessed. There, through interaction with other OCF members, they gained an understanding of what it meant to be a fellowship of students reaching out to their friends and preparing to serve God in the future. It breathed new life into their regular meetings.

In 1997, Fiona Teo[150] stepped up to serve as the OCF Hobart chairperson. To further strengthen recently renewed links with OCF Australia, she invited Aunty Merrilyn to speak at their Easter camp. Their unofficial advisor also attended this camp. He had no official appointment in OCF, as the 1997 local centre advisor guidelines had not been implemented in Hobart yet. However, many of the students attended the church where he was a leader and they regarded him as a good Bible teacher. He was also a staff worker with another Christian group.

After the camp, this unofficial advisor strongly criticised the running of the camp and Aunty Merrilyn. Although Fiona disagreed with him, she did not speak up due to an ingrained culture of respect for people in authority. Although severely shaken herself, Aunty Merrilyn did her best to comfort Fiona. Aunty Merrilyn realised the vulnerability of her position: there

---

[150] A pseudonym, requested due to the traumatic and sensitive nature of events described.

was no one more senior in OCF Australia to defend her. When she returned to Adelaide, she gave an account of what had happened to her church pastor Rev Ng Sin Thong, and to the EXCO chairperson Tuck Yean. Subsequently, EXCO members Tuck Yean and Barry Wee met with Rev Ng for advice on how to approach discussions with the unofficial advisor and also on how to strengthen OCF's organisational structure.

Following this, Tuck Yean and Barry flew to Hobart. Tuck Yean, Barry, and Fiona met with the unofficial advisor. Starting with the doctrinal statements of OCF and the evangelical position, a common understanding of the gospel was established. EXCO then explained that Aunty Merrilyn's role as the EXCO resource person had been confirmed unanimously by the GC, the governing body of OCF Australia. Her appointment was based on invitation and was not a self-appointed role or imposed by any other external organisation.

The unofficial advisor expressed his concern about women in pastoral and teaching roles. EXCO explained that OCF, as a fellowship consisting of members of different church denominations, did not restrict women from senior leadership roles. While all agreed that this was not a core issue, the discussion sentiment suggested that he would voluntarily choose not to continue with OCF Hobart if the centre leadership maintained their ties with Aunty Merrilyn. After Tuck Yean and Barry left, there was no one close at hand from OCF Australia to continue supporting Fiona. Many

Sundays at church, the unofficial advisor continued to ask Fiona to choose between Aunty Merrilyn and all the resources he had to offer. Due to the ongoing pressure, Fiona could not focus on her studies.

Many thoughts crowded her mind. Some of the more pleasant ones were memories of an EXCO visit the previous year. From these visitors, Fiona had heard about Melbourne ministry households. It seemed as if serving God together as a household could be a great blessing. Fiona also read the *OCF (Australia) Handbook*. She was amazed by what students before her had accomplished. Though they were young and inexperienced, they had come together to form OCF Australia with a vision of preparing to serve God in the future. When she read the 1983 *OCF Guidelines on the Charismatic Movement*, she marvelled at students coming together to deal with issues facing their generation. She became more conscious of OCF's spiritual legacy. In fact, Fiona's predecessor Lisa was the daughter of Jonathan Parapak, the founding president of OCF Hobart. Since God had started something in Hobart, Fiona reasoned that they should not wrap it up without first exploring the possibility that God might also have a mandate for them at the present time.

After almost two years of uncertainty, Fiona and some others decided that OCF Hobart would remain part of OCF Australia. They started attending a different church. After this, OCF Hobart enjoyed greater connection with OCF Australia. From this, Fiona noticed how OCF members took personal responsibility for their faith and for reaching their friends.

Sadly, by this time, around half the members of OCF Hobart had left, due to the fallout from the Easter camp.

In the second half of 1998, Fiona and her brother Simon found two new five-bedroom houses on a subdivided plot near the university. Fiona and Simon told the owners they wanted to start two ministry households, one for boys, and the other for girls. The owners readily agreed to rent the homes to them, and to allow them to sublet rooms to other students. By the following January, the ten students had signed lease agreements for two adjacent houses on View Street. They became known as the View Street boys: Simon, Oliver, Brian, Abraham and Calvin; and the View Street girls: Fiona, Ann, Sing Loong, Elizabeth, and Georgina. Soon after moving in, they hosted a Chinese New Year reunion dinner. They set up tables and chairs outdoors in the cool summer breeze. Their simple hospitality brought much joy to students, many far from family for the first time.

In the following months, they learned many life lessons together. Most were supported by parents, though some had bursaries or part-time jobs. They pooled their money, time and resources to give back to the fellowship. At household meetings, they organised cooking and washing up duties, or addressed high electricity bills. They often hosted birthday parties. People used to drop by freely. Their homes became a place for connecting and building up God's people.

In this nurturing environment, God healed wounds of the previous months. Simon took over from Fiona as president. He attended Church of Christ and approached the pastor there, Pastor Clinton Wardle, to teach committee members how to handle the Word of God. Pastor Wardle was generous with his time, teaching students even though some did not attend his church. He became the first official advisor of OCF Hobart. OCF Hobart members started forming connections with the pastors of the different churches that they each attended—Assemblies of God, Anglican, Baptist. Church leaders started to trust the ministry of OCF and encouraged their members to attend the fellowship. Apart from official advisors, there were other Australian Christians who joined them, such as Uncle Frank Cole and his wife Aunty Jenny. (Georgina was their niece.) Uncle Frank often affirmed members as they served in OCF, 'I can see you've got this gift; you did this really well.' Aunty Frances Hearn from the Brethren church, volunteered as an English teacher. She would bring her homestay students to OCF.

Gradually, OCF Hobart became a more well-connected and well-resourced group. Returning to the foundations of sound Bible study in small groups and regular corporate prayer put the group on a firm footing. They became united under God's word, and they progressed to outreach. Later, leadership development was added into the training ministry as well.

In 2000, when an influx of international students arrived at the University of Tasmania, OCF Hobart had the capacity to befriend many and welcome them into fellowship. Soon, six cell groups were formed, including one for students who preferred to speak Mandarin, and another for very young believers or people just exploring Christianity. Many faithful Christian workers and leaders emerged out of OCF Hobart from this period.

By 2003, OCF Hobart had grown to a healthy size, capable of hosting the convention, which for the first time was held in Tasmania. By this time, Fiona had graduated and relocated. However, she flew back to attend the convention, heartened to see the outcome of her decision to remain in OCF Australia.

Formation of OCF UniSA

In 1997, a new centre was formed—OCF University of South Australia (UniSA). The university had seen an increase in student numbers since the early 1990s. The first breakthrough in OCF's outreach attempts at UniSA had come three years earlier when a small group of like-minded students began to pray every Wednesday at UniSA's City East campus. A growing number of UniSA students began attending OCF Adelaide University (AU) as both campuses were located in the city centre.

In March 1996, UniSA students began holding their own meetings and were supported by Aunty Merrilyn and several other AACC uncles and aunties. About fifteen OCF Adelaide University (AU) members, or a quarter of its membership, transitioned to this new centre. OCF AU spent the next five years strengthening their ministry at Adelaide University. OCF UniSA became a very multicultural group, with members not only from Malaysia and Singapore, but also from the Netherlands, South Africa, Russia, Hong Kong, Indonesia, Brunei and the United States. The University of South Australia was very supportive of OCF members being involved with the orientation of newly arrived students. When they were fully affiliated in 1997, OCF UniSA had 30 members as shown in the table below.

Average Weekly Attendance	1995	1997
OCF Adelaide	70	40
OCF Uni SA	-	30
OCF Flinders	40	25
Total in South Australia	110	95

Table 1: Average Weekly Attendance in OCF centres in South Australia

At first glance, the total number of attendees dropped slightly in 1997, even though there were three centres, as compared to 1995 before Uni SA was formed. However, the number of people reached through the OCF ministry cannot be estimated by attendance alone. The average length of their time in OCF must also be taken into consideration. Indeed, the length of time in OCF was diminishing by this stage, largely due to the rise of twinning programs, where students undertook the initial portion of their degrees in off-shore campuses but completed their degrees in Australia.

Chairpersons carrying chairs, 1996 South Australian Easter Camp.
From left: Yong Tuck Yean, Herman Chua and Haryady Chandra,
chairpersons of OCF Adelaide Uni, Flinders Uni and UniSA respectively.
Photo supplied by Herman Chua.

If, in 1995, the average time spent in OCF was 3 years, it meant that OCF had to replace a third of its membership yearly (110/3 = 36 new members needed). If the average time in OCF dropped to 2 years in 1997, OCF would then have to replace half of its members annually (95/2 = 47 new members needed). With this in mind, it is likely that OCF in SA had at least maintained its reach in the second half of the 1990s, even though membership numbers had dipped slightly.

In South Australia, OCF began developing a state identity. The three centre chairpersons—Herman Chua (Flinders), Haryady Chandra (UniSA) and Yong Tuck Yean

(Adelaide Uni)—came together regularly for mutual encouragement and support. Hosting EXCO from 1997 to 2000 further strengthened this bond, as each centre had to release leaders for EXCO and manage their own leadership resources carefully.

The fruit of the three centres was more evident in the 2000s when all three South Australian centres flourished. By God's grace, total membership was over 120. Easter camps were attended by more than 100 full-timers. Many of these OCF members blessed churches around Adelaide. The three OCF SA centres worked closely with, and received support from, the local churches AACC and Paradise AOG. And more significant than these numbers, many were equipped for future pastoral work in churches or missions, and others for their witness through their vocational profession.

The formalisation of OCF Australia's supporters put in place a process for building a network of support for OCF Australia. In 2023, Tuck Yean wrote his personal reflections:

> I am impressed that OCF Australia and OCF centres existed for a good part of 40 years without any of these documents. Many partnerships between OCF and advisors flourished without them. OCF has now operated with the existence of these documents for the past 25 years but the fellowship in this period has not genuinely become more effective than the preceding 40 years. My apprehension with these documents is that they can be used in a legalistic way when not applied correctly, which in turn suffocates the organisation. OCF must grow in realisation that

God's work extends beyond what man can frame in a few pages. Minimally, these documents should provide guidance and safeguard, but strong partnerships need to grow with the work of the Holy Spirit through God's word.

From the *1978 Declaration* to the *1997 Standing Orders for Resource Persons*, many reams of paper were used up over articles added to the Handbook. They provided information to articulate the stand of the fellowship, or to encourage members or leaders in some aspect, but overall did not have a huge impact in passing on vision or solving problems, as prescriptive guidelines inevitably failed to anticipate new situations.

The more significant help for students came from pastors, informal supporters and advisors who invested time into the ministry. However, there were fewer supporters in this period compared to the founding years, fewer Australians in the fellowship, and the use of associate members to describe them fell into disuse. As a result, OCF Australia as a student-led organisation struggled to deal with issues it faced at a national level.

At a local and state level, however, growth in this period was significant. Many centres grew around a love for God's Word and a dependence on the work of the Holy Spirit, with many members forming deep long-lasting Christian friendships through serving together in OCF. Local centres were free to organise themselves as they saw fit, and this worked well when coupled with state level collaboration and leadership. Many student leaders, who were exemplary in their Christ-like character, inspired younger students to give themselves wholeheartedly to God.

OCF AUSTRALIA IN THE LATE 1990S

Section 3: Recent Times, 2000 and beyond

To celebrate its 40th anniversary, the annual OCF convention was held outside Australia, and opened to the alumni for the first time. The high turnout in Melaka, Malaysia, especially among the alumni, highlighted a characteristic of OCF whereby bonds formed through the fellowship often lasted a lifetime. The essence of the ministry, a spiritual family away from home for overseas students, facilitated deep connections with God and with one another. Correspondingly, the fruit of the ministry can only be fully appreciated through the lives of young people, whose brief time in OCF cause them to surrender self-determination to God's plans and purposes for them.

However, the brevity of their time in OCF resulted in a transience that made it harder for OCF Australia to capitalise on opportunities or respond to challenges of the 21st century. Citizens and permanent residents played an increasingly important role in resourcing local centres. Yet the constitution placed time limits on the leadership of students who were not from overseas. In trying to fix these challenges, OCF Australia leaders were pulled in two directions: a determination to stay true to the vision and methods of founding members, and a growing awareness of the inadequacies of the present system. Solutions were hard to find and execute because no one person, church, or organisation held the reins of OCF Australia. Year after year, committee after committee, OCF Australia was entrusted to young people, who made their mark on the fellowship and then handed it on to the next batch of students.

When Australia closed its borders due to the COVID-19 pandemic, the viability of the ministry was in doubt. Yet, through the challenging months that followed, OCF Australia found ways to care for overseas students who were isolated from family and sometimes even from other students. The seriousness of the situation helped OCF Australia to distinguish between dispensable ideology and indispensable Christian principles.

17. Formal Support

OCF Australia entered the 21st century with an awareness that it needed to adapt to meet the challenges of the new millennium. In 1997, the EXCO chairperson Yong Tuck Yean had discussed this in his paper *Contemporary Issues and Challenges for Overseas Christian Fellowship (Australia)*. He observed increasing affluence among international students due to marked increases in international student fees. He also highlighted how new initiatives in tertiary education led to more competition for students' time and attention. For example, summer courses made it hard for members to attend the OCF annual convention, which had been a major bonding and training opportunity. Furthermore, twinning

The 40th OCF Australia convention in 1999. For the first time, the convention was held outside Australia, in Melaka, Malaysia so that OCF alumni as well as current OCF members could gather. Since then, the 50th and 60th conventions have also been opened to the alumni.

programs at offshore campuses allowed international students to start their degrees in their home countries, shortening the time they would spend in Australia.

On the positive side, the numbers of international students were increasing rapidly, and they were coming from a greater diversity of countries. The overall picture was that there were a greater number of international students to minister to, but OCF Australia had to work more strategically to make an impact on them.[151] Since Tuck Yean presented his paper in 1997, the EXCO and GC had discussed possible solutions over several AGMs, but it was hard to find solutions that everyone agreed to.

No Consensus

At the AGM held in Adelaide in December 1999, the OCF Australia Strategic Review committee presented a verbal report. This committee had been formed eight months previously in response to Yong Tuck Yean's report on challenges facing the fellowship. Each state was invited to set up a forum and bring their findings back to the review committee. Pastors and advisors were also invited to make submissions.

Pastor Allan Webb, formerly of Swanston Street Church of Christ, had moved to Sydney as the OMF national director. He urged OCF to foster closer associations with local

---

[151] Yong Tuck Yean, 'Contemporary Issues and Challenges for OCF (Australia)' (OCF Australia, 31 Oct 1997), 1-3.

churches rather than other parachurch groups, since they would face the same challenges as OCF. The staff worker Errol Smith, however, proposed closer ties with the Australian Fellowship of Evangelical Students (the IVF had been renamed), and a reemphasis on the Doctrinal Statement, which OCF shared with AFES. In Victoria, Moses Khor, a Clayton Church of Christ pastor and former EXCO chairperson, suggested a centralised organisational structure for efficiency, even if it meant giving up a measure of local centre autonomy. In Western Australia, the state advisor Ross Nancarrow and Curtin chairperson Donny Lim suggested that full- or part-time resource persons were needed in every centre, or at least, every state.[152] In South Australia, however, Rev Ng Sin Thong of the Austral-Asian Christian Church urged for a close working relationship with the church. Aunty Merrilyn and the elders of AACC felt that there was no need for a staff worker. Queensland did not make a submission.

    Each state proposed arrangements that had worked well for them. Everyone agreed something had to be done to arrest the decline in membership, but there was no consensus. The OCF Curtin chairperson Donny Lim chaired the Review Committee. Yong Tuck Yean, whose 1997 paper had sparked this review, was the co-chair, but he believed that the committee had already veered off-course because it failed to study challenges and propose solutions in a systematic and objective way. Instead, focus had been on the uniqueness of the OCF ministry and challenges in fulfilling its

---

[152] Ross Nancarrow and Donny Lim, *The Challenge Before Us* (Perth, 1998), 4.

vision. Submissions hardly considered issues around membership, leadership, support personnel, relationship with local churches and changes in the education scene. In 2000, when the committee was meant to hand in its formal report, Donny Lim was preoccupied with local Curtin matters. No written report was ever submitted.

Western Australia Staffworker Organisation

In 2000, OCF Murdoch and Curtin were on the brink of closure. Three years prior, Donny Lim had put in place a plan to 're-engineer Curtin'. The essence of this plan was for OCF Curtin to train overseas students in reaching out to others, but to encourage them to find fellowship and support from whichever church they attended in Perth. The thinking was that OCF should avoid overlap or duplication of function with the local church. OCF Murdoch supported Curtin's initiatives, but the group of twelve final year students there had in mind to fold up the centre when they graduated.

OCF Perth did not want to accept Donny's suggested changes, even though he had the support of the state advisor. According to David Liaw, the 1999 OCF Perth chairperson, the fundamental flaw to the re-engineering was that OCF Curtin relegated the basics of discipleship, fellowship and follow-up to these churches. As a result, students no longer identified with OCF as their home fellowship away from home. Many chose to be part of the church fellowship groups only, leading to a sharp dive in membership.[153]

The 2000 EXCO treasurer from Sydney, Ong Chong Wei, visited Perth seeking to reconcile the WA centres. He did not want to see fellowship in Christ broken over differences in organisational structure. However, he could not do much because OCF Murdoch dissolved later that year. OCF Curtin had two members left, and they asked to be accepted back into OCF Perth. One of the OCF Perth graduates, Dominic Voon, recalled how God had orchestrated the founding of these two centres (see Chapter 12 Perth, *The Formation of OCFs Murdoch and Curtin*). He pleaded with the Curtin members to persevere. OCF Perth sent some of their members to help them out, including Curtin pharmacy student Jonathan Liaw. Through hard work and by God's grace, OCF Curtin pulled through. Jonathan became OCF Curtin's chairman. He found a young seminary student, Rob Robayna, originally from Spain, to be their advisor.

Around 2002, when Rob Robayna was about to graduate, he informed OCF of his plan to become an AFES staff worker. Dominic Voon and a few OCF WA alumni asked Rob if he was willing to serve in OCF instead, as he had a good relationship with the Curtin students. At this time, eight past presidents of OCF Perth were residing in Perth. They put their heads together to propose an OCF WA Staffworker Organisation Inc (WASO). This organisation would be the vehicle whereby OCF WA alumni could give back to OCF by

---

[153] David Liaw, Email to author, 6 August 2023.

financially supporting a staff worker. The role of the staff worker was first, to help struggling centres, and second, to pioneer new centres.

The WASO constitution was carefully worded to preserve OCF's student leadership ethos. OCF centres were not obliged to accept the services from a staff worker. Student leaders would need to opt-in, to avail themselves of the services of a staff worker. A Staffworker Oversight Committee, comprising graduates and student leaders, detailed the day-to-day operations and specific role of the staff worker. They elected a Staffworker Executive Body to employ the staff worker, and to provide spiritual and moral support for the person. AFES helped WASO by managing accounts, accepting donations and forwarding salaries. In 2002, Dominic presented the WASO concept to OCF Australia. At the following AGM, the proposal was accepted.

WASO employed Rob, who served as a full-time staff worker for four and a half years, which strengthened OCF in WA. In 2004, OCF Murdoch reformed through the combined efforts of Hui Mun Tzin and Lydia Wei. They were Murdoch students who were attending OCF Curtin and Perth respectively. One of the students who benefited from Rob's service was Ang Chin Wee, the 2006 OCF Curtin chairperson. Chin Wee had become a Christian through the ministry of OCF.

Chin Wee's mother was a Buddhist. He enjoyed visits to the temple as fun family outings but did not believe the teachings. As an overseas student, he joined OCF Perth for the friendship they offered. But when they asked him, a self-confessed atheist, about his religious beliefs, he started investigating the claims of Christianity. As a result, Chin Wee became a Christian on Easter Sunday 2004. He was full of enthusiasm to serve God, and advisor Pastor Max Graieg encouraged him to serve in various OCF roles.

In 2006, none of Chin Wee's peers wanted to be the Curtin president, so he stepped up. But he found that being president was not easy. His committee once spent a whole day discussing possible themes for the year without reaching a conclusion. In hindsight, Chin Wee admitted that he had caused the waste of time because he had not wanted the burden of responsibility that came with decision-making. Fortunately, Rob's consistent presence gave Chin Wee much assurance to step up as a young leader.

Chin Wee recalled an incident when Rob's handling of a serious pastoral matter was crucial. A student leader announced that he and his girlfriend were stepping down from leadership because she was pregnant with their child. As staff worker, Rob affirmed OCF's support for the two young people. However, because of their conduct, they could not continue as leaders. This incident made a deep impression on Chin Wee about how these major things should be handled, with grace and truth.

In retrospect, as a pastor now himself, Chin Wee acknowledged the difficulty that Rob must have faced, only being able to advise, but not direct, the students. As a result, the ministry suffered at times because of the poor choices or inexperience of its leaders. From the outside, it is hard to see what staff workers do, as they support students at the forefront of the ministry. On occasions, Rob expressed frustrations to the Staffworker Executive Board when the students did not take his advice. However, the board seldom intervened because the WASO constitution had safeguards to protect the student leadership ethos of OCF. The founders of WASO hoped that through service, and the pressures of leadership, students would experience God's deliverance and providence first-hand, and emerge stronger.

To make matters more challenging, OCF WA leaders and Rob fielded many questions about Rob's role at OCF Australia AGMs. Perhaps these questions came about because Rob was not known to the other students personally. Perhaps the questions reflected a fear that paid staff would jeopardise student leadership and initiative. In 2007, Rob resigned due to personal commitments and moved to Sydney. Although WASO employed several other part-time staff workers after Rob, there were often gaps as not all student leaders chose to have staff workers. Some leaders also did not see the point of attending quarterly Staffworker Oversight Committee meetings, which hiring a staff worker would necessitate.

In the absence of answers at a national level, it was a natural and positive step for Western Australia to create its own solution in the form of WASO. The alumni members who carefully designed this formal entity were motivated by a reluctance to see OCF Curtin close when it had been birthed through the faith and faithfulness of earlier members through God's providence. They were also motivated by their own experience in OCF. They wanted current and future students to have the same opportunities to be blessed.

However, it introduced a point of difference between WA and the rest of OCF Australia (apart from OCF Sydney, which also had local staff workers). At some AGMs, this difference churned up unnecessary angst, when it was a local solution to a local problem. Looking back, former EXCO member Chong Wei said that large and well-resourced centres have different needs from small centres on the brink of closure. Now a practising doctor, Chong Wei reflected on how the advice he gives a healthy patient is different from the advice given to one who is sick. To the first, he advises regular exercise and a healthy diet. To the other, he encourages them to get strong enough in order to receive further treatment. He said, 'The more I think of it now, it is not a one-size-fits-all.'[154]

Such a realisation would have benefited the ministry in the coming years. But to think in this way required a confidence and clarity in the essential nature of OCF Australia, so as not to be threatened by differences in organisational structures and resourcing methods.

---

[154] Ong Chong Wei, Interview with author, 2022.

18. Informal Support

Since the early years of OCF Australia, one of the ways EXCO had helped local centres was through administration, sharing resources and ministry trips. As EXCO members were full-time students, the addition of Aunty Merrilyn in 1986 as their resource person had provided much needed help.

Since then, there had been no increase in the number of people doing this work of support, although the number of local centres had increased from thirteen in 1986 to twenty-four by 1997. As has been described, several of these centres were struggling in 1997, such as Hobart, Murdoch and Curtin. OCF Armidale in New South Wales was also struggling and EXCO had sent people to help them. However, this help did not prevent the centre from closing in 2000.

OCF Armidale was the first OCF centre to close since OCF Geelong dissolved in 1966. However, OCF Geelong had been revived in the early 1980s when members from the larger centres of Parkville and La Trobe drove down regularly to encourage the small group. With Armidale, the nearest centre of considerable size was OCF Sydney. (The word 'nearest' is misleading because Armidale is 475 kilometres from Sydney, while Geelong is 75 kilometres from Melbourne.) In 2000, with OCF Sydney struggling to resource itself, it could not support smaller centres in its vicinity—Armidale, Newcastle, Wollongong and Canberra—to the extent it had done in the past.

This chapter contains a snapshot of centres in New South Wales in 2000 when it hosted EXCO. Taken together, these stories highlight how informal support, for example by OCF alumni moving for work, can play a crucial role in the health and growth of OCF centres. Informal support networks can complement formal support structures, which struggle to keep up with the pace of change in the 21st century.

Sydney

In 2000, Philip Ji became the first and only OCF Australia chairperson so far to come from China. He was from the Fujian province. By this stage, Sydney had many students from China. Although quite a few came into contact with OCF, not many remained in the fellowship. Perhaps, as OCF WA advisor Pastor Ronald Nugent once observed, the worldview of the typical OCF member from South East Asia had less in common with students who had grown up in a communist country compared to, say, African students educated in a post-colonial education system in English.

Although Philip was a fifth-generation Christian, his family did not attend church services. Instead, he had worshipped at home with his parents and grandmother. He arrived in Australia in 1992 to study for his Higher School Certificate. He attended the West Sydney Chinese Christian Church and was baptised there. From 1993 to 2001, he studied at the University of New South Wales and joined OCF.

During this time, he lived in Kingsford, sharing a flat with other OCF members.[155] Philip recalled his OCF experience:

> At that time when I joined [OCF Sydney], there were six district groups, and each one was about 30 people, more or less. I was there for eight to nine years. It changed [over the period of time]. When I first went there, we met on the Saturday evenings. I think that's also a difference between Sydney OCF at that time and other centres because we met on Saturday night, while other OCF centres met on Friday night. But it's also a good thing for me because I was able to attend the church fellowship on Friday, and then OCF on Saturday.
>
> We usually met at about 7.00 pm. Before that we had about fifteen minutes, so some people could come earlier to pray. And then at seven o'clock, we started sings-piration for fifteen, twenty minutes and then broke into small groups to do Bible study. We usually had maybe about four or five [Bible study] groups [in each district group]. There was always one group doing the evangelistic Bible study, for the gospel friends [friends interested in the gospel]. And for the rest, we divided into different groups, based on different needs. Every semester we reshuffled.
>
> Our flat, as I mentioned, had five bedrooms. That's how we could have at least four or five Bible study groups. We sat on the floor, and it was student-led. We were very close. We prepared the study materials, [usually] studied one chapter at a time. Basically, we did a topic every semester. After that we had

---
[155] Phillip Ji, Interview with author, 2022.

refreshment always and chit-chat and fellowship—pretty typical meeting.

In 1997, Sydney University changed its medical degree from a six-year undergraduate degree to a more intensive four-year postgraduate degree. Previously, most of the OCF Sydney chairpersons were medical students, and most held this term for three consecutive years. It became increasingly difficult to find students who could provide mature spiritual leadership.

Two years later, in order to deal with the student leadership shortage, OCF Sydney trialled an Administrative Board to replace the Executive Board. The Administrative Board was less demanding, as it only handled admin matters, not spiritual oversight and direction as the Executive Board had done. The Sydney leadership hoped it would free up senior student leaders to care for the spiritual needs of members. Three years later, in evaluating the trial, it was noted that certain things had fallen by the wayside. For example, the OCF Sydney chairperson had not visited churches supportive of OCF. Opinion was divided on the way forward. Finally, against the wisdom of their predecessors, OCF Sydney reverted to the Executive Board.

By 2000, the North District Bible study group based around Macquarie Uni had only had one postgraduate student. OCF Sydney staff worker Errol Smith had been supporting the group near Macquarie Uni that met close to his home. The following year, he withdrew as staff worker due to family commitments. In his long association with OCF, as a member then staff worker and General Secretary, he had served faithfully and selflessly.[156]

When Philip took on the role of OCF Australia chairperson, each issue of the OCF Australia newsletter *Koinonia* focused on one point from the doctrinal statement. The purpose was to reunite OCF Australia around these statements, which the EXCO in Sydney saw that as the glue holding the fellowship together. In 2001, EXCO, still in Sydney, was reduced from five to three people because of difficulties in filling the posts. The EXCO treasurer Chong Wei was concerned that some of the other centre advisors were not teaching the doctrinal basis to members. Consequently, when students signed the membership form, would they understand what they were signing up to? In OCF Sydney, guarding purity of doctrine, and understanding the implication that flowed out of that was very important.

In 2007, Dr Vincent Chin helped to compile a booklet to celebrate OCF Sydney's golden jubilee. It described how, after a period of great growth, OCF Sydney first brought onboard two staff workers in 1979. They were Meleane Moala, who served two days a week, and Chris Chua the Honorary General Secretary. He had declined a salary because he was already drawing a wage from church. Meleane served as administrative assistant, while Chris oversaw the teaching program and some district group visitation. They helped OCF

---

[156] *OCF Sydney 1957-2007*, 49-53.

Sydney at a time when the fellowship had almost 300 members.

Since then, OCF Sydney had employed various staff workers, to meet certain needs or to take advantage of certain opportunities. For example, in 1983, Graham Cocks was employed to help out with the Indonesian Bible study group as he was preparing to serve in Indonesia. In recent times, however, staff had been employed to stabilise the group as numbers dwindled. In 2004, St Barnabas Church in Broadway hired catechist, or Christian teacher, Denesh Divyanathan to help OCF. Sadly, the St Barnabas Church building burned down in 2006. With that, OCF Sydney lost its regular venue, and perhaps some other forms of support while the church leaders dealt with their loss.

By the time the golden jubilee booklet was published in 2007, Sydney had two staff workers. The OCF Sydney staff worker Esther Lukabyo had been there for some time. She raised her own support and sent regular newsletters to her supporters. The most recent appointment was the OCF UNSW staff worker Rob Robayna. Earlier that year, Vincent and Mary had a chance encounter with Rob. They learned that he just moved from Perth where he had served as a full-time staff worker for four years. They took his openness to work with OCF and his experience to be divine providence, because they had found out that the OCF group at Macquarie University was on the verge of closing—there was one OCF leader Jack Lim, and five non-Christians in their discovery group.

Vincent Chin, Peter Chin and Conrad Chang spearheaded a fundraising committee to raise financial support for Rob. An early member of OCF Sydney felt that asking for donations was out of step with the faith-based nature of OCF but contributed nonetheless for old time's sake. One semester later, by the time Rob was employed, the Macquarie group had grown from fifteen to twenty members. However, the group at UNSW was in a dire position with only three or four members. So, Rob became a staff worker primarily for them instead. With increased support from staff, alumni, and advisors, OCF Sydney seemed to turn a corner. After three years, however, the committee suffered fundraising burnout. Without significant growth to highlight, and little personal connection between financial backers and Rob, ongoing support was hard to raise. Rob served until 2010. There were no staff workers the following year.

Armidale

OCF Sydney and OCF Australia had been showing concern for the students at the University of New England in Armidale since the 1960s, with trips to gauge the possibility of forming an OCF centre there.[157] The 1975 OCF Australia chairperson, Yong Chen Fah, had also visited the Bible study group there

---

[157] Benjamin Tan, EXCO treasurer and convention chairman from OCF Sydney, 'Report of Visit to the New England University, Armidale, NSW,' *OCF Australia Newsletter*, no. 2, 1 July 1966, 7, 8.

regularly from Sydney.[158] The geographical location of Armidale was challenging, having to travel by road or rail for around six hours from either Sydney or Brisbane. Despite these difficulties, OCF Armidale had been affiliated in 1984.

In 2000, the University of New England had several hundred international students but few stayed for more than two to three years. OCF Armidale had not sent delegates to several AGMs before this, clear signs of distress and struggle at a local level. In 1998, Aunty Merrilyn visited Armidale, and spoke at one of the OCF weekly meetings. At the request of EXCO 1998, who could not make a trip, the previous OCF Australia chairperson Yong Tuck Yean made a three-day visit in late September 1998 to encourage the group and invite them to attend the 1998 OCF convention in Canberra. Ronald Mugamu from Africa was the centre chairperson.[159] He was to complete his study in the middle of the following year, but there was no evidence of any succession plan for 1999. The centre closed in 2000.

Newcastle

In 2000, OCF Newcastle had twenty members. At the end of the year, six members returned home. Their annual report paints the picture of a vibrant centre. Blessings of the year were listed as:

1. Many regular non-Christians attendees

---

[158] Yong Chen Fah, Interview by author, 2021.
[159] *OCF Australia National Prayer Day Booklet, 1998, 22.*

2. Highly diverse group from many countries
3. Working people willing to help OCF
4. Regular Saturday prayer meetings
5. Three new Christians.[160]

The group was clearly vibrant but faced difficulties in sustaining the ministry of OCF there as a student-led group. This was even clearer in 2002, when they had only three overseas Christian students, but ten non-Christian students, five advisors and five more local Australian helpers. An email from supporters Lee and Akiko Fung suggested scaled-down methods of evangelism through friendship instead of big events like Chinese New Year dinners.[161] By 2008, OCF Newcastle had closed.

Casting our minds back to 1987, the OCF Newcastle chairperson at the time, Denis Lu recalled his experience. After completing Year 12 in Sydney, he was accepted by the University of Newcastle to study commerce. When he moved to Newcastle, he found out that it was an industrial city, where the wind occasionally carried the smell of sulphur. The university was outside the city, in a working-class environment. Students seldom ventured to the heart of the city by the seaside.

---

[160] Frans Sahureka, 1999/2000 president *OCF Newcastle 2000 Annual Report*, 2.

[161] Lee and Akiko Fung, Email to several people, 12 March 2022, with handwritten notes by Aunty Merrilyn.

On Friday nights, Denis attended OCF. The group varied from 30 to 80 people during his time there. They would set up chairs in the front, supper at the back, and books for sale at the book table—humble jobs but very much part of gospel ministry. Quite a few older Australians also joined them. A loving couple, Doug and June Poetschka, were at OCF almost every Friday and they became like a father and mother to the students. They guided the committee; and invited students to their house for long lunches, or tea and biscuits in the living room.

Most students attended Islington Baptist or Mayfield Church of Christ. Towards the end of his studies, Denis remembers a renewal in prayerfulness and a responsiveness to God. When the Doulos ship visited Newcastle in 1989, he

Supporters of OCF Newcastle, June and Doug Poetschka.

Celebrating returning students of OCF Newcastle at Islington Baptist circa 1990. Photos supplied by Denis Lu.

responded to the challenge issued there, writing his commitment on a card. Aunty Merrilyn also visited them, and wrote him a card with many Bible verses, which he treasures to this day.

Over the years, it was a highly diverse group, with students coming from Taiwan, Korea, Africa, Pacific Islands, and Australia, as well as the usual South East Asian groups. At one point, they had a high portion of ELICOS students; that is, short-term language students, some staying for only six months. Because many were not proficient in English, and only stayed on for a short time, it was hard to sustain the ministry of OCF in Newcastle.

Wollongong

OCF Wollongong had been affiliated in 1987. In 1993, Kenneth Tan was the chairperson. There were several other active seniors, and the group was small but growing. Shu Wern Sze attended OCF Wollongong from 1993 to 1997. Kenneth told her that at one time, he was the only attendee at a meeting, and he would still worship with his guitar and pray by himself.

The following year, Kenneth moved to New Zealand where he started a new Bible study group at Auckland University. Sill'a Kilepoa took over the leadership of OCF Wollongong. There were twenty members, predominantly from Malaysia and Singapore, and also people from India, Taiwan, PNG, Tonga, Western Samoa, Fiji, Indonesia and Korea.[162] Pastor John Kohler from the Lighthouse Church helped out in OCF, and many OCF members attended this church. By the time Wern Sze left, the group had between thirty to forty members. However, by 1999, the group had shrunk to six members.[163]

In 2000, there seemed to be a turnaround. Although it only had five official members, occasionally up to twenty-one people attended. Two people came to know the Lord through their ministry that year, and one more had been baptised. However, by 2004, no one was attending OCF Wollongong. The chairperson was bogged down with studies and could

---

[162] *OCF Australia 1994 Prayer Booklet, 1994, 41.*

[163] *OCF Australia National Prayer Day Booklet, 1999, 23.*

OCF Wollongong with Bronwyn Tully, a missionary volunteer, January 1996. Photo supplied by Shu Wern Sze, seated at the very front, in white.

not carry out proper orientation programs. As a result, there were no newcomers. OCF Wollongong had closed their accounts and sent their money to OCF Australia. Musical instruments had been sent to Sydney for safekeeping. In 2008, after several years of non-attendance at AGM, OCF Wollongong officially closed.[164]

Canberra

In the early 2000s, OCF Canberra had a close relationship with OCF Sydney. Several medical doctors from OCF Sydney moved to Canberra for their internship: Roopesh Dhar, Ong Chong Wei, Douglas Chan, Steven Yew and Cheah Poh Lin.

---

[164] *OCF Australia 2004 AGM Minutes Session 6, 2005, 6, 7.*

Roopesh, Chong Wei and Douglas had served together in the 2001 OCF Australia EXCO and Steven was a former OCF Sydney chairperson.

When they saw how Bible studies were conducted at OCF Canberra, they said, 'There is a better way to study the Bible.' They started training the students in inductive Bible study methods. They also taught the students to write their own Bible study materials. One of the students at that time, Jessica Wong, had been a Christian for some years, yet realised for the first time that Ephesians was a letter! She later served as a part-time WASO staff worker in Perth, with the WASO fund subsidising her study at Bible College. Many OCF Canberra members developed a high regard for the Scriptures, a fear of the Lord, and a lifelong love for God's word.

Over time, the flagship activity in OCF Canberra became writing their own Bible studies. This culture of writing tailor-made studies for overseas students and for OCF can be traced back to the three-year study developed by Chris Chua in the late 1970s, and more recently to Errol Smith's two-year Bible study in the 1990s. They were both postgraduate students or part-time staff workers serving several small Bible study groups.

Although much smaller in size, the Canberra group followed suit whole-heartedly. Student leaders would spend all of Saturday mornings studying a passage of Scripture, with the help of concordances and dictionaries, taking it as seriously as if they were Bible College students writing up essays. Saturday night was for writing up Bible Study material—observation, interpretation, application—often to the wee hours of the morning. One person would vet the material that had to be sent out to Bible study leaders by Wednesday at the latest. This was to ensure Bible study leaders had sufficient time to prepare to lead the Friday night study. In later years, students found it too onerous to write all their Bible study materials from scratch, comparing the workload to the equivalent of one extra university subject, and started buying Bible study material instead.

In 2011, OCF Canberra went through a very fruitful period under the leadership of Joseph Ting. Apart from the Bible studies, there was sports ministry, campus outreach during Jesus Week, BBQ sausage sizzles when OCF members surveyed people waiting in line to find about their spiritual beliefs, and evangelistic meetings during Orientation Week. At this time, OCF Canberra members came not only from Malaysia and Singapore, but also from Thailand, Mongolia, New Zealand and Indonesia. Most members studied at the Australian National University, but some also came from the Australian Defence Force Academy. There was regular prayer in small and large groups, training in worship leading, and an initiative called Every Member Ministry whereby senior OCF leaders approached juniors to identify which ministries they wanted to serve in OCF. OCF Canberra's centre report at the AGM that year was a highlight and an encouragement to all.[165]

---

[165] OCF Australia AGM Minutes (Sydney, 2011), 10, 11.

There were similarities in how the OCF Sydney and the OCF Perth alumni contributed to the ministry of OCF Canberra and Curtin respectively (Chapter 17 Formal Support *Western Australia Staffworker Organisation*). They were both helpful, even though one provided formal support, and the other informal. This highlights that there are many ways to strengthen the ministry. Not everything needs to be done at a formal organisational level. Too much focus on organisational solutions can lead to stagnation.

To counter over-reliance on institutional mechanisms, focus should be on forming relationships with and encouraging students in their faith. In this, the help of local Christians is invaluable because they can provide regular and consistent input. This helps students focus on what is important, so that the centre is geared towards growth, rather than survival. Small centres demonstrate how the ministry can be of great value in isolated areas where there tends to be less support for overseas students. Although Armidale, Wollongong and Newcastle have since closed, their impact continues through the lives of the students who have been touched. For example, Denis Lu is now a pastor at Hope Kuching and Joseph Ting is leading a mid-week fellowship group and part of the leadership team at Gungahlin Bible Church in Canberra.

19. Spiritual Mothers and Fathers

In 2004, the EXCO under the leadership of Tan Hui Ling, published standing orders for the Board of the Advisors (BOA). For the first time in its 45-year history, OCF Australia had an organisational chart. It categorised the advisors of OCF into local, state and national levels, three tiers in parallel to student-led bodies.

OCF AUSTRALIA STRUCTURE

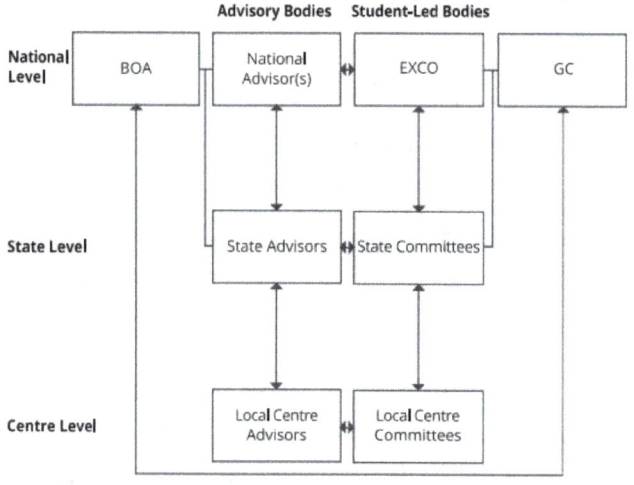

Overall structure of OCF Australia. Arrows indicate a mutual commitment and expectation of ongoing dialogue between both groups.

OCF Australia is composed of two main bodies: Advisory and Students. There are three types of advisors: National, State, Local Centre; National Advisor(s) and State Advisors (one from each state) form the Board of advisors.

State Committees are typically formed by Local Centre Chairpersons of the constituent centres, plus additional dedicated Steering Committee members (if any).

OCF Australia structure from the 7th edition of the OCF Australia Handbook, 2004.

In its original 1997 concept, the board comprised of resource persons to support student leaders in EXCO and the GC who were in the formative period of their lives. No organisational structure had ever been drawn up as the EXCO did not want hierarchy to weigh down OCF, which was a student-led organisation. (Chapter 16 Catalyst and Safeguard, *A Board envisaged*).[166] However, the 2004 EXCO created the structure to meet their current needs, including preparation for the eventual retirement of OCF Australia's single resource person up to that point, Aunty Merrilyn.

A Board Established

In 1999, each state with an OCF centre presented one BOA nominee to the GC. The first nominees were: Kerry Nagel for NSW, Dorothy Mathieson for Queensland, Pastor Hon Hoh (former Parkville chair) for Victoria, and Rev Ng Sin Thong of AACC for South Australia.[167]

---

[166] Yong Tuck Yean, Email to author, 31 July 2023.
[167] OCF Australia AGM Minutes (Adelaide, 1999), 3.

Western Australia did not nominate anyone, and so, OCF Sydney suggested that they invite Rev Allan Webb. He was the current OMF National Director and the previous senior pastor of Swanston Street COC. When WA asked for more time to consider this, Aunty Merrilyn suggested that Rev Webb be invited to be part of the BOA as a national advisor. This was in view of Rev Webb's love for the students and long association with OCF. The GC unanimously agreed. In 2000, when the first OCF Australia Board of Advisors was formed, Rev Webb became the first OCF Australia national advisor. He recalled his time in this role.

> Allan Webb: I feel as if I did very little, to be very honest. Truthfully, I look back upon those years and I think, 'Well, I really didn't do anything very meaningful or effective.' I would attend EXCO meetings sometimes, but very few. I would be asked for some advice about a certain matter and I would provide some counsel. But really, I really don't think I contributed very much at all. Again, I can only give a huge plug for Aunty Merrilyn Teague. I mean, she has been the person that has done so much to hold OCF together. And she has been the one that the students have looked to, both male and female, not just female, but she has counselled so many students over the years and she is greatly loved and respected and trusted.[168]

---

[168] Allan Webb, Interview with author, 2021. Transcript p. 16.

Rev Allan Webb stepped down after a year or so. In 2004, Aunty Merrilyn then stepped into the role of national advisor, a term that superseded the previous title of resource person.

At the age of 62, she was still travelling for six months of the year to minister to OCF centres and sought out godly people whom she trusted to be local and state advisors. Anticipating her retirement, EXCO created a formal structure with state advisors in charge of appointing new local centre advisors and stepping in temporarily if a local advisor had left and a replacement had not yet been found. In formulating the BOA standing orders, these were some of EXCO's considerations.

EXCO 2004. Front row, from left: Tan Hui Ling (2nd), Aunty Merrilyn (3rd). Photo supplied by Tan Hui Ling.

Tan Hui Ling: I think one concern for us was—it probably links a bit with the staff worker issue—a lot of the local centres are crying out or seeking support from someone senior, locally, where they are. We noticed some of the centres did not have appointment of advisor, or there was a gap, but someone came, but someone left. So, with that, we came with a formal structure to have a board of advisors at each state. It is also a form of accountability so that we know who these advisors are and they are accountable to each other within the state and as well as nationally.[169]

A Board Functions

Aunty Merrilyn held the national advisor role from 2004 to 2022. Other state advisors stayed in their roles over varying periods of time. Examples of their contributions follow.

Pastor Timon Bengston served as OCF SA's state advisor for about ten years from 2011 to 2021. He contributed to the ministry by welcoming many OCF members to his church and had a close relationship with some of the leaders, especially those who attended his church. In 2014, when OCF SA staged the musical Prince of Egypt as an outreach and fundraising event, Pastor Timon allowed OCF to use the Oakden Baptist auditorium for rehearsals and performances.

In 2016, the WA state advisor Pastor Ang Chin Wee gave a talk at the AGM on visionary leadership, about having a vision from God and passing it on to members and newer leaders. In this sense, seeking committee members was not

---

[169] Tan Hui Ling, Interview with author, 2021.

about finding people to do administrative work, but asking them to develop their gifts in line with God's purposes for the ministry on campus and for their own lives as well. After this talk, one of the GC members said that she had not realised that this was the role of spiritual leaders and had not realised the importance and meaning of vision. Meanwhile, in Victoria, Dr Chan Chee Kai encouraged OCF Clayton to develop a Chinese cell ministry. In NSW, Pastor Boon Quah encouraged some of his best people to take on EXCO in 2020 and 2021, even though OCF UNSW was not a large centre.

OCF UNSW attendees at the 2019 AGM. From left: Hannah Chi, Huey Nin Woon, Julian Han, Dansen Cho, Bob Rick Looi, Marcus Gan, Pastor Boon Quah, who was the NSW state advisor.

As many state advisors were pastors or returned missionaries of repute, their support for OCF gave the ministry legitimacy, and they could speak to other Christian leaders in a city, in a way that local centre advisors, who were mostly lay people, could not. Also, state advisors helped by providing support counsel when students and local advisors faced situations beyond what they felt capable of handling.

The main limitation in how the BOA contributed to the OCF ministry was the lack of time. Since they had to be theologically trained, and many already had good relationships with OCF members, many state advisors were pastors of growing churches. As their churches grew, they had less time for the OCF ministry. Also, OCF Australia, which functions like a spiritual family, did not naturally communicate along organisational lines, although it was necessary for the appointment of local and state advisors.

Furthermore, the importance of leadership of the group remaining with students had been emphasised by EXCO: '... a part of the ministry of OCF Australia is to train the student-members to be leaders by providing opportunities for leadership responsibilities. Therefore, the formation of the BOA must not remove the training opportunity. The process of decision-making and management of OCF Australia will still remain with GC.'[170] Because of this emphasis, both students and advisors became very conscious that advisors should limit their input to giving advice when asked or

---

[170] *BOA Explanation Documentation 2000*, report distributed as part of the 2005 AGM papers.

providing some service when invited to do so. The 1997 recommendation of not more than five advisors per centre, became concrete restrictions of not more than five local centre advisors, and one state advisor per state.[171] Because the term Associate Member now referred to students who were permanent residents and citizens, there was no clear role for non-students who were not advisors.

As a result, the leadership of OCF Australia remained firmly with the students. However, to flourish, OCF Australia needed many godly supporters. Deep friendships enable mature Christians to speak into the lives of young students. Since the establishment of OCF Australia, many godly men and women played the role of spiritual fathers and mothers to overseas students. Many of the older Australians have already been acknowledged in earlier chapters. Here are more examples of their contributions.

Aunty Merrilyn modelled to Hui Ling how a godly female Christian leader carries herself and ministers to others. Another example is the long-term input of Pastor Stewart Rae and Graeme Tonkin who made an impact in OCF Geelong, Parkville and Melbourne University. Pastor Stewart Rae was a gifted teacher of the Word, who also helped OCF Melbourne Uni to learn how to use the gifts of the Spirit wisely. To attend Friday night meetings, he used to travel weekly by train from Geelong to Melbourne, and then take a tram from the Southern Cross Station to OCF Parkville, and or Melbourne.

---

[171] *OCF (Australia) Handbook*, (7th ed., 2004), 20, 23.

From left: Sue and Graeme Tonkin (OCF Melbourne Uni advisors), Tan Hui Ling, circa 2004.

Through their life example, these men and women demonstrated godliness through countless small decisions and words spoken throughout the day, week in week out. Close association is necessary for the formation of godly character and to learn how to respond in situations that are more complex than one-word answers. The formalisation of the advisory bodies gave necessary structure to the fellowship. However, after this period, the number of mature Christians involved closely with the group, and also the way they were involved, became more limited.

Overall, state advisors occasionally helped to resolve situations of need and conflict. The student leaders appreciated their state advisors who took up these voluntary unpaid roles.

Aunty Merrilyn attended almost every AGM, while state advisors made every effort to attend the triennial BOA planning and strategising sessions with the GC. However, it would be misleading to think of the OCF BOA as a board comparable to a church board, or the board of AFES. OCF Australia BOA members did not know each other well, and meeting once in three years was too infrequent for them to function as a team to guide OCF Australia.

While the formation of the BOA was a good and necessary initiative, it created a clearer distinction between student-led bodies and advisory bodies that was not always helpful. Occasionally, help beyond advice would have been profitable, for example at times of crises or when longer-term solutions were needed. To an extent, the BOA served as a safeguard and a catalyst at the state level. At the national level, however, it did not help OCF Australia with big-picture long-term planning.

20. The Struggles and Significance of Being Small

This chapter is a snapshot of OCF Australia in the period from 2005 to 2010. In December 2005, there were 22 OCF centres in total. Nine had 20 members or less, eight had between 25 to 60 members, and five centres had over 70 members. While the vitality of some small centres was evident, they faced a more precarious existence due to the difficulties of finding suitable students to take up leadership positions every year.

Strategic Growth Officer

In 2005, Penny Kee was the new EXCO chairperson. Both Penny and her predecessor Hui Ling were medical students from OCF Melbourne Uni, at that time the largest OCF centre at 160 members. The outlook of members from large and thriving centres could be quite different from small and struggling centres. Perhaps because of this, the EXCO under Penny's leadership had two goals. The first was to establish an OCF centre in every sizeable campus by 2020. The second was to strengthen and grow existing centres. Crucially, they identified the following eight centres with less than fifteen members as needing special attention.

Victoria	OCFs Geelong, Frankston, La Trobe, Kew
Queensland	QUT
NSW	Newcastle, Wollongong
Tasmania	Launceston (provisionally affiliated 2003)

A year on, growth was reported, and larger centres had helped smaller ones through prayer and practical support, such as sending teams to build relationships with newcomers during orientation.[172]

With regards to the establishment of new centres, small groups had been meeting unofficially for several years in Launceston and in Bristol, United Kingdom. In 1999, Chen Mei Ching from EXCO had visited a small group in Launceston to encourage them. That same year, Aunty Merrilyn had flown to Bristol at the invitation of a former OCF Melbourne Uni member. A small group of four students grew to 40. In her 1999 *Resource Person Report*, she said, 'Asians in [the] UK are lonely with the best of churches. Pray for OCFers and Christians in the UK. They are interested in being affiliated to OCF.'[173] By 2004, OCF London had also been formed.[174]

Hence, the period in 2000 to 2005 was one where there were centres struggling to be viable, but also the possibility of new OCF groups being established. By 2009, several unaffiliated centres were listed in the National Prayer and Mission Month booklet—OCF Berwick in Victoria; OCF London; and International Christian Fellowship Canterbury and OCF Palmerston North in New Zealand. Sadly, however, with the exception of OCF Swinburne, all centres identified for extra support had closed. A notable difference between OCF Swinburne and the other centres was the continuity of

---

[172] OCF Australia Ministry Overview (2005), 72.
[173] OCF Australia AGM Minutes (Adelaide, 1999), 15.
[174] OCF Australia AGM Minutes, Session 4, (Brisbane, 2004), 2.

support by the Swinburne University chaplain Rev Chris Gibson.

OCF Swinburne

Since its formation in 1989, the Swinburne University chaplain Rev Chris Gibson had been actively involved in what started as OCF Kew, but later became known as OCF Swinburne. At the 2010 AGM, Aunty Merrilyn spoke of Rev Gibson's ill-health by which time he was wheelchair bound: 'He disciples the leaders and watches over BS [Bible Study] meticulously as a godly man in his role as an advisor. However, he is getting tired and his mother is sick. [He] is not giving up because of himself but because of responsibilities to his widowed mother. He will be honoured one day for being faithful. Please pray for Swinburne, the new team

OCF Swinburne's 20th anniversary celebration, 2011. Front row from left: Levene Wong (1st), Rev Chris Gibson (2nd). Photo supplied by Levene Wong.

there, and for a new advisor'. Rev Gibson's passing two years later was recorded in the AGM minutes as 'a very great loss to us. He has been a friend, advisor and mentor to us.'

OCF Caulfield

OCF Caulfield had always been a small centre, but with a close association to OCF Clayton. In the early 2010s, they started a South East Asian Food Fest as a means of outreach. The university recognised OCF's contribution to campus life. Through this food fest and the invitation of friends, Mulyadi Robin joined OCF Caulfield and later became its president.

Mulyadi came from a Christian family in Indonesia. He arrived in Australia determined to enjoy his freedom. Yet, through the persistent invitation of friends, he joined OCF and became serious about his faith. OCF Caulfield was a close-knit group that took turns to cook and ate dinner together every evening. Through strong fellowship, they managed to nurture new leaders.

On Friday nights they had Bible studies and a pastor from Compass Church was a great help. There was one supper place in the Glen Waverley area and it used to be a race for both OCF Caulfield and OCF Clayton to see which group would reach there first. After Friday night sessions, drivers would take people home, and a lot of sharing happened during long talks in the car. One anointed car saw twenty salvations.

OCF Caulfield circa 2010. Front row from left: Mulyadi Robin (2nd).

Later, Mulyadi did a PhD in organisational leadership at Monash University. He said that even in big corporations, they have around six months to transmit the culture of an organisation. So, it is possible, to raise up leaders in OCF in a short time.[175]

OCF Hobart

Prayer was a big part of OCF Hobart. In the late 2000s, three to six students met on alternate mornings for house prayers and devotions. The idea of gathering like-minded Christians to live together, had begun in 1999. So, this legacy of faith was passed on from one generation of students to another.

---

[175] Mulyadi Robin, Interview with author.

In 2009, when OCF Sydney declined to host the 2010 convention because of lack of resources, Leslie Lew and Caleb Chandra stepped up to co-chair the convention committee. Convention committee members were paired up with graduates to guide them. Nine or ten graduates were very involved. In December 2010, Hobart hosted the convention at Camp Clayton Ulverstone in Tasmania.

OCF Curtin

In 2008, Cheryl Weng was the OCF Curtin chairperson. The centre had been going through a difficult time, with the previous student leaders feeling very tired as most of the students were on twinning programs. However, in 2009, there were several positive developments. Aunty Carol, from Vose Seminary, became their local centre advisor. Through WASO, Jessica Wong served as a part-time staff worker for OCF Murdoch and OCF Curtin.[176] Some OCF members (from various centres), invited by education agents, gave pre-departure talks in Malaysia and Singapore. This yielded new contacts.

Despite low attendance, the committee persevered with Wednesday evening prayer meetings at a ministry household. Slowly, some very young pre-university students from Canning College started attending. Members bonded over hanging out together, sharing their needs and praying for

---

[176] OCF Australia AGM Minutes, (Kuala Lumpur, 2009), 16.

one another. They also prayed for missionaries and other countries. They became more outward looking. OCF Curtin became very lively, and there was a renewed sense of joy in serving. At the state level, Cheryl worked with Jeremy Ong, the Murdoch chairperson, in convention fundraising. Despite their best efforts, they fell short of their target. A day later, the airline had reduced fares by the amount that they lacked, so that their members were able to attend the convention. Once again, God had answered their prayers.

Vital Church Support

In 2010, Cheryl became the OCF Australia chairperson, the first time Western Australia hosted EXCO. The first job of Cheryl's EXCO was to update the handbook. The new article titled *Local Churches and OCF Members* in the 8th edition described principles of partnership between local churches and OCF centres whereby 'strong growing partnership …[was] essential.' Benefits of that partnership between OCF and local churches, in Australia and overseas, flowed both ways. The new article stated that the partnership between local churches and OCF was a very dynamic one. As such, this article is 'unable to prescribe every aspect necessary for this partnership.'[177]

Former OCF Australia chairperson Yong Tuck Yean had contributed to this updated article. One year previously, in

---

[177] *OCF (Australia) Handbook (8th ed., 2010), 29, 30.*

Members of OCF WA leading worship, circa 2010. From left: Jeremy Ong (3rd), Cheryl Weng (4th).

2009, Tuck Yean and Danny Wong (then EXCO secretary) represented OCF Australia at the Lausanne International Student Ministry (ISM) working group meeting. This meeting was attended by other ISM leaders from the US, Canada, Singapore, Malaysia and the UK. Danny and Tuck Yean spoke there about the student-led model of ministry with the support of advisors and surrounding local churches. In OCF, students experienced the challenges and joys of ministry. When they turned to God in prayer and expectancy to provide, they encountered him in a way that went beyond attendance at a Christian meeting organised for them. The Lausanne Movement had been started by Rev Billy Graham and Rev John Stott in the early 1970s. It is closely associated with IFES and many evangelical churches/organisations that are in turn linked with OCF. Within the Lausanne Movement, there is an active group seeking to strengthen international student ministry globally.

Through the Board of Advisors, OCF Australia had formalised links with individual supporters. However, no formal means had been created for local churches. This was left to students and their advisors. Although advisors can and do support students in their own capacity, this support grows when they also form bridges with their own local church and connect the students with a wider faith community.

Many centres in OCF Australia continued to provide a spiritual home for overseas students. The agency that transient overseas students had in OCF to reach their friends was unique. However, that transience required great intentionality and effectiveness in passing on vision and training up leaders. For smaller and more isolated OCF groups, continuity was harder to ensure. Relying on students and advisors alone might not sustain the group. An additional source of support could be local churches, especially in lean years, when there are too few student leaders to reach out or train up leaders for the following year. Without such support, the gains of establishing new groups are easily lost.

21. Drift Apart

Relationships have ebbs and flows. The strength of the relationships between OCF centres and various local churches, and OCF centres with one another, are affected by a variety of factors such as past experiences, alignment in styles of worship and ministry practices, and the personal connections. Over time, some centres become closer to their churches, others drift away. Similarly, some OCF centres become closer to the OCF Australia family, others drift away.

When the energy it takes to sustain a relationship outweighs the benefits derived, a reasonable conclusion is that the partnership is no longer beneficial. In 2015, OCF Sydney and OCF Carlton became youth fellowship groups of the churches that had been supporting them and left OCF Australia. However, the circumstances leading up to both departures were very different.

Sydney Breaks Away

By 2013, there were encouraging signs in Sydney. OCF Sydney had recovered from several years of struggle to the point that they could host EXCO again. Dr Vincent Chin and his wife Mary continued to open their home for camps such as a Servant's Retreat and a combined camp between Sydney and UNSW. Mary drove every week to Macquarie, Sydney, and UNSW to minister to the girls.

One of the girls she connected with was Rachel Chan. Rachel first arrived in Australia from Mauritius in 2009 to study medicine. She joined OCF, attracted by the student-run nature of the group. Rachel benefitted from Aunty Mary's support. Together they found innovative ways of outreach, such as sessions for girls on make-up and another one on making mooncakes. Support from churches, the alumni, and advisors stabilised numbers. In 2012 and 2013, Natania Chue served as a self-funded staff worker for eight hours per week for OCF Sydney.

EXCO 2013 at the OCF AGM in Victoria. Photo supplied by Rachel Chan, who is in the centre.

In 2013, Rachel Chan served as the OCF Australia chairperson. However, at the end of the year, NSW could not continue with EXCO due to a shortage of leaders and handed it on to Victoria. At this AGM, the incoming OCF Sydney chairperson Prashaanth Rajandran listened to other leaders presenting their centre reports. He realised that each OCF centre had a unique set of problems. He saw EXCO and Aunty Merrilyn trying to support and encourage all centres across Australia and concluded that the organisational structure of OCF Australia was not ideal.

In 2014, Prashaanth took up a second term as chairperson because no one else wanted the job. Melissa Yong from the OCF NSW Steering Committee said, 'We are struggling as student leaders and we do need help from other resources. Barneys is willing to train us up and be under the ministry.' (Barneys was the nickname for Saint Barnabas Church.) By this time, Nathania Chue had finished her two-year term as part-time staff worker for OCF Sydney. Eddie Yoon was the NSW state advisor, but Prashaanth was not in his church. In week-to-week matters of running Friday night meetings, OCF Sydney relied on support from St Barnabas.

Prashaanth did not attend the 2015 AGM. He wrote a letter, which was read out:

As the president of OCF Sydney University, I decided to speak to OCFers who had gone before me and gather their thoughts on a potential 'break away' from OCF Australia. The new model we came to agree upon was not very different from the one we had before. Simply put, above the committee, there would now be St Barnabas staff.

The 2 benefits that are of significance here:

a. *Increased support for the committee*

b. A level of constancy/consistency in the ministry where there is a high turnover.

In the letter, he went on to explain that one of his pastors advised him to consult his committee first and then the whole fellowship. He did so, and as there was no disagreement, the committee decided to proceed.

In 2015, the OCF group at Sydney University officially terminated its affiliation with OCF Australia and became the International Christian Fellowship (ICF) at St. Barnabas Broadway. By this stage, OCF UNSW was the only remaining group out of the conglomeration of district Bible study groups and campus ministries that had once existed at the Universities of Sydney, Macquarie and NSW. Therefore, OCF Sydney was renamed OCF UNSW.

One year later, when Prashaanth was no longer chairperson of the group, he observed that the committee members were receiving more input from the pastors at St Barnabas. Although he acknowledged that the assimilation of ICF members into the church could be improved, 'these things take time'. OCF UNSW maintained unofficial contact with ICF and had four joint events with them in the following year.[178]

---

[178] OCF Australia AGM Minutes (Canberra, 2016), 29.

Section 3: Recent Times, 2000 and beyond

Parkville Moves Out of Swanston Street COC

Since its formation, OCF Parkville had been closely associated with Swanston Street Church of Christ. Over the years, the nature of the relationship changed. Increasingly, OCF Parkville members attended a variety of different churches, and Swanston Street Church of Christ also grew and established new ministries.

From 2001 to 2004, the International Student Ministry of Swanston Street Church of Christ grew from 50 international students to around 200 members.[179] However, the church still encouraged and supported ministries such as OCF Parkville and Asian Navigators. Eventually, it became too crowded and noisy for two meetings for international students in one venue, and OCF Parkville decided to move to a nearby shop.

In 2008, OCF Parkville changed their name to Melbourne City. The leaders felt that God had led them to use RMIT as a 'beachhead' into other inner Melbourne institutes of education such as Latrobe Uni, Victoria Uni and Central Queensland Uni's Melbourne campus.[180] With a sense of excitement, OCF Melbourne City registered with RMIT.

At the 2008 AGM, OCF Melbourne City thanked OCF Carlton for their cooperation.[181] For three decades, OCF

---

[179] Calvin Ma, *The Church in the Heart of Melbourne* (Melbourne, 1995), 72. 74.

[180] Jason Song, 'Victoria State Representative Report', *OCF Australia 2008 AGM Handbook, 121.*

[181] OCF Australia AGM Minutes (Adelaide, 2008), 17.

Carlton had been ministering to RMIT students, for example, by setting up a club's booth at orientation, sending out witness pairs to share the gospel, and holding free English classes. Since formation, OCF Carlton had met at the Lygon Street Church of Christ, now called Lygon Christian Chapel, where they were well-supported.

Carlton Steps Aside

Sadly, OCF Melbourne City struggled to remain viable. In 2014, they had only six members, too few for reaffiliation with the RMIT Student Union. Furthermore, RMIT would only allow one OCF group to operate on campus and required that all registered clubs operate on campus.

The state committee of OCF Victoria, VicComm, therefore asked OCF Carlton to meet on campus, at least every fortnight, in view of its university-affiliation. OCF Carlton responded that they did not have the capacity to devote their energy solely to RMIT, or to hold regular meetings on campus. Their main priority was not to relocate, but to be effective in sharing the gospel with young people, irrespective of their place of study or work.

Revisiting this period, VicComm and OCF Carlton have different recollections. To VicComm, both groups agreed to separate due to the different ways they operated. This was around the meaning of campus ministry and the OCF identity. To VicComm, the OCF identity meant students from various churches working together to serve other students at their campus. The locus of OCF activity, as far as possible, should be on campus. Furthermore, campus ministry called for students to take responsibility for the day-to-day operation of the ministry as far as possible.

OCF Carlton felt they had been given no choice but to leave OCF Australia simply because they could not meet on campus. They were loyal OCF Australia members, attending annual conventions, even if they did not attend OCF Victoria Easter Camps. OCF Carlton became the young adult fellowship of the Lygon Street Christian Chapel, but continued association with OCF in other ways, such as by supporting the ministry of former OCF leaders.

In 2015, both OCF Carlton and OCF Melbourne City ceased operations. After this, there was a delay in establishing a new group at RMIT as there was no one to lead this venture. Eventually, it was established by OCF Melbourne Uni leaders with the help of the International Student Ministry of CrossCulture (the new name for Swanston Street Church of Christ). At the 2017 AGM, complete handover to RMIT students was noted in the OCF RMIT centre report.[182]

OCF Sydney felt that the administrative requirements of being a part of OCF Australia was not commensurate with the benefit they derived. This was probably true. Likely they derived little benefit since not many delegates from Sydney had attended OCF AGMs or conventions for many years. As a

---

[182] *OCF Australia 2017 AGM Handbook*, 97.

result, there was little friendship, mutual encouragement and cross-fertilisation of ideas. It had been a slow drift away.

Some may say that OCF Carlton had been functioning like the international young people's arm of Lygon Street Chapel. However, in the early years of OCF, this was true for OCF Parkville with Swanston St COC, and OCF Clayton with Clayton COC, maybe even OCF AU with AACC. However, over time members of Parkville, Clayton and AACC started attending different churches, and ties between those OCF groups and their traditional church partners loosened, while their ties with OCF Australia were maintained. In contrast, Carlton maintained a strong relationship with the one church that had supported it since its establishment. This is neither right nor wrong. It is just how churches and OCF centres changed both internally and in the way they related to one another over time.

Let us imagine for a moment that the kingdom of God is like a walled city, and both church youth groups and OCF centres are gates in the wall. Citizens of the kingdom interact most frequently with foreigners near their respective gates. Each opening in the wall enables those on the outside to look into the wealth and comfort within the city walls, and perhaps encourages them to step in and become citizens themselves. Regardless of group names and affiliation, may all who minister in the name of Christ continue to faithfully bear witness in this world.

22. Regroup

In the years immediately following the departure of OCF Sydney and OCF Carlton in 2015, EXCO took active steps to unite remaining centres around the OCF Australia vision and identity. Out of this came good initiatives such as leadership training and inter-state prayer groups that fostered closer ties between centres. However, attention on membership and leadership rules detracted focus from the more fundamental problem whereby constant change in student leaders made it hard for OCF centres to minister effectively in a stable on-going fashion.

Pass on Vision, Raise up Leaders

At the 2016 AGM, EXCO Strategic Officer David Tai presented a talk on 'OCF 101 and the handbook'. When David Tai became the EXCO Strategic Growth Officer earlier that year, he had to ask around for a copy of the OCF Handbook. He had heard of it, but not many of his peers had read it. When David finally located a copy, he was amazed at the wealth of information it contained.

In his presentation to the GC, David summarised four core characteristics of OCF Australia from the constitution, which were:

1. A constitutionally enshrined doctrinal basis (Sections 3, 6.1, 6.2, 9.2).

2. Interdenominational (Section 4).

3. Student-led and run (Section 5.6, 6.5).

4. Internationally focused (Section 5.6, 6.5).

The doctrinal basis firmly describes OCF Australia as an evangelical Christian fellowship. The interdenominational character describes a welcome of Christians from different denominations, in Australia and from the home churches of overseas Christians. If OCF Australia is to be a spiritual home

2015 EXCO at the AGM that year. From left: Megan Ong, Serene Chew, Jennifer Setiawan, Alexander Thong, Daryl Tan, David Tai. The returneees officer Kangdi Peng is not in the picture. Photo supplied by David Tai.

to these Christians from around the world, it must be interdenominational.

David coined the phrases 'student-led and run' and 'internationally focused' out of the following two clauses in the handbook.

Section 5.6 No one Associate Member shall hold office in the General Committee, except under extenuating circumstances and then for not more than an aggregate of two years.

Section 6.5 Pertaining to membership:
a. Full membership shall be open to all overseas students on declaration of their faith.
b. Associate membership shall be open to all others on declaration of their faith.

That is to say that OCF Australia, formed by overseas students, put safeguards in their constitution so that leadership of the group would remain with overseas students as far as possible.

David highlighted how leaders had to sign the Doctrinal Statement to indicate agreement with it before taking office. This elicited some surprise, as not many centre leaders had read the Handbook and fewer still followed its rules. David explained, 'Membership is not a prerequisite to fellowship, but it is a prerequisite for leadership. It is a step of commitment. OCF wants committed members and leaders. Time and again, I have seen people saying 'yes' to committing or cell leading and then they disappear and don't continue.

Membership is a commitment in two ways. It is a commitment to the doctrinal basis and it is a symbol of commitment to submit to the local centre leadership. Membership is important to the proper running of the centre.'

Joel Han from OCF Melbourne Uni said, 'It will be difficult to find people to be committed to serve. We are already scraping the barrel with the current membership procedure. Also, what if they sign the form, but disappear?'

David said, 'About scraping the barrel, we have to decide whether we want more committed leaders or more leaders? Our founding fathers said that having more committed leaders is the way to go.'

Emmy Baru, the OCF Adelaide Uni chairperson, said that many members had leadership potential, but not many wanted to step up to serve. This may have been due to a generational wariness of religious institutions and clubs, resulting in few members wanting to take on leadership positions. However, this could be overcome, as explained by OCF Melbourne Uni chairperson Judah Chew.

During the AGM, Judah facilitated a workshop on leadership training. Their training had been extended and refined over decades. It ran for four Saturdays, ending with a weekend retreat whereby members were asked to consider how they wanted to live their university days, and the rest of their lives. It had helped them mobilise around half of their 110 members to serve in some way, to pass on a 'culture of commitment'. Part of its effectiveness was the ministry night of prayer and affirmation, whereby members encouraged one another in what their giftings were, and all saw the ministry as a body whereby each part had a role to play.

After Judah's presentation, the OCF Curtin delegate Jeremy Lee observed that most centres, which were smaller in size, would not be able to run such a comprehensive training, but 'the two main principles are the preparation and maintaining the unity of different ministries and leaders.' Jeremy put this to good effect in WA and in 2018 he ably led a team to organise the 2018 OCF Australia convention. In 2018, Melvin Teo from OCF Hobart thanked the GC for supporting their Leadership Training Course and mentioned his surprise that all the members who attended had stayed on in OCF.

Prioritise Overseas Student Leadership

In 2016, the GC decided to plan for a special leaders' meeting, to strengthen unity and help leaders to connect with one another across Australia. By the time the event took place in mid-2018, a potential constitutional change needed attention. The EXCO treasurer Eugene Rodrigo explained, 'The constitution says no one associate member shall hold office in the GC except under extenuating circumstances and then for not more than an aggregate of two years. We want to hear your views on this. Do you think this needs to be changed?'

Aunty Merrilyn said, 'There is no discrimination at all in OCF Australia. However, we are a body called the Overseas Christian Fellowship. A permanent resident or a citizen has different goals in life. This is to be sure that the vision of OCF and the vision of sending back is maintained.'

The OCF Melbourne Uni chairperson Jedidiah Watt said, 'Sometimes though, international students may not catch the vision as well as a local student. For example, I am an Australian citizen but I want to go back to Singapore.' It was also questionable if limiting the leadership of OCF to overseas students would safeguard the 'send back' aspect of the OCF vision when some overseas students came with the intention of seeking a migration pathway.

Eugene said, 'Wouldn't the clause "extenuating circumstances" allow you to serve as chairperson?'

Jedidiah replied, 'The past four presidents of Uni Melbourne have been citizens or PRs [permanent residents].' Not only at Melbourne Uni, but across Australia, many permanent residents and citizens, especially those with a heritage other than Anglo-Celtic, were attracted to the ministry of OCF. In recognition of the reality of the day, the GC agreed that EXCO would draft a possible amendment for consideration.

At the 2018 AGM, the OCF Australia chairperson Emmylyn Baru introduced this draft amendment. She said, 'This issue has been brought up for four years since 2015. We realised that year that we had so many associate members in official

Leaders of OCF centres gathering for a special meeting in Adelaide in the middle of 2018. Photo supplied by Emmylyn Baru, who is the front row, far right.

leadership positions, be it EXCO or as centre chairpersons. We've come to a point where it needs to be changed to suit the current climate. We have many associate members and they don't necessarily implement the OCF vision. It is about how we can change the Constitution if something like this arises. It is a difficult procedure to get through. To get it officially changed, we have to bring it to the local committee level, have it approved, and come back next year to finalise it at AGM. By then it will be five years in the making.'

By 2019, the GC decided that the hard limit of two years could be removed in extenuating circumstances. EXCO and the local committee should decide what 'extenuating circumstances' warranted associate members holding office for more than two years. If they could not agree, the final decision rested with the EXCO.

Unfortunately, this amendment to the constitution was lost when the EXCO moved from South Australia to NSW. The new EXCO took a different approach to addressing the need for support by focusing on guidelines for advisors. Despite the huge amount of time spent on the topic, the problem of a lack of suitable people to carry out the work of the ministry was not addressed.

Since the associate membership criteria were written in 1959, Australian society had changed drastically. Back then, citizenship status was mostly a direct correlation with cultural identity. This no longer held true. OCF's membership categories were based on outdated ways of thinking about citizenship and culture, identity and belonging. Sixty years ago, a person might hold the same citizenship status throughout their lives, and work in the same job too. At the present time, the legal status of overseas students might change while they were studying. A great motivation was the vast difference between local and overseas student fees. So, an overseas student could become a permanent resident before the end of their course, all the while being a member of OCF. Membership criteria, apart from faith, had never been strongly enforced in OCF.

Since formation, Australian-born Chinese had been a vital part of the fellowship. In 1979, their contribution had been acknowledged. Discussions had been ongoing to a greater or lesser degree since then. The protracted discussion around membership criteria detracted OCF leaders from addressing the most serious problem of too few people to do the work of the ministry.

OCF is a fellowship of overseas Christian students. Overseas students, newly arrived themselves, best understand the needs of other overseas students, but need support to minister to them. Possibly, the original reason for limiting the leadership to overseas students was to safeguard the direction of the group, to remain relevant and concerned for overseas students, rather than to ensure that the 'send back' portion of the vision was perpetuated.

When OCF Australia was first established, all full members would be sent back, as migration was not an option. When migration became possible, this natural progression was recast as a challenge to go home where the needs were greater, rather than to stay on in Australia. Later still, with the proliferation of other on-campus student groups, preparing members to be sent back became a defining feature of OCF, almost a justification for its existence. This became problematic when it prevented OCF from seeing overseas students as they were, in their many concerns, hopes and dreams, which for some included a hope of migration. While the 'send back' portion of the vision has resulted in many going back and serving God effectively, it is better understood as one of the many choices each disciple of Christ must make prayerfully, in submission to God, rather than as a more spiritual option.

The OCF Australia constitution preferences the leadership of overseas students, who, being transient, will be less likely to assume higher positions of leadership unless the fellowship prioritises them. OCF Australia needed greater maturity and flexibility to prioritise overseas student leadership while welcoming the contribution of local students and non-students, especially in a fast-paced, constantly changing context. Local students, non-students, pastors and local churches have a vital role to play in the ministry, without which many of the small centres might close, and those that could remain would not enjoy the blessings of being connected and welcomed into Australian homes and churches. Historically, both overseas students and locals have been blessed by working together in humility and unity, fellowship and service centred in the Lord Jesus Christ and his gospel.

23. The Essential Nature of the Fellowship

As the problem of inadequate support had not been solved, a push to employ staff workers came from two centres. When a motion to explore the staff worker option was defeated, EXCO designed an *Advisor-Student Commitment Statement* to facilitate discussion and agreement between students and advisors on how the advisor should contribute. But could one actually ask advisors for greater commitment when they were not paid like staff workers, and were giving time and service to OCF over and above other family, work and church commitments?

Staff Workers

OCF Perth

At 7 am on Easter Sunday in 2018, the OCF Perth chairperson Andrew Yan called Aunty Merrilyn. She was with OCF Canberra at the time for their Easter camp.

Andrew said, 'I am having great difficulties with my studies and leadership responsibilities. I am drowning and need help. I need a staff worker.'

'We will pray for you,' replied Aunty Merrilyn. 'But, no, you don't need a staff worker.' She had explained her view at the 2016 AGM, 'OCF Sydney had a non-OCF Australia paid staff worker who was financed by AFES to work with OCF.

However, the issue was that with the staff worker's presence, the students did not step up to serve or lead, which is why I do not approve of paid staff workers in OCF Australia.' (It is more likely that AFES did not actually finance the staff worker but provided the means to transfer funds to the staff worker. Funds were usually raised either by staff workers themselves, or by fundraising committees associated with OCF alumni.)

After the phone call, Aunty Merrilyn arranged to fly to Perth. In WA, it was determined that a staff worker would be sought after all. Their state advisor, Pastor Chin Wee helped OCF WA to search for a suitable staff worker. Within a week, Pastor Rob Kane, a retired Baptist pastor, had been approached to fill the role of a part-time staff worker. When Aunty Merrilyn arrived in Perth, she attended an OCF WA combined meeting where Pastor Rob spoke, 'I have been a failure at certain times and I know what it's like to fail as a leader. So, I will help you. I want to pass on the knowledge of how to negotiate these hurdles of failure and disappointment when they do come along'.

Aunty Merrilyn was moved to hear him speaking so candidly. She left Perth with the assurance that he was doing a good work among the students.[183]

---

[183] OCF Australia AGM Minutes (Perth, 2018), 9.

OCF Melbourne University

Also in 2018, the OCF Melbourne Uni chairperson Jedidiah Watt sought more support for his centre. He had joined OCF one year previously and had seen Pastor Stewart Rae walk out alone at the end of a session for the last time one night to catch his train back to Geelong, as he retired from being an advisor for the centre. Given Pastor Stewart's contribution, Jedidiah thought that he deserved a better send-off. This contributed to Jedidiah's view that OCF Melbourne Uni was largely run by students, without supervision from more mature adults.[184]

The vision of OCF to send people back to their home countries struck a chord with Jedidiah. He approached

2018 OCF Melbourne University committee planning retreat at the Belgrave Heights Christian Convention Centre in Victoria. From left: Thomas Tai, Jen-Li Eng, Whitney Wong, Jedidiah Watt, Deborah Eu, Phoebe Goh, Esther Lim, Annabelle Teo, Jiawei Wong, Ivander Lay.

---

[184] Jedidiah Watt, Interview with author, 2023.

chairperson Lionel Lee with suggestions on improvements. To his surprise, Lionel asked him to become the next chairperson the following year despite Jedidiah's lack of leadership experience in OCF. Jedidiah accepted the role and worked with other Christian student leaders on Easter outreach activities through the Melbourne University Campus Christian Network. He saw the close relationship between student leaders and their staff workers and longed for that sort of guidance. He visited local churches near Melbourne University and invited their pastors to partner with OCF. To Jedidiah's disappointment, his efforts did not result in any formal partnership with any churches.

As a result, he drafted a *Graduate Strategy Working Paper*. He described how OCF's three-part vision to reach out, build up, and send home was currently viewed as equal in importance. He proposed that this should be changed to one where reaching out and building up were both for the purpose of sending home. Jedidiah's analysis was that OCF could not fulfil the vision of sending back with the current resourcing. Students, having not returned themselves, could not prepare others. Advisors, as unpaid volunteers, lacked the time commitment of staff workers. Therefore, he suggested employing staff workers to address this problem.[185] He sent this proposal to EXCO for consideration at the 2018 AGM.

---

[185] Jedidiah Watt, 'Graduate Strategy Working Paper', 2018, 7,8.

Staff Worker Proposal Defeated

At the 2018 AGM in Perth, the GC discussed Jedidiah's proposal. EXCO treasurer Eugene pointed out that Perth and Melbourne Uni both wanted staff workers, but for different reasons. Perth, which had been on the brink of closure, wanted a staff worker to support the students and the ministry. In contrast, Melbourne Uni was a large centre, but wanted a staff worker to better fulfil the vision, especially that of sending back.

Jedidiah proposed tapping into the OCF alumni and overseas churches to raise funds for OCF staff worker salaries. In his report, Jedidiah referenced the 2018 AFES financial report on budgeted staff salaries. In contrast to what was a significant figure in that report, OCF Australia did not currently employ anyone. OCF Australia's main source of funds was university grants (for centres affiliated to universities), the membership fee of $10 collected annually, and fundraising used mainly to subsidise camps and conventions.

In earlier years, Aunty Merrilyn's travel costs were paid for by OCF centres that invited her to minister. Only when smaller centres could not raise the money, did OCF Australia use the common pool to pay travel costs. Whatever students lacked in money, they made up for in hospitality. They gave up their beds and shared their food. Many helpful conversations took place outside the formal program, in the course of doing the mundane things of life together, washing the dishes or waiting for a tram. OCF was operating on the model that it had adopted from IVF (as AFES used to be known) in the 1950s—students and graduates bore the responsibility for staff salaries, for their meals and accommodation when they were on ministry trips.

At the 2018 AGM, Jedidiah described his proposal. Following his presentation, EXCO asked the GC to vote if they wanted EXCO to explore the possibility of employing a staff worker. Various delegates spoke up, some with questions, others with the pros and cons of employing a staff worker. The main fear was that it would hamper student leadership. The main benefit was a dedicated person or people to invest into the ministry, hopefully over several years, to mitigate the high turnover of student leaders. OCF WA alumni stalwart Lawrence Peh said that staff workers would not provide continuity. WASO had employed several staff workers, who left after serving a few terms. A salary alone was insufficient to ensure longevity of service as staff workers in OCF did not have a pathway of longer-term full-time service the way that AFES ministry apprenticeships often evolved into a career in church or in missions. Around the AGM table, the mood in the room was heavy, students sensing it was an important decision, but not all able to understand or contribute to discussions. There was no unanimous agreement, and so the motion was defeated.

Although disappointed, Jedidiah continued to serve a second term as the OCF Melbourne Uni chairperson. In 2019, he

Section 3: Recent Times, 2000 and beyond

OCF Melbourne Orientation Booth, 27 February 2019

OCF Melbourne University Orientation Night, 1 March 2019. Photos supplied by Jedidiah Watt.

wrote letters to his centre advisors, inviting them to serve another term, listing seven items on their job description, and a redress procedure for reconciliation. He wrote that although OCF was student-led, it was not wholly student-run, and advisors had an important role to play in ensuring continuity as they generally outlasted the student chairperson's term of one year. He had in fact envisaged this as a key role of staff workers, but after the previous AGM, that option was not available.

The 2019 OCF Australia chairperson Rachel Leong was also disappointed that the GC could not agree on merely exploring the staff worker option. In her role as the previous OCF Flinders leader and then the OCF Australia chairperson, she had felt keenly the lack of support that students faced. She said to the GC that being student-led and run is not in the constitution, which might have sounded shocking to some. Rachel's statement might have sounded contradictory to the presentation by the EXCO Strategic Growth Officer David Tai in 2015.

Although both used the phrase 'student-led and run', Rachel and David were referring to different aspects of the ministry. David's statement was based on the decision-making body of OCF being the GC. As far as possible, the GC had to be full members, thus overseas students. Rachel, however, pointed out that there was nothing in the constitution that forbade the employment of paid staff by OCF Australia. In fact, in 1959, the first OCF Australia secretary Tan Eng Seong had flagged the idea of a paid staff worker to help stabilise the student-run body, and also to travel to various centres that would likely be beyond the capacity of students. Indeed, Aunty Merrilyn had been serving in this capacity for many years, travelling to each centre and supporting student leaders.

The 2020 EXCO expanded the advisor guidelines to a form that both the advisor and the local committees had to sign after both parties discussed how they would work together. For example, could the advisor come each week? And so on. However, on a practical level, apart from highlighting the need to communicate better, this had little impact on the ministry.

Due to the challenges facing the ministry, OCF Australia came under increased pressure to consider hiring staff workers, despite a long-held fear that staff workers would diminish student initiative because they were paid. Often, the difference cited between staff workers and advisors is that the former is paid, while the latter are volunteers. As such, students can ask more of a staff worker than an advisor.

However, in 1997, these words had been penned, 'In recent years, the EXCO has benefited from the assistance provided by advisors who have been genuinely interested in the welfare of OCF (Australia). These [advisors] have either been made available by churches or Christian organisations in the hosting states or have been requested by the EXCO to perform the role.'[186] This earlier document acknowledged that advisors or resource persons unpaid by OCF Australia are still paid in some form, whether by local churches or mission organisations, or God had provided them personal funds so that they could serve without financial remuneration.

As such, perhaps the more pertinent difference is not whether supporters—staff workers or advisors—are paid, but whether OCF Australia receives help provided as a gift or an entitlement. If it is an entitlement, students will be less motivated to serve. On the other hand, if it is received as an unmerited gift, students will be spurred towards greater involvement. In fact, one of the hallmarks of true discipleship is to serve God and others out of a heart of gratitude for all that Christ has done. If OCF members are growing in their faith, they will continue to serve God, regardless of how the supporters of OCF are resourced.

Another concern in OCF was that staff workers would be viewed as experts in ministry, and this would also reduce student involvement. However, this can be avoided by a proper understanding of their role to support and equip students, and by the selection of suitable people. Although supporters may have more theological training or ministry skills, students are closest to other students and best understand their needs. Effective supporters will seek to learn from the students before they try to teach them. They

---

[186] 'The OCF (Australia) Standing Order for the Selection and the Conduct of Resource Persons for the EXCO', *OCF (Australia) Handbook* (6th ed. 1997), 21, 22.

will learn about the mindset of the next generation, the culture of their homelands, and the way Christianity is practised there. Out of this understanding, they will be better able to impart lessons on Christian living, hermeneutic and ministry skills.

Instead of asking 'should OCF employ staff workers?' it may be helpful to broaden question to 'how can OCF cultivate mutually beneficial relationships with its supporters?' How those supporters are resourced is just one aspect to consider. In the past, various ways of resourcing have been used. In the early 1960s, IVF travelling staff workers were OCF graduates who served under the oversight of the IVF General Secretary. Their travelling expenses were paid, but they did not receive a wage. In the late 1960s, the Church Missionary Society provided OCF Australia with the services of Dr Janet Plummer, a returned missionary from Hong Kong. In the late 1970s, when OCF Sydney first employed Melanie Moana as a part-time staff worker, the roughly 300 members of OCF Sydney provided her salary. At the same time, Chris Chua served as the OCF Sydney Honorary General Secretary. He declined a wage from OCF because his church was employing him. Many local churches have released their pastors to serve OCF. In some cases, this was informal, such as with Pastors Pat Kavanaugh, Allan Webb and Bruce Morton, and they contributed to OCF over and above their church responsibilities. Other churches, such as AACC, released Aunty Merrilyn formally to serve OCF for six months of the year. On occasions, OCF alumni raised funds for staff worker salaries, for example, through the West Australian Staffworker Organisation. Some staff workers in OCF Sydney raised their own financial support.

The other aspect linked to employment is how these supporters are themselves supported and under whose oversight they served. Often the organisation or church making these supporters available also took responsibility for their pastoral care. The creation of the OCF Australia Board of Advisors was intended as a way for advisors to support and hold one another accountable.

It is likely that OCF Australia will be better supported if it were open to a range of resourcing options, including employing staff. As it does this, it must carefully cultivate Christ-like relationships of humility and mutuality with its supporters. When students and supporters are relating in this way, students, who are away from home, will gain agency to reach and bless their friends on campus.

Staying true to our vision

The vision of OCF summarised as Reach Out, Build Up, Send Back evolved over many years. When OCF Sydney was first formed, and articulated a vision, it was to stimulate members to faith growth and spur them to reach out. The original vision was by overseas students, to help other overseas students around them. In fact, the early days of growth in OCF could be attributed to how students could help fellow students, both Christian and non-Christian. Sharing the gospel was part of that help, alongside assistance with transport, accommodation, studies and so on. The longer-term objective of wanting to be equipped to serve God in the future was a natural progression as students became serious in their faith. The third part of the vision 'send back' was only explicitly stated after 1978 when migration was an option.

The supporters of OCF can only build up those who are Christians. The impetus to make a difference on campus comes from these overseas Christians. They do the work of outreach. That is why the strategy of establishing new OCF centres does not work apart from having a desire, prayer, and waiting for a Christian overseas student to be enrolled there, and they spearhead any venture. Going back is again a natural outworking of a life-vision to serve God wherever He calls. Along with the student-led aspect, it has been one of the most distinctive aspects of OCF, but also the most contested.

In gathering material for this book, our researchers asked interviewees about their opinion about 'sending back', the third part of our vision. There were a range of views—from 'you can serve God anywhere' to 'the decline of OCF is due to losing the courage to make a strong stand on going home'. Where we live, serve and observe the world affects our point of view. Archdeacon Yong Chen Fah has a perspective shaped by his long and fruitful service in the Sabah Anglican Church, but also from three years of ministry to the Chinese diaspora in Sydney. He had done so at the invitation of the archbishop of Sydney, Peter Jensen, whom he knew from his student days. In response to our research question, Archdeacon Yong said:

> Our God is bigger than what we can see. Leave it to people to decide on permanent residency or taking up citizenship. Whatever it is, leave them to them, their conviction. But ask for deeper conviction from everyone, whatever you are, 'What is God calling you to do? Otherwise, you will be drawn into this world today.
>
> If there are more Chinese, minister to them meaningfully in a Chinese way. Do not minister in a Western way. It is not easy nowadays to even minister to people, basically you need to adjust; it is a very complicated world, right? Very split, you know, thinking wise, feeling wise. The human soul needs peace in order to bring in the gospel to their heart. Otherwise, they cannot see it because there are too many issues that keep bothering them. So why worry about that among ourselves?
>
> Leadership is identifying if something is an important issue or not an important issue. The important issue is the gospel-issue. The gospel-issue is live or die. That is a gospel-issue. That is something that you cannot let go. But other than that, personal likes or dislikes, some things that you can or cannot get used to, those are secondary issues. Secondary issues are no issues at all. We must not allow secondary non-issues to dominate or hinder our relationships.

In this modern world, creating relationships is one of the key areas for ministry. It is important to understand different backgrounds, different people, different thinking. Therefore, the wider your interests are, the better you will be able to understand people. Rather than my way or your way, it is better for me to move one step towards you, to understand you, to win your heart. That is what the gospel is—it is a bigger heart. Even though as human beings, our heart is not so big like Jesus. Before he died, he said, 'Father, forgive them for they know not what they do. That is the biggest heart we can see in life.

Let the gospel come first. Let the Lord Jesus be Lord in our lives, so that we can share with almost everybody young and old. We are one in the gospel. We move forward. One extra witness is better than nothing.'

Archdeacon Yong's view is reflected in the constitution of OCF Australia. The doctrinal statement, which represents the gospel, is the only item in our constitution that can never change. All other matters of governance in the constitution can be changed if it will allow us to minister more effectively. However, push for change did not succeed and alumni and students started to fear for the future of the OCF Australia ministry.

OCF Australia is a spiritual family out of which ministry flows. It was formed by overseas students who wanted to enjoy fellowship and work together to reach out to their friends. Local Australian Christians supported them in their endeavour. When overseas students experienced deep spiritual fulfilment in Christ, they naturally sought to serve the Lord further. This included greater involvement in churches, a concern for their families and their own people, and for cross-cultural gospel work internationally. OCF Australia works well when overseas students are cared for like family first. Joy in service and vitality naturally follows. From personal observation, the fellowship struggles to minister effectively if the order is inverted, if overseas students are asked first to shoulder responsibility for the ministry, to embrace the idea of being sent back, or behave in a certain way, in order to become a spiritual family.

24. Reset

In 2019, OCF Australia held its 60th convention in Melaka, Malaysia. Once again, it was open to the alumni. Jerad Tan led the convention committee which welcomed around 300 students and former OCF members. Many used the journey from Kuala Lumpur or Singapore to Melaka as an opportunity to car pool and catch up on news of intervening years or decades. As joint alumni and student conventions happened only once per decade, students and alumni also prayed together and discussed the future of the ministry.

The Sixtieth Convention

During the convention, OCF Canberra leaders received an email from a church they had been closely associated with for the past fifteen years. The church would no longer supply advisors or support OCF, because they believed that the student-led and run model of OCF was no longer working. The church had just started a Mandarin Bible study group led by church staff. That group was growing, while OCF struggled to remain viable with two committee members. The church's conclusion was that OCF needed church staff on board to turn things around. If OCF refused to do this, they would be taking up valuable church resources to little end.

To the OCF leaders, however, this was a choice between remaining in OCF Australia, or becoming an outreach arm of the church. They did not think that they could call themselves

OCF, a student-led group that was interdenominational, and relinquish decisions on leadership appointments and programs to a single church.

With that, the previously close relationship between OCF and the church came to an end. It was painful not only because of their shared past, with many fond memories, but also because some church leaders had once been OCF members. OCF Canberra became divided—some stayed with the church and others with OCF. The survival of OCF Canberra was in doubt. A very small group was left, and now it had no advisors.

Joint panel session on OCF at the convention. From left: Bob Rick Looi, Dominic Voon, Calvin Ma, Lawrence Chia, Rachel Leong, Hannah Chi, Joshua Sim. Both Bob and Joshua were on the convention organising committee and went on to be part of the OCF Heritage team.

Section 3: Recent Times, 2000 and beyond

Photos of the 60th convention, clockwise from top left: Games, main speaker Pastor Jeremy Ong (formerly OCF Murdoch chairperson), sticking flowers onto a collage at the thanksgiving dinner, OCF Canberra, small group discussion for Bible studies, worship.

The EXCO and the alumni jointly presented a panel session on OCF. On stage were the outgoing and incoming EXCO chairpersons, Rachel Leong and Hannah Chi, as well as alumnus Dominic Voon, Calvin Ma, and Lawrence Chia. Their student involvement took place in the 1990s in Perth, 1970s in Melbourne, and 1950s in Sydney respectively.

Calvin Ma the 1978 OCF Australia chairperson and former NSW state advisor said, 'Yes, OCF is now smaller and perhaps not as strong as before. Yet, we must affirm that the vision that was given to our forefathers—to reach out, to build up, and to send back or perhaps better phrased to send forth (into the world, either back home or in the Australian society)—is not yet realised.'

He affirmed the place of OCF despite the proliferation of other Christian groups, which together, were still only reaching a very small proportion of the overseas student population. He said that he was speaking out of his personal opinion, and that other alumni might have different viewpoints. In different ways, the past and the future of the ministry exercised the minds of delegates. Former OCF Melbourne Uni leader and current Adelaide Uni advisor Lee Joon Chong organised a prayer gathering for each of these two centres. Spiritual forebears and spiritual descendants shared a moving time of prayer.

At the thanksgiving dinner on the last night of the convention, generation after generation of OCF members, from founding members to current students, walked up to the stage to place a flower on a board as a symbol of sowing

The 60th OCF Australia Convention at Melaka, Malaysia, December 2019.

into the ministry. Each generation built on the work of those who had gone before and handed it on to those who came after. It was a wonderful night of singing, laughter and reminiscing. Many had become firm friends through their service together in OCF.

Innovation and Increased Partnership

On 11 March 2020, the World Health Organisation declared COVID-19 to be a pandemic. Before the end of the month, Australia shut its borders to all except citizens and permanent residents. Strict social isolation rules were imposed to curb the airborne disease. As a result, seven OCF Easter camps were cancelled. Aunty Merrilyn flew back from Queensland where she had been ministering to OCF UQ and quarantined in her home. For the rest of 2020, OCF moved to online meetings.

Meanwhile, Jason Ang Woon Seng from OCF Clayton led the 2020 convention organising committee. In the first half of 2020, the program and publicity officer Donovan Koh believed that a cure for COVID would be found, and that OCF Australia would be able to meet in person for the convention. However, from July 2020, Victoria entered the longest stay-at-home lockdown of any state—262 days in the next eighteen months. As the lockdowns dragged on, many people struggled to find the energy to carry out daily tasks. Donovan found himself sleeping at dawn and waking at dusk. His housemate had to wake him up on Sundays by saying, 'Hey, let's watch this livestreamed church service together.' It was as if his body was waiting for COVID to be over so that real life could resume.

Finally, in the second half of 2020, the convention committee accepted that an in-person convention was impossible and they moved the AGM and convention online. The unprecedented circumstances encouraged innovation. Donovan's OCF household at Arnott Street set up a live streaming hub for planning and meetings. Several states recorded worship sessions for online playback during the convention. Despite many challenges, they saw the goodness of God in helping them to meet online as OCF Australia.

As no overseas students flew into Australia and graduates continued to leave, centres became very small, some barely surviving. In this difficult climate, EXCO prioritised caring for one another and for centre leaders. The 2021 OCF Australia chairperson Dansen Cho explained:

> Part of the challenges of COVID was us starting to realise that the ministry and the students were basically crumbling under the weight of trying to do everything by ourselves. Maybe in years past, when you have a couple of hundred students nationally, then you have the critical mass to do events. But then, when the numbers start getting into the low hundreds and the number of people in centres are basically single digit for a lot of the centres, then you are really just spread so thin that the students can't do everything.[187]

2021 EXCO. From left: Kimberly Gan (returnees officer), Dansen Cho (chairperson and prayer officer), Timothy Tan (secretary), Marcus Gan (treasurer and missions officer).

EXCO emphasised that even when fruit is not evident, and the survival of OCF is in doubt, God calls us, first and foremost, to be faithful. EXCO also forged partnerships with

---

[187] Dansen Cho, Interview with author, 2023.

Reach Out, Build Up, Send Back

Screenshots from the 2020 AGM. Photos supplied by Dansen Cho.

other Christian organisations because they saw that the students needed more help. Notable partnerships were with publishing company YMI that provided Christian tracts and booklets, City Bible Forum that provided training on being a witness in the workplace, and with the OCF Alumni Network through financial support and support in other ways, such as to upgrade the website using professional services. Although students faced increased isolation on a personal level, OCF Australia became more connected to local and overseas Christians and groups.

The Blessing of Meeting Together

As restrictions eased in 2021, various states and centres found their own ways to meet together again. In Victoria, large indoor gatherings were still prohibited. So, OCF Victoria

OCF Victoria Easter event 2021. Photo supplied by Donovan Koh.

held a two-day outdoor event during Easter instead. On the first day, they had a barbecue, following by a speaker session on 'Amazing Grace'. The next day, they put into practice what they had learned, by inviting their friends to an amazing race with stations across the city.

In Western Australia, the Perth, Murdoch and Curtin groups had combined to meet as one. Similarly, in Adelaide, UniSA OCF joined Adelaide Uni (AU). Only one AU student, Benjamin Lim, remained in the local committee. There were another two regular members, who helped out significantly in Bible study leading and in worship, but for personal reasons declined committee involvement. Although I was their local advisor and not a student, I supported the group by running prayer meetings and writing Bible studies for summer. In the past, I would not have volunteered or taken the initiative to make suggestions, as these were not considered part of an advisor's role. Similarly, the OCF Caulfield advisor Yeoh Seng Hock started leading Bible studies. This was contrary to the perception that only students should lead Bible studies so that they could develop such skills, useful for future ministry. The pandemic gave us permission to put aside cherished traditions and respond to needs as best we could.

The 2021 convention was conducted in a hybrid format. In South Australia, people travelled daily to Adelaide Uni from where the event was livestreamed. Other states organised themselves according to what their social distancing laws allowed. For example, Victoria had a camp where they watched the sessions together, but some students participated online from Australia or from their home countries.

Finally, in 2022, overseas students began arriving again. By this time, there were few senior OCF members to mentor new OCF members to take responsibility for the day-to-day running of the ministry, such as how to organise meetings, approach speakers, or even set up a PA system. The pandemic caused OCF to lean into advisors and other external bodies to a greater extent, strengthening the partnerships that Hannah's and Dansen's EXCO had envisaged.

Donovan Koh welcoming delegates to the 2022 AGM in Upper Plenty, Victoria.

In 2022, EXCO moved to Victoria, a year before NSW completed their three-year term, because many OCF UNSW members were graduating and they did not have enough people to take on the role. Even in Victoria it was not easy to find suitable students because they had to know the OCF ministry well. Despite having never been a local centre chairperson before, Donovan accepted the role of OCF Australia chairperson. Realising how the previous year had been marked by a personal inward focus of trying to stay safe through physical distancing or social isolation, and local centre challenges, the EXCO under his leadership decided to focus on 'Missions—to fill ourselves with a renewed sense of looking outwards …'

In December 2022, forty-six students and advisors gathered for the 64th OCF Australia AGM at a valley in Upper Plenty, Victoria, around an hour's drive out of Melbourne. This was the first in-person AGM since 2019. Thirteen of the fifteen existing OCF centres were represented. Apart from local Victorians, students and advisors had come from Western Australia, South Australia, Queensland, NSW and the ACT.

Looking at the delegates, Donovan said, 'We're back again, once again, face-to-face. I can see you. I can talk to you. Not through a screen, but I can see absolutely everyone, all the centres represented here. It is such a wonderful thing to be able to experience being part of EXCO, GC and the convention committee.' For Donovan, the joy of so many leaders meeting together dispelled any doubts as to whether OCF should exist.

Throughout the AGM, centre leaders presented reports. The closure of international borders resulted in a sharp drop in attendance. Several centres had merged and some were struggling to meet university club requirements. Others reported growth, such as Curtin and Murdoch being large enough to separate from OCF Perth and meet as one group south of the river. Caulfield would separate from Clayton. OCF UQ was small but would organise the next convention. The convention chairperson was Jeremy Lee, formerly from WA, who was about to graduate. It was timely that the GC created a new Graduate Member category for recent graduates. A sunset clause ensured that this provision would be reviewed in two years.

It had been two years since OCF Canberra had lost the support of a church. Since then, Pastor Mark Warren from Momentum Canberra had come onboard as their local advisor. In view of their recent struggles, it was encouraging to have Alex Titus and Naomi Yong represent the group. They had twelve members—students from Singapore, India (Tamil Nadu and Kerala), Sri Lanka, Papua New Guinea, Malaysia and Australia. In his centre report, Alex described his learning points: 'Connection to communities external to the church is essential for making connections and evangelising in a way that is not predatory. Respect people's culture and be careful not to make Christianity a westernising endeavour. This is not well-received and will not work. Work with people in other communities and attempt to empower them.' Alex and Naomi were domestic students. Naomi had a Malaysian Chinese heritage, while Alex had a Sri Lankan Tamil one. Alex urged the leaders to get involved in their local community clubs and to go to where the people were.

At EXCO's invitation, I presented a workshop on the 'Relationship between Church and OCF'. In preparation, I had read Jerry White's 1983 book *The Church and the Parachurch: An Uneasy Marriage*. Having studied OCF's history for three years, I reflected on past criticisms of OCF, and how we have sought to address these. Looking at the leaders seated around the AGM table, I said, 'Tensions are not necessarily bad. Think of tension across two points keeping the clothesline taut. The heavier the load, the stronger the forces required to maintain functionality. Similarly, some tensions that we face when working with others can keep us true to our calling and faith, if we can identify the concerns driving those tensions and address them effectively.'

Following this introduction, I outlined four main areas of tensions between churches and parachurch organisations—legitimacy, authority, loyalty and finance—and OCF's response to each.[188]

1. Legitimacy: Although OCF members serve primarily in OCF during their student days, the importance of being a member of a local church is constantly emphasised. All OCF leaders and advisors, as

---

[188] J. E. White, *The Church and the Parachurch: An Uneasy Marriage* (Portland, Oregon: Multnomah Press, 1983).

individuals, come under the authority of their local churches.

2. Authority: OCF Australia relies on the collective peer leadership of the GC and EXCO, local centre advisors and the Board of Advisors comprised of the national and state advisors who must be theologically trained.

3. Loyalty: OCF asks local churches to release its members to serve primarily in OCF while members are students. However, OCF members are exhorted to hold their local churches close to their heart, in prayer and involvement where possible. OCF has contributed much to the church in Asia and Australian during and after the student days of its members.

4. Finance: This has not been a big factor of contention in OCF. OCF has historically operated on a very low financial budget. It is energised by youth and harnessing the unstructured or flexible schedule that students typically have.

Since its formation, OCF Australia has provided a simple but effective framework to support overseas students who want to fellowship with other Christians, and to reach their friends. Supporters for this ministry come from various local Australian churches during term time, and churches in the home countries of members.

On the last night of the 64th AGM, EXCO and GC celebrated Aunty Merrilyn's 80th birthday. EXCO presented her with a

Celebrating Aunty Merrilyn's 80th birthday on the last night of the AGM, 2 December 2022.

bouquet of flowers. The OCF AU advisor Lee Joon Chong spoke on behalf of OCF Australia. He said:

> In OCF's 63-year existence, Aunty Merrilyn has been involved for 41 years—36 years at the national level, with 19 years as national advisor. She has attended countless OCF AGMs and conventions, walked alongside many student leaders, preached at many OCF meetings, counselled many OCFers, conducted many pre-wedding counselling sessions, and joined many in holy matrimony. The total number of lives that she has touched through the ministry of OCF will only be known on the other side of eternity.
>
> For me, the word that sums up her ministry in OCF is FAITHFULNESS. She has ministered faithfully in the ministry that the Lord entrusted to her, through the

good times, and especially the bad ones. I will end with some of Aunty Merrilyn's lingo familiar to us: To the biggest "Jesus lady" that I know, who "never ever ever ever" gives up on her sheep, "bless your lovely heart" Aunty Merrilyn for your faithful ministry and unceasing love for the OCFers.

Then the lights in the chapel dimmed. The projector whirred to life, and on the screen, generations of OCF members past and present wished Aunty Merrilyn a happy birthday. Thus, on Aunty Merrilyn's 80th birthday, she retired from OCF to spend time with her family. That night, the few advisors who were at the AGM agreed to organise themselves to meet quarterly to support one another and to pray. Perhaps this was the start of a move towards the pool of resource people that had originally been envisaged.

Praying for the incoming student leaders at the end of the 2022 AGM.

Section 3: Recent Times, 2000 and beyond

2022 OCF Australia convention at Upper Plenty, Victoria.

Through the pandemic and in the aftermath, OCF Australia regained an awareness of its essential nature as a spiritual family, formed to meet the needs of overseas students away from home. Increasingly, this included domestic students. As an organisation of over sixty years, OCF Australia has developed organisational structures and guidelines, but OCF Australia does not look to these as the primary growth agents. Instead, investment and the main work is in personal connections and building up the faith of individual students in godliness, Spirit-illuminated study and meditation on the Word of God, and in a loving community of faith. By working on godly relationships in a prayerful manner, there is trust that they will take the fellowship in the right direction and make the right decisions, so that the fellowship can grow, not because of its rules and dogma and tradition, but because disciples of Christ are continually being called and equipped to further the good work.

OCF has always been more than an on-campus Christian club. We have said that we are not a church. Sometimes we have described ourselves as an on-campus missionary group. But really, we are a fellowship. The word is in our name. Fellowship is a homely word. And because most are overseas students or domestic students away from home, this fellowship looks like a spiritual family away from home. It is spiritual in nature because we come together based on what we already have in common, our faith in Jesus Christ. The wonder of OCF is that in and through our simple fellowship, we can make a difference, even if we are young, or timid, or not particularly gifted or well-connected.

Involvement in OCF requires people to give time and energy to help others when they themselves are in need of help, serving with little monetary reward or recompense. The reward instead is in the relationships we formed as we served. These made up the fabric of some of our best years and led us to our closest friends and most trusted gospel partners. It was in the experience of attempting to do something for someone else, that we saw God provide a place where we could serve meaningfully. To have a part to play, to serve the purposes of God, to share his heart concern for others, that is unmerited favour, that is the grace of God.

OCF AUSTRALIA IN 2022

 Western Australia
OCF Curtin
OCF Murdoch
OCF Perth

 South Australia
OCF Adelaide Uni/
 Uni of South Australia
OCF Flinders

 Queensland
OCF UQ

 New South Wales
OCF UNSW

 Australian Capital Territory
OCF Canberra

Victoria
OCF Caulfield (Monash)
OCF Clayton (Monash)
OCF Melbourne Uni
OCF RMIT
OCF Swinburne

 Tasmania
OCF Hobart

25. The Next Chapter

With the conclusion of the previous chapter, the history of OCF Australia has been written and summarised up to 2022. The next page has intentionally been left blank, for you, the reader, to sign your name or to write a few words about anything the Lord has placed on your heart with regards to the ministry.

If you are a student, you are invited to consider if the OCF vision of 'reach out, build up, send back' is something that the Lord is inviting you to embrace. If so, there are many opportunities for you to serve, from being a friend to someone, to hospitality, teaching, leading, administration, music, communication and so on.

If you are a recent graduate, OCF Australia is trialling a category of graduate membership. The brevity of time many students have in Australia and the frenetic pace of change today mean that the ministry will benefit from the support of experienced OCF members who are recent graduates.

For advisors, alumni, and anyone with a heart for international students, you can help by making your homes, workplaces, and churches places of welcome for these young people as they move between countries. On the OCF Australia website, you can sign up to receive newsletters to support the ministry through prayer and intercession, and any other way God impresses on your heart.

Section 3: Recent Times, 2000 and beyond

Epilogue

OCF Australia is a fellowship for overseas students. This fellowship is a Christian family away from home, where international students find a place to belong, to grow, to serve. Through four years of research, my conclusion is that OCF was formed, and continues, out of a concern for overseas students. We collaborate among ourselves and with others in order to minister to and serve all overseas students —Christians and non-Christians. Sharing the gospel is part of that help, along with practical assistance with accommodation, friendship etc. When there is good collaboration, fellowship and partnership, the ability to minister is strong, and vice versa. Ministry flows naturally out of the strong friendships formed in this place of fellowship. The word fellowship in the Bible comes from the Greek word *koinonia*. It speaks of a connection with God and one another.

To function, the fellowship established a rhythm and took a concrete form—a constitution with a doctrinal statement; a rotating EXCO to serve the decision-making body, which was the General Committee—all young people in the transience of their student years—who met once a year at an AGM. For over sixty years, this has continued unchanged. The second standout characteristic of OCF was that members found coming together to be profitable. Although it is costly to serve and to care for others in a fallen world, we serve a risen Christ. Yet, he does not call us servants, but he calls us friends. As we come together to serve in this ministry, we become firm friends. OCF is a place of deep friendship with God and one another. Probably the biggest impact of the ministry apart from awakening faith, is providing cherished, often lifelong, friends.

The fellowship remained, for a large part, strong in its core nature. But at key points, student leaders had to wrestle with the identity and categorisation of OCF, how it related to local churches and other on-campus groups, and how it resourced itself. Some of these were painful. Some hurts linger. In this, we mirror real-life families, where the bond is deep, relationships are tested by the vicissitudes of life and closely-held views and strong personalities.

In dealing with conflicts, we have a choice. We can ignore them. We can try to find a silver lining. Or we can examine them. The OCF Heritage team chose to examine them. Researching and writing this book has led me to many new friends—former OCF members from the 1950s to current students. My life has been enriched by their stories. Thank you for the time you spent talking to me, recollecting as best you could, what happened in your OCF days and what impact it had on your life. In seeking to understand how OCF evolved, I asked people to remember some difficult events too, where there were conflicts and tensions. I thank those people for their forbearance, trusting me to tell me things that they had long not spoken of. It led me down some surprising side roads with new insight and revelation as to what OCF is and is not. If the pain of the past generation can be distilled into lessons for the future generation, then we haven't wasted the pain. We hope that as an organisation,

OCF Australia can mature and grow through these honest reflections.

We have included events that shaped OCF Australia at a national level. In writing up these accounts, I have sought to present both perspectives, and also to stand back to try to understand the context in which it all happened. Although OCF had an immense impact on us and was such a large part of our student lives, it is actually a very small organisation that exists within nations and churches and in universities. Many things affected the decisions we had to make. Although every effort has been made to verify facts and to be accurate, errors may still be in the text. I apologise if anyone finds this is so. Omissions have been many, because I tried to tell one unified story that would not tax too greatly the patience of the reader. And out of all that, you have the book you hold in your hands. I hope that you will take away something helpful from it.

Researching and writing has been enriching, but not an easy task. I thank those who bore with my repeated emails, messages and texts asking for clarifications or probing deeper into some matter. When the manuscript was almost done, I walked to a lookout. After a steep ascent, I had a vantage point on a hill that was above a sandstone war memorial and above a line of white clouds. A stillness of mind and a quietness of soul came over me. I took in the view of the city spread out to the sea. Nearer to me, in the valley below, I saw a mud lane above a green bank. At the bottom lay a small vineyard, the vines were barren as it was winter.

Away from the noise of everyday living, I heard magpies, parrots, and crows. I gazed ahead to the vast expanse of sky. There on the hilltop, I gained a perspective I had not had before. With the sounds of God's creation in its diversity, I appreciated the manifold wisdom of God, displayed in the calling on our lives. He used OCF for a brief period in our lives, to mould us as he saw fit—missionaries and pastors, politicians and civil servants, accountants and business owners, parents and grandparents, homemakers, intercessors and worshippers. To God be the glory, great things he has done.

Acknowledgements

I would like to express sincere thanks to the OCF Heritage team members, especially the core team of Seet Ai Mee as Barnabas-encourager, Joshua Sim as historian and archivist, Bob Rick Looi as digital archivist, and also the members involved at various times of the project—Christina Chew, Esther Siong, Gavlen Lee, Peh Yan Ting, Eugene Rodrigo, Jedidah Watt, Joshua Chan. Thank you to generous donors, whose contributions enabled us to involve current students in transcription work and to use online interviewing platforms. Their funding also enabled me to make a week-long research trip to Moore Theological College in Sydney.

Thank you to Moore College and the Senior Archivist Erin G. Mollenhauer who made documents available to us, to the staff and students of Moore College who made me feel welcome, and to Bernice Shen and Pastor Boon Quah who helped me to scan boxes and boxes of documents. Each morning, we walked down the stairs into the basement to digitise archives. Each day, when the library closed, we ascended those stairs back to present-day ground-level life. In the following months, I read all those documents; and wrestled to understand the actions, thoughts and motivations of men and women who had written letters, designed pamphlets, and discussed challenging issues in their meeting minutes. Even though many of them have gone to be with the Lord, their faith still speaks to us who remain, and forms a substantive part of the first section of this book.

In Sydney, I also visited Shirley Au-Yong, the first secretary of the Asian Fellowship, formed in 1956, mentioned in the Prologue under the section of *Adelaide*. We shared a wonderful time of fellowship together. When I was facing many challenges in the final stages of this book, Aunty Shirley supported this project through prayer and intercession. Thank you, Hia Chek Phang for putting us in touch with our graphics designer, Naw Day Day. Sincere thanks also to Helena Stretton who proofread the final manuscript. Thank you to the alumni who published and distributed *Pioneering with a Purpose*, a collection of testimonies, which I was able to refer to for some of the history of the early years. Collectively, the alumni—ever-willing to help in a multitude of ways—form a great cloud of witnesses, speaking to us through their lives of faith and their continued friendship.

Thank you to the Oral History Association of South Australia for awarding the OCF Heritage Project the Lizzie Russell Grant to support the intergenerational manner in which our interviews were conducted. Where possible, an OCF member accompanied a more experienced interviewer, a collaborative intergenerational approach suggested by Galven Lee. Students were invited to work on transcription and also reflected on the significance of the material to them today. Their insights helped me to identify the important and timeless truths out of all that has taken place.

Sincere thanks to my husband Lee Joon Chong for his support and encouragement, and to our children Joel, Charlene and Jordan on whom I can always count for honest feedback. Thank you to the past and present members of OCF AU and UniSA who journeyed with me and prayed for the successful completion of this project. May it help us remember God's goodness and lean on His faithfulness all the days of our lives.

Appendix A OCF Australia Chairpersons

Year	Headquarter State	Convention & AGM venue	OCF Australia Chairperson
Early 1959	South Australia		Charles AW
Late 1959	South Australia	Adelaide	Panusunan SIREGAR
1960	New South Wales	Melbourne	HAN Chow Fong
1961	Queensland	Brisbane	Deo NARAYAN
1962	New South Wales	Sydney	Bill LIM
1963	Victoria	Melbourne	SHEN Dah Cheong
1964	Victoria	Adelaide	SHEN Dah Cheong
1965	Queensland	Brisbane	WONG Toh Sing
1966	New South Wales	Sydney	John TAY
1967	Victoria	Melbourne	Steven TEO
1968	South Australia	Brisbane	HIA Chek Pang
1969	South Australia	Adelaide	Melville SZTO
1970	Queensland	Perth	Edward CHUI
1971	Tasmania	Perth	HWA Yung
1972	New South Wales	Hobart	YONG Chen Fah
1973	Victoria	Sydney	PHUA Kwee Sin
1974	South Australia	Adelaide	Thomas LEE Seng Hock
1975	Unknown	Unknown	Unknown[189]
1976	New South Wales	Perth	Chris CHUA
1977	New South Wales	Hobart	Chris CHUA
1978	Victoria	Sydney	Calvin MA/YUE Chee Yoon/Max ONGKILI
1979	Victoria	Melbourne	Calvin MA/Freddy BOEY/Daniel WONG
1980	New South Wales	Adelaide	KOO Tuk Su
1981	New South Wales	Sydney	KOO Tuk Su/Chris CHUA

---

[189] From as early as the third edition of the OCF Australia Handbook (1984), the 1975 chairperson was erroneously recorded as Yong Chen Fah, who had already returned to Malaysia by this time.

Year	State	City	Name
1982	New South Wales	Melbourne	Colin LEE
1983	Victoria	Adelaide	Calvin MA
1984	Victoria	Sydney	Peter TEO
1985	Victoria	Brisbane	Peter ONG
1986	South Australia	Melbourne	Mark GOH
1987	South Australia	Adelaide	CHEW Kim Yong
1988	South Australia	Sydney	Peter TING
1989	Victoria	Katoomba, Newcastle[190]	TAN Loke Mun
1990	Victoria	Melbourne	TAN Loke Mun
1991	New South Wales	Adelaide	James WONG
1992	New South Wales	Brisbane	Hendry WAN
1993	New South Wales	Perth	Samuel WONG
1994	Victoria	Sydney	Moses KHOR
1995	Victoria	Melbourne	Raymond LEONG
1996	Victoria	Adelaide	LEE Chee Keat
1997	South Australia	Brisbane	YONG Tuck Yean
1998	South Australia	Canberra	LEONG Hoi Hoong
1999	South Australia	Melaka/Adelaide	Andrew OW
2000	New South Wales	Melbourne	Philip JI
2001	New South Wales	Sydney	Roopesh DHAR
2002	Victoria	Adelaide	Alvin CHUNG
2003	Victoria	Hobart	TAN Hui Ling
2004	Victoria	Brisbane	TAN Hui Ling
2005	Victoria	Perth	Penny KEE
2006	South Australia	Melbourne	Gillian FOO
2007	South Australia	Melbourne	Gillian FOO
2008	South Australia	Adelaide	Janice KWOK
2009	South Australia	Kuala Lumpur/Melaka	Moses KOH
2010	Western Australia	Tasmania	Cheryl WENG

---

[190] The OCF Australia convention was held in conjunction with *Douloi*. The convention was jointly hosted with AFES at Katoomba, New South Wales.

2011	Western Australia	Sydney	Janesa WONG
2012	Western Australia	Perth	Maxwin CHONG
2013	New South Wales	Melbourne	Rachel CHAN Moy Fat
2014	Victoria	Adelaide	Makarios WONG
2015	Victoria	Perth	Daryl TAN
2016	Victoria	Canberra	Alexander THONG
2017	South Australia	Perth	Emmylyn Takung BARU
2018	South Australia	Perth	Emmylyn Takung BARU
2019	South Australia	Adelaide/ Melaka	Rachel LEONG
2020	New South Wales	Online via Zoom	Hannah CHI
2021	New South Wales	Hybrid, live from Adelaide and online	Dansen CHO
2022	Victoria	Melbourne	Donovan KOH
2023	Victoria	Brisbane	Donovan KOH

Appendix B Oral history interviews

In conducting research for this project, the team prioritised the interviewing of OCF Australia chairpersons, national advisors and staff workers. However, where possible we also interviewed local centre chairpersons or former members who had contributed in some significant way. In addition, many informal conversations and phone calls, emails and messages have been exchanged.

Transcripts of the interview are given to interviewees for review, and permission to publish are signed and countersigned between interviewer and interviewee. In some cases, current OCF members accompanied an experienced interviewer from the OCF Heritage team to conduct the interview.

Clockwise from left: Lim May Kuan, Melville Szto, Daniel Chieng.
Online interview of Melville on 11 February 2021.

Appendix B Oral history interviews

Only interviews with the permission to archive and publish forms signed will be kept in the OCF Digital Archive created by the OCF Heritage team and lodged in several theological colleges upon the completion of the OCF Heritage Project.

Interviewee(s)	Interviewer(s)	Location	Date
Alexander Thong	Lim May Kuan	Online	4 Jul 2021
Allan Webb	Lim May Kuan	Online	18 Feb 2021
Alvin Chung	Lim May Kuan	Online	11 Jan 2022
Andrew & Sok Hui Chew	Lim May Kuan & Michelle Tan	May Kuan's home	13 Dec 2020
Ang Chin Wee	Lim May Kuan	Online	27 Feb 2023
Bob Rick Looi	Lim May Kuan	Online	27 Oct 2022
Calvin & Joyce Ma	Lim May Kuan	Online	4 Aug 2021
Cheryl Weng	Lim May Kuan	Online	19 May 2021
Chew Kim Yong	Lim May Kuan & Benita Loh	Online	2 July 2021
Chia Chek Kwang	Lim May Kuan	Online	8 & 9 Apr 2022
Chris Chua	Lim May Kuan	Online	1 Jun 2021
Clive Murdoch	Lim May Kuan	Clive's home	22 Jul 2022
Dansen Cho	Lim May Kuan	Online	29 Mar 2023
Daryl Tan	Lim May Kuan	Online	27 Jul 2021
David & Jessica Liaw (neé Wong)	Joshua Sim	Online	14 July 2021
David Tai	Lim May Kuan	Online	18 Feb 2023

Denis Lu	Lim May Kuan	Online	20 Dec 2022
Dominic Voon & Lawrence Peh	Joshua Sim	Online	28 Dec 2020
Donovan Koh	Lim May Kuan	Online	21 Mar 2023
Edward Cheah	Joshua Sim & Lim May Kuan	Online	30 May 2021
Edward Chui	Lim May Kuan	Online	28 Jan 2022
Emmylyn Takung Baru	Lim May Kuan	Online	17 Jul 2021
Freddy Boey	Lim May Kuan & Carmen Ho	Online	22 May 2021
Geoff Sunstrom	Lim May Kuan & Joshua Chan	Online	14 Dec 2021
Gillian Foo	Lim May Kuan & Nethinim Wong	Online	28 Dec 2020
Helena Stretton	Lim May Kuan & Goh Shu Xuan	Helena's home	7 July 2020
Hendry Wan	Lim May Kuan	Online	3 Jan 2021
Hia Chek Phang	Lim May Kuan & Peh Yan Ting	Online	9 Apr 2021
Hon Hoh	Lim May Kuan	Online	26 Apr 2022
Hwa Yung	Lim May Kuan	Online	10 Mar 2021
Janice Kwok	Lim May Kuan	Online	7 Jan 2022
Jedidiah Watt	Lim May Kuan	Online	14 Mar 2023
Jimmy Kuswadi	Joshua Sim & Bob Rick Looi	Online	20 Oct 2021

Appendix B Oral history interviews

John & Ivy Tay (neé Goh)	Lim May Kuan	Online	5 Feb 2021
Koo Tuk Su	Lim May Kuan	Online	10 Jan 2022
Lawrence Chia	Joshua Sim & John Kiew	Lawrence's home	2 Sept 2020
Lee Chee Keat	Lim May Kuan	Online	17 Jan 2022
Lim Kim Bew	Lim May Kuan & Tess Teo	Online	12 Oct 2021
Mark Goh	Lim May Kuan	Online	18 Jan 2022
Maxwin Chong	Lim May Kuan	Online	16 Aug 2021
Melville Szto	Lim May Kuan & Daniel Chieng	Online	11 Feb 2021
Merrilyn Teague	Lim May Kuan & Eugene Rodrigo	Merrilyn's home	Part One 31 Aug 2020 Part Two 12 Jul 2022
Moses Khor	Lim May Kuan and Joy Wong	Online	21 Dec 2021
Moses Koh	Lim May Kuan	Online	28 Jan 2022
Mulyadi Robin	Lim May Kuan	Online	11 Nov 2022
Neoh Sim Hee	Lim May Kuan	BCSA[191]	21 May 2021
Ong Chong Wei	Lim May Kuan	Online	3 Nov 2022
Pat Kavanagh	Lim May Kuan	Phone Call	3 May 2021
Penny Kee	Lim May Kuan	Online	24 Jun 2021
Peter & Amy Cheng (neé Hew)	Lim May Kuan	Peter's home	9 Jul 2020

[191] Bible College of South Australia, Adelaide

Peter & Abby Ting (neé Lim)	Lim May Kuan & Tess Teo	Online	30 Dec 2021
Peter Teo	Lim May Kuan	Online	8 Feb 2022
Philip Ji	Lim May Kuan	Online	6 Jan 2022
Phua Kwee Sin	Lim May Kuan	Online	15 Mar 2021
Rachel Chan Moy Fat	Lim May Kuan	Online	26 Jan 2022
Rachel Leong	Lim May Kuan	Online	24 Mar 2023
Raymond Leong	Lim May Kuan	Online	24 Mar 2023
Ronald Nugent	Joshua Sim & Lim May Kuan	Online	3 Jun 2021
Samuel Wong	Lim May Kuan	Online	15 Jan 2022
Seet Ai Mee (neé Ling)	Lim May Kuan	Online	15 Jul 2021
Simon Sie, Ricky Lee, Leong Sea Heng, Yeoh Seng Hock	Lim May Kuan	Online	19 Apr 2022
Shen Dah Cheong	Lim May Kuan & Timothy Lim	Online	27 Apr 2021
Tan Hui Ling	Lim May Kuan	Online	17 May 2021
Tan Loke Mun	Lim May Kuan	Online	31 May 2021
Vincent Chia	Galven Lee	Vincent's home	10 Jul 2021
Vincent & Mary Chin (neé Yan-Carruthers) & Peter Chin	Lim May Kuan	Vincent & Mary's home	15 May 2022

Appendix B Oral history interviews

Wong Toh Sing	Lim May Kuan	Online	25 Feb 2021
Yong Chen Fah	Lim May Kuan	Online	25 Mar 2021
Yong Tuck Yean	Lim May Kuan	May Kuan's home	28 Aug 2021
Yue Chee Yoon & Tracy Yue (neé Tsen)	Lim May Kuan	Online	5 Jul 2021

In addition, members of the OCF Heritage team also spoke to Andrew Chin, Ann Choo, Ben Lee, Charles Aw, Eddie Yoon, Henry and Juliana Kong (neé Chiam), Ho Wey Jing, Lee Bee Teik (by email), Lim Jit Cheng, Lionel Yap, Oh Teik Gee and Tan Teng Teng, Peter King.

Bibliography

Primary Sources

OCF Australia Annual General Meeting Minutes 1959, 1961, 1963, 1964, 1966, 1968, 1969, 1997-2000, 2002-22.

OCF Australia Annual Prayer Booklet 1990, 1993-1996, 1998, 1999, 2009.

OCF (Australia) Handbook editions 1st (1964), 3rd (1984), 5th (1992), 6th (1998), 7th (2005), 8th (2010), 9th (2014), 10th (2018), 11th (2020).

OCF Australia Extraordinary General Meeting Summary Notes 1994.

OCF Australia Extraordinary General Meeting Minutes 2018.

OCF Australia Newsletter 1/1, 1983; 1989/4 and 90/1, 1990.

OCF Australia Newsletter *Koinonia* Spring and Winter editions from 1997-2001.

Burke, Donald, ed., *Historical Notes OCF (Melbourne) 1957-1977*, March 2019.

Yong, Tuck Yean, ed., *OCF (Australia) 40th Anniversary 1999*, (Published by OCF Australia, 1999).

Liew, Jia Ching, ed., *OCF Fifty Years of History 2009*, (Published by OCF Australia, 2009).

Wong, Pollyanna, ed., *The History of the Overseas Christian Fellowship, Perth*, (Self-published,1983.)

Lee, Colin, Lim Chin Aun, William Lim, Hendry Wan and Roopesh Dhar, *OCF (Sydney) 1957-2007*, (Published by OCF Sydney Alumni, 2007).

OCF [Adelaide] 25 years 1956-1981 (Self-published by OCF Adelaide, 1981).

Pioneering with a Purpose, (Published by OCF Alumni Network, 2022).

Papers of the IVF General Secretary Ian Burnard in Series 159/11, 159/24, Collection 277, Collection 278, Samuel Marsden Archives, Moore Theological College

Secondary Sources

'Ecumenism' in Vol.1-4 of *The Encyclopedia of Protestantism*, edited by H. J. Hillerbrand, Routledge, 2004.

Anderson, Allan, *An Introduction to Pentecostalism.* Cambridge, UK: Cambridge University Press, 2004.

Chee, Wilfred, *His Hand on My Life.* Self-pub., 2010.

Cole, Keith, *The History of the Church Missionary Society of Australia.* Melbourne: Church Missionary Historical Publications Trust, Victoria, 1971.

Fraser, 'Overseas Students in Australia: Governmental Policies and Institutional Programs.' *The University of Chicago Press* 28, no.2 (1984): 279-299.

Howe, Renate, *A Century of Influence: A History of the Australian Student Christian Movement 1896-1996.* Sydney: UNSW Press, 2009.

Ma, Calvin, *A Church in the Heart of Melbourne.* Published by CrossCulture Church of Christ, 1995.

Portelli, Alessandro, 'Living Voices: The Oral History Interview as Dialogue and Experience.' *The Oral History Review* 45, no. 2 (2018): 239-248.

Prince, John and Moyra, *Out of the Tower.* Sydney: ANZEA Publishers, 1987.

Robertson, Beth M., *Oral History Handbook.* Published in Adelaide by the Oral History Association of Australia, South Australia branch, 2013.

Szto, Melville, *Where Your Treasure Is.* Singapore: Armour Publisher, 2017.

White, Jerry E., *The Church and the Parachurch: An Uneasy Marriage.* Portland, Oregon: Multnomah Press, 1983.

Wong, Jason, *Trash of Society.* Self-published, 2017.

www.ingramcontent.com/pod-product-compliance
Lightning Source LLC
Chambersburg PA
CBHW071953290426
44109CB00018B/2005